OLD TESTAMENT MESSAGE

A Biblical-Theological Commentary

Carroll Stuhlmueller, C.P. and Martin McNamara, M.S.C.

EDITORS

Old Testament Message, Volume 11

Ezekiel
with an Excursus on
Old Testament Priesthood

Aelred Cody, O.S.B.

Michael Glazier, Inc.
Wilmington, Delaware

ABOUT THE AUTHOR

Aelred Cody, O.S.B. did his biblical studies at the Pontifical Biblical Institute, and at the Ecole Biblique, and received his doctorate from the Pontifical Biblical Commission. He has taught at St. Meinrad Seminary, at Pontificio Ateneo di Sant' Anselmo and at the Pontifical Biblical Institute. He is Novice Master at St. Meinrad Archabbey.

First published in 1984 by: MICHAEL GLAZIER, INC., 1723 Delaware Avenue, Wilmington, Delaware 19806
Distributed outside U.S., Canada & Philippines by: GILL & MACMILLAN, LTD., Goldenbridge, Inchicore, Dublin 8 Ireland

Library of Congress Cataloging in Publication Data

Cody, Aelred.
    Ezekiel, with an excursus on Old Testament priesthood.
    (Old Testament message; v. 11)
    Bibliography: p. 264
    1. Bible. O.T. Ezekiel—Commentaries. 2. Priests,
Jewish-Biblical teaching. I. Title. II. Series.
BS1545.3.C63 1984   224'.4077   84-13629
ISBN 0-89453-411-4
ISBN 0-89453-245-6 (pbk.)

Gill and Macmillan ISBN 7171-1175-X

Cover design by Lillian Brulc
Typography by Richard Reinsmith
Printed in the United States of America

CONTENTS

Part Two
Judgement on Foreign Nations

Part Three
Deliverance for the House of Israel

Part Four

A Vision of the Restoration

Editors' Preface

Old Testament Message brings into our life and religion today the ancient word of God to Israel. This word, according to the book of the prophet Isaiah, had soaked the earth like "rain and snow coming gently down from heaven" and had returned to God fruitfully in all forms of human life (Isa 55:10). The authors of this series remain true to this ancient Israelite heritage and draw us into the home, the temple and the market place of God's chosen people. Although they rely upon the tools of modern scholarship to uncover the distant places and culture of the biblical world, yet they also refocus these insights in a language clear and understandable for any interested reader today. They enable us, even if this be our first acquaintance with the Old Testament, to become sister and brother, or at least good neighbor, to our religious ancestors. In this way we begin to hear God's word ever more forcefully in our own times and across our world, within our prayer and worship, in our secular needs and perplexing problems.

Because life is complex and our world includes, at times in a single large city, vastly different styles of living, we have much to learn from the Israelite Scriptures. The Old Testament spans forty-six biblical books and almost nineteen hundred years of life. It extends through desert, agricultural and urban ways of human existence. The literary style embraces a world of literature and human emotions. Its history began with Moses and the birth-pangs of a new people, it came of an age politically and economically under David and Solomon, it reeled under the fiery threats of prophets like Amos and Jeremiah. The people despaired and yet were re-created with new hope during the Babylonian exile. Later reconstruction in the homeland and then the trauma of apocalyptic movements prepared for the revelation of "the mystery hidden for ages in God who created all things" (Eph 3:9).

While the Old Testament telescopes twelve to nineteen hundred years of human existence within the small country of Israel, any single moment of time today witnesses to the reenactment of this entire history across the wide expanse of planet earth. Each verse of the Old Testament is being relived somewhere in our world today. We need, therefore, the *entire* Old Testament and all twenty-three volumes of this new set, in order to be totally a "Bible person" within today's widely diverse society.

The subtitle of this series—"A Biblical-Theological Commentary"—clarifies what these twenty-three volumes intend to do.

Their *purpose* is theological: to feel the pulse of God's word for its *religious* impact and direction.

Their *method* is biblical: to establish the scriptural word firmly within the life and culture of ancient Israel.

Their *style* is commentary: not to explain verse by verse but to follow a presentation of the message that is easily understandable to any serious reader, even if this person is untrained in ancient history and biblical languages.

Old Testament Message—like its predecessor, *New Testament Message*—is aimed at the entire English-speaking world and so is a collaborative effort of an international team. The twenty-one contributors are women and men drawn from North America, Ireland, Britain and Australia. They are scholars who have published in scientific journals, but they have been chosen equally as well for their proven ability to communicate on a popular level. This twenty-three book set comes from Roman Catholic writers, yet, like the Bible itself, it reaches beyond interpretations restricted to an individual church and so enables men and women rooted in biblical faith to unite and so to appreciate their own traditions more fully and more adequately.

Most of all, through the word of God, we seek the blessedness and joy of those
who walk in the law of the Lord!...
who seek God with their whole heart (Ps. 119:1-2).

Carroll Stuhlmueller, C.P.   *Martin McNamara, M.S.C.*

INTRODUCTION

I. How the Book is Put Together

There is in the Book of Ezekiel an orderly structure, the result of an editorial process, which makes it fairly easy to distinguish four parts, each with its own characteristics.

The first part (1:1-24:27), after an introductory account of the way in which God called Ezekiel to be his spokesman (1:1-3:15) and to be a watchman for the house of Israel (3:16-21), contains narratives and oracles condemning Israel's behavior and attitudes. God's judgement will soon lead to the havoc of a Babylonian invasion and exile. In this first part we find the long report of Ezekiel's vision of cultic abominations in the Temple of Jerusalem, a vision which culminates in the sight of God's glory departing from the Temple (8:1-11:25). Oracles of judgement on the house of Israel are characteristic of this first part of the book, but some of the oracles of judgement are concluded with oracles of deliverance.

In the second part of the book (chapters 25-32) we find more oracles of judgement, but in these oracles judgement is spoken, and punishment threatened, not to Israel but to Israel's foreign neighbors, Ammon, Moab, and Edom across the Jordan east of Judah, the Philistine city-states along the Mediterranean coast west of Judah, the Phoenician coastal cities of Tyre and Sidon, and, finally, Egypt.

In what we find in the third part (chapters 33-39), the historical perspective is usually that of the years following the Babylonian destruction of Jerusalem. After an introduction which is really a new account of Ezekiel's call to be a watchman with a new oracle on repentance (33:1-20), there is an oracle on lack of repentance (33:21-33), but then chapters 34-37 in a series of oracles of deliverance and new life for the house of Israel. These are contrasted with the punishment to be meted out to the wicked who are a menace to Israel, whether from within or from without. Chapters 38-39 stand apart in certain respects. In them is prophecy announcing God's protection of his people from an invasion from without, not, however, from clear contemporary neighbors but from vague peoples of the distant north, in an equally vague future. The contents of this third part often invite comparison with the contents of the first part. A number of topics and themes appearing in the first part reappear in the third. While the first part is characterized by oracles of woe, the third is characterized by oracles of salvation or deliverance, and just as some of the oracles of woe are followed by an oracle of weal in the first part, so are some of the oracles of weal in the third part preceded by an oracle of woe.

In the fourth and final part of the book we find the extensive report of Ezekiel's vision of the new Temple to be built in Jerusalem, with provisions for the roles of the clergy and the secular prince in its liturgical functions. This section is followed by his vision of the river flowing from the new Temple out over the land, and finally by idealized dispositions for a new apportionment of the land among the tribes of Israel, their clergy, and their prince, and for a new system of gates in the walls of the holy city. This entire fourth part is a sort of counterpart to the earlier vision reported in 8:1-11:25 of the first part. In both, Ezekiel is taken from Babylonia to Jerusalem in vision. In the earlier vision, he sees abominations in the Temple and the departure of God's glory; in the final vision, he sees a Temple which will be kept holy and the return of God's glory to the new Temple, to remain there forever (43:1-12).

This well planned structure, with its neat groupings of content, its balance and contrast, its thematic links, cannot conceal the fact that the parts of the whole — the single narratives and oracles — do not flow smoothly along, one after the other. The practiced eye can see phrases, or even whole passages, which can only be understood as explanatory notes or as supplementary additions to a more embryonic form of the original passage. Both the unity given to the disparate parts of the book in the general structure and the insertions and supplements added to those parts show clearly that an editor, or successive editors, put the individual parts together. Was Ezekiel the prophet both the author of the individual parts and the editor who put them together, perhaps in successive stages? Did Ezekiel himself actually write the individual parts, for that matter, or did someone else set down in writing what the prophet said? Soundly critical scholars disagree among themselves in their answers to such questions. All agree that Ezekiel did not write everything in the book bearing his name. Some attribute to him most of the book, others attribute relatively little to him. There is general agreement on the presence of editorial work in the organization of the various components of the book, whether most of the components were set down in writing by Ezekiel himself or not. There is also general agreement on the conceptual homogeneity of the book, the additions being on the whole made in such a way that the ideas of the basic texts are developed and expanded by the additions. In some cases, though, the additions introduce new concepts, new interpretations or points of view, even new concerns.

The purpose and the brevity of a commentary like this one make it impossible for the commentator to deal at any length with literary questions like these, or with the questions of authorship which depend upon them, but the reader has a right to know the working hypotheses which the commentator adopts in such matters. In this commentary it is accepted that the editor or editors of the Book of Ezekiel collected and arranged oracles and narratives which had been composed by Ezekiel at various moments in his life and which had at first been kept as small independent compositions without any intrinsic relation to one another. It is also accepted that the editor or editors not only assembled those small compositions of Ezekiel into a book with a plan but that they added to them and supplemented them. The ideas contained in the additions are often further elaborations of the ideas contained in the earlier texts; the conceptual similarity of the additions and the oracles or narratives to which they are added leaves it quite possible, for that matter, that the additions were composed by Ezekiel himself, at a later moment in his prophetic life, and that it was he who expanded some of his earlier texts with later elaborations. In such cases it is often difficult to distinguish the additions from the original texts with certainty. Efforts to do so would call the reader's attention to subtleties and contribute to his depth of understanding, but they would be out of place in a commentary of this nature. In other cases, however, the editorial work has given an original text a new turn, or has even introduced an element of discrepancy or contradiction into the book. In many of these cases, we shall point out the results; once they are noticed, the passage is easier to understand. It was the final product, the finished Book of Ezekiel, which was received into the canon of inspired books, but alterations of the text were still being made when Greek translations of Ezekiel were appearing in the last pre-Christian centuries.

II. The Historical Setting

Ezekiel must have been born sometime in the last half of the seventh century B.C., but we know neither the year of his birth nor the year of his death, sometime, perhaps many years, after the most recent date mentioned in his book, which is a date in 571 (all years in this commentary are B.C.). We do know that he was of a priestly family, and we presume that he had himself been functioning as a priest in

Jerusalem when the Babylonians took Jerusalem the first time and took him off into the Exile in 597. It was in Babylonia that he functioned as a prophet, and it must have been in Babylonia too that he died. The events of his own lifetime shifted the political shape of the entire Near East and profoundly affected the destinies of the Jewish people. Some of these events were the occasions of oracles and actions recorded in the book which bears Ezekiel's name.

In the generation or two before Ezekiel reached maturity, dominant power in the Near East lay in the hands of the rulers of Assyria. Long before, in 722, the northern kingdom of Israel had been suppressed outright by Assyria, and the southern kingdom, Judah, had had to accept the necessity of political accommodation to Assyrian hegemony. Ezekiel kept alive the memory of the northern kingdom, but he associated it closely with Judah, so that in his oracles both kingdoms constituted a single "house of Israel," in sin, indeed, but also in the promise of a coming restoration in the promised land after a new exodus in a new spirit. Assyria, beset by disruptive forces from within and without, began to fall on hard times in the last quarter of the seventh century, and the resulting political vacuum made it possible for King Josiah of Judah (640-609) to run his country as he saw fit, and to extend his effective sphere of influence into the territory of the former northern kingdom. Among the accomplishments of his forceful reign was a religious reform carried out around 622 in conformity to the ideological and practical norms found in the Book of Deuteronomy. His reform included measures leaving the Temple in Jerusalem the sole legitimate place of public worship in the realm. A heightened sense of the Temple as God's sole earthly dwelling place was enlisted in support of these measures. This intensified sense of the Temple as the focal point of the presence of God on earth governs some of Ezekiel's oracles and many of the visionary plans for the restoration in chapters 40-48. It gives to Ezekiel's visions of the departure of God's presence from the Temple (11:23) and of its return (43:5-7a) their full meaning as visions of transcendental events heavy with consequences for earthly history.

The fall of Nineveh, capital of Assyria, in 612 left Assyria's southern and ethnically related neighbor, Babylonia, the major power to the northeast of Judah. To the southwest, Egypt had been consolidating its strength anew, and under the Pharaoh Necho II (610-595) Egypt became active in Western Asia, in competition with Babylonia for power and influence over the petty states in Syria and Palestine. Rulers of those small states, among them Jehoiakim of Judah, who had been placed on his throne through Necho's imperious intervention in 609, needed a great deal of political astuteness and diplomatic skill if they were to shift their own political alliances opportunely and thereby retain a certain amount of autonomy in the face of both Egypt and Babylonia. Serious errors of judgement in this respect were soon to lead to disaster in Judah.

Late in 605 Nebuchadrezzar II (605-562), who was to have a fateful role to play in the destinies of Judah, became king of Babylonia. (Ezekiel uses the form Nebuchadrezzar, closer to the Babylonian form of the name, rather than the form Nebuchadnezzar which is more common in the Old Testament; for consistency's sake we shall conform to Ezekiel's usage in this commentary.) For three years, probably 603-600, Jehoiakim accepted the position of a vassal king with Nebuchadrezzar as his suzerain, but he then began to behave as a fully independent monarch, in the knowledge, no doubt, that both the Babylonians and the Egyptians had sustained heavy losses in a battle with one another in 601. By 598 Nebuchadrezzar was again imposing his suzerainty on the petty states up in Syria, and at the end of that year he set out with his army for Judah. About the same time Jehoiakim died and was succeeded by his son Jehoiachin. The Babylonian army besieged Jerusalem, which surrendered on the 16 March 597. The precise Babylonian date, easily convertible into the Julian date B.C., is indicated in the recently found Babylonian Chronicle for that year.

After that first conquest of Jerusalem by Nebuchadrezzar's army, Jehoiachin, who had reigned for only three months, was taken off with his family and his entourage to exile in Babylonia. He was replaced in Jerusalem by his uncle Zedekiah, Nebuchadrezzar's choice as vassal king of Judah, expected to be properly compliant to the will of his suzerain. His royal legitimacy was suspect in the eyes of many Judeans, and the dates in the Book of Ezekiel are reckoned not according to the regnal years of Zedekiah but, significantly, according to those of Jehoiachin, whose regnal year 1 was the Babylonian year beginning the 13 April 597, just after the surrender of Jerusalem. Other persons of power and prestige in Judean society, and those craftsmen and workers whose activities might be useful to fomenters of sedition in Judah, were also taken off to exile in Babylonia, many of them to be settled in the irrigated area around Nippur, where they were allowed to live together in colonies and to enjoy a certain freedom of communication and assembly. Among these members of the influential classes taken into exile in 597 were members of the priestly families of Jerusalem. One of them, who took up residence among the exiles in the region of Nippur, was Ezekiel.

In Judah itself, secular and religious life continued with some adjustments. The kingdom suffered relatively little after the surrender of the capital in 597, and many of the people had a false sense of security in the ability of their leaders and in the protection of God, whose earthly residence was in their capital, and whose chosen people they were. Their smug confidence, allied to their lack of profound religious and moral spirit, is the object of frequent condemnation in Ezekiel's oracles of judgement. Politically, there were pro-Egyptian and pro-Babylonian factions in Judah. Whether the kingdom of Judah was allied with Babylonia or with Egypt, the terms of the alliance would entail a curtailment of the kingdom's autonomy, for neither Nebuchadrezzar nor Necho was accustomed to thinking of alliances with a petty state except in terms of vassalage with the payment of an annual tribute to the foreign suzerain and with mutual obligations to render military aid when it might be called for. The rural gentry and the leading persons left in Jerusalem, all of them chafing at the Babylonian bit, tended quite naturally to feel that Judah's interests lay in establishing ties with Egypt, in the hope that with Egyptian military backing Judah might cast off the Babylonian yoke. Such expectations were neither realistic nor prudent, and in Jerusalem the prophet Jeremiah made himself unpopular with a large part of the citizenry by saying so. So did Ezekiel in Babylonia, after he had received his prophetic vocation in 593. Nothing negative is said of Babylonia anywhere in the entire Book of Ezekiel, not even in the second part (chapters 25-32) which comprises an entire series of oracles against Judah's neighboring states.

In the oracles of the first part of the book, which reflect conditions in the latter years of Zedekiah, there is insistence on political prudence on the part of Judeans no matter where they are, in exile or in the homeland; they should examine their own consciences if they want to find the reasons for their misfortunes, for the Babylonian army, in Ezekiel's proclamation, is merely the instrument of punishment wielded against the house of Israel by God in his righteous wrath.

In 589 a new pharaoh, Apries, called Hophra in the Bible, began his reign over Egypt. That same year the political behavior of Zedekiah and the inhabitants of Judah must have become overtly rebellious, for in January of 588 the Babylonian army moved into Judah and began a second siege of Jerusalem, which lasted much longer than the siege of 597. Zedekiah eventually sent to Hophra for Egyptian military aid, which was provided and which caused the Babylonians to lift the siege of Jerusalem for awhile, early in 587 probably. The Babylonians bested the Egyptians and began the siege anew. In the summer of 586 (according to the solution of the chronological problems which is adopted in this commentary) Jerusalem was taken, and this time the Babylonian vengeance was far more ferocious than it had been in 597. Zedekiah and those close to him escaped from the city but were caught at once and taken to the Babylonians' western headquarters at Riblah in Syria, where Zedekiah's sons were killed and he himself was blinded before being taken to Babylonia, never to be heard of again. About a month later, the palace and the Temple in Jerusalem were destroyed, the city was burnt, and its walls were partly torn down, while some leading persons, including priests and scribes, were taken to Riblah and put to death there. Others were taken to Babylonia to increase the number of exiles there, and further deportations followed in later years.

Not long after the destruction of Jerusalem the Babylonians began a thirteen-year siege of the Phoenician city of Tyre, probably from 585 until 573, which is reflected in Ezekiel's oracles against Tyre. The siege of Tyre was in fact inconclusive, and Tyre was not destroyed. It continued to exist as a city-state, in vassalage, no doubt, to Babylonia.

The fall of Jerusalem in 586 meant the end of Judah as an independent kingdom, and for the next half century the program of full, regular, public worship in the Temple ceased. Before the national disaster of 586 neither government nor worship nor the moral life of the people was as it should have been in the eyes of God, and Ezekiel took pains to point that out, countering the general smugness and foolishly sanguine hope with oracles of condemnation and threats of imminent punishment. After the disaster, he countered the general despair with oracles of hope and promise. In the first decades after 586 the exiles had little reason to hope for return to Judah, but Ezekiel's oracles from that period, found particularly in chapters 34-37, announce a national restoration of the house of Israel in its homeland, under the secular leadership of a Davidic prince, and in chapters 40-48 we have visionary plans and sanguine provisions for such a restoration.

The possibility of return from exile for those who cared to return was opened when the Babylonian empire fell in 539 to Cyrus of Persia, whose treatment of subject peoples was relatively benign. In 538 he issued an edict permitting the Jewish exiles to return to Judah. Whether they began returning in large numbers soon afterwards or not is disputed. A new sacrificial altar was constructed in Jerusalem late in 538, according to Ezra 3:3, and foundations for the new Temple were laid in 537, according to Ezra 3:8 and 5:16, but construction lagged for years and it was only around March of the year 515 that the Temple was finished and ready to be consecrated. At least by 520 there were in

Jerusalem a Jewish governor or civil commissary (Zerub-babel, grandson of the exiled King Jehoiachin) and a high priest (Hag 1:1); a fairly large number of exiles must by then have returned to their homeland. Some scholars would like to date parts of Ezek 40-48 (the cultic laws especially, but also the plan of the Temple) to the period when the new Temple was nearing completion or had been completed. It is true that much of Ezek 40-48 is later than the original visionary core of that part of the book and that much of it may not be Ezekiel's own work, but in this commentary it is accepted as a working hypothesis that chapters 40-48, and the Book of Ezekiel as a whole, were for all practical purposes completed probably before the arrival of Zerubbabel the civil governor and Joshua the high priest who were in Jerusalem by 520, and in any case before the restoration of the regular round of worship in the reconstructed Temple in 515.

PART ONE

JUDGEMENT ON THE HOUSE OF ISRAEL

A PREFACE TO THE CALL-NARRATIVE AND TO THE ENTIRE BOOK
1:1-3

> **1** In the thirtieth year, in the fourth month, on the fifth day of the month, as I was among the exiles by the river Chebar, the heavens were opened, and I saw visions of God. **2** On the fifth day of the month (it was the fifth year of the exile of King Jehoiachin), **3** the word of the LORD came to Ezekiel the priest, the son of Buzi, in the land of the Chaldeans by the river Chebar; and the hand of the LORD was upon him there.

In the bare information provided here on the prophet who is at the center of the entire book, the tragedy in his life is implicitly communicated. Along with the prophet's name and patronymic, we receive the information that he was a priest, or at least the son of a priest (the Hebrew text can be understood either way). Israelite priesthood had by then become a prerogative of certain families anyway. We are also told that when he received his call to be a prophet he was in Babylonia (the "land of the Chaldeans"), in a settle-

21

ment on one of those waterways — not rivers, really, but canals — near the ancient city of Nippur which were important for irrigation and for commercial transportation in that part of Babylonia. Ezekiel was, then, living in exile in a heathen land far from God's house, the Temple in Jerusalem, which by that time was the only place where an Israelite priest could exercise most of his priestly functions.

This brief introduction is not all of a piece. In v. 1 Ezekiel speaks in the first person, and the verse leads directly to the account of the vision in vv. 4-28. This connection is interrupted, however, by vv. 2-3, in which Ezekiel, introduced now by name, is spoken of in the third person; these verses point more directly to the divine word which does not begin until chapter 2. V. 1 gives a date in a thirtieth year of an unspecified era. In vv. 2-3 there is a date in the fifth year of an era reckoned, as dates in Ezekiel regularly are, from King Jehoiachin's first full regnal year (beginning a few days after the surrender of Jerusalem in 597), which happens also to be the first year of his exile, as the text puts it. The text becomes clearer when we realize that v. 1 is the original introduction to 1:4-3:15, not to the entire book, and that vv. 2-3 have been added editorially, to give us the introductory information which is appropriately found at the beginning of an entire prophetical book, but also to date the account of Ezekiel's prophetic call in the year which corresponds to the period between 30 April 593 and 18 April 592. Different explanations of the thirtieth year of v. 1 have been offered. None of them imposes itself as an explanation which is demonstrably the right one.

EZEKIEL'S INAUGURAL VISION
1:4-28

⁴As I looked, behold, a stormy wind came out of the north, and a great cloud, with brightness round about it, and fire flashing forth continually, and in the midst of the fire, as it were gleaming bronze. ⁵And from the midst of it came the likeness of four living creatures. And this was their appearance: they had the form of men,⁶ but each had

four faces, and each of them had four wings. [7]Their legs were straight, and the soles of their feet were like the sole of a calf's foot; and they sparkled like burnished bronze. [8]Under their wings on their four sides they had human hands. And the four had their faces and their wings thus: [9]their wings touched one another; they went every one straight forward, without turning as they went. [10]As for the likeness of their faces, each had the face of a man in front; the four had the face of a lion on the right side, the four had the face of an ox on the left side, and the four had the face of an eagle at the back. [11]Such were their faces. And their wings were spread out above; each creature had two wings, each of which touched the wing of another, while two covered their bodies. [12]And each went straight forward; wherever the spirit would go, they went, without turning as they went. [13]In the midst of the living creatures there was something that looked like burning coals of fire, like torches moving to and fro among the living creatures; and the fire was bright, and out of the fire went forth lightning. [14]And the living creatures darted to and fro, like a flash of lightning.

[15]Now as I looked at the living creatures, I saw a wheel upon the earth beside the living creatures, one for each of the four of them. [16]As for the appearance of the wheels and their construction: their appearance was like the gleaming of a chrysolite; and the four had the same likeness, their construction being as it were a wheel within a wheel. [17]When they went, they went in any of their four directions without turning as they went. [18]The four wheels had rims and they had spokes; and their rims were full of eyes round about. [19]And when the living creatures went, the wheels went beside them; and when the living creatures rose from the earth, the wheels rose. [20]Wherever the spirit would go, they went, and the wheels rose along with them; for the spirit of the living creatures was in the wheels. [21]When those went, these went; and when those stood, these stood; and when those rose from the earth, the wheels rose along with them; for the spirit of the living creatures was in the wheels.

²²Over the heads of the living creatures there was the likeness of a firmament, shining like crystal, spread out above their heads. ²³And under the firmament their wings were stretched out straight, one toward another; and each creature had two wings covering its body. ²⁴And when they went, I heard the sound of their wings like the sound of many waters, like the thunder of the Almighty, a sound of tumult like the sound of a host; when they stood still, they let down their wings. ²⁵And there came a voice from above the firmament over their heads; when they stood still, they let down their wings.

²⁶And above the firmament over their heads there was the likeness of a throne, in appearance like sapphire; and seated above the likeness of a throne was a likeness as it were of a human form. ²⁷And upward from what had the appearance of his loins I saw as it were gleaming bronze, like the appearance of fire enclosed round about; and downward from what had the appearance of his loins I saw as it were the appearance of fire, and there was brightness round about him. ²⁸Like the appearance of the bow that is in the cloud on the day of rain, so was the appearance of the brightness round about.

Such was the appearance of the likeness of the glory of the LORD. And when I saw it, I fell upon my face, and I heard the voice of one speaking.

The account of God's calling Ezekiel to be a prophet has two principal parts: first the description of a transcendent vision (1:4-28, which we shall now consider), then the report of the words and actions which constitute the actual call or commission, with the whole account followed by a visionary conclusion (2:1-3:15).

Ezekiel's call-narrative is not unique in beginning with a vision of divine transcendence. The visionary overtures to the verbal divine calls of Moses (Exod 3:1-4) and of Isaiah (Isa 6:1-7) also contain imagery expressing God's powerful separation from this profane and common world. Fearful natural phenomena like thunder and earthquake, lightning and fire, regularly accompany theophanies or manifestations of God in the Old Testament. They lend themselves well to descriptions of God's appearance in this world because they elicit our feelings of awe, and because they express God's power and his intangibility. God's being carried along through the skies on storm-clouds moved by the wind entails an image of physical, spatial distance above the cosmic earth which suggests his metaphysical transcendence, as well as an image of ethereal natural phenomena, clouds and wind, which suggests his incorporeality. The vision is designed to show something of the awesome power of God breaking into Ezekiel's life and consciousness as he receives his prophetic commission. It serves as a preparatory confirmation of his prophetic role: as a spokesman for God, he perceives heavenly realities hidden from the eyes of other mortals.

What Ezekiel sees in his inaugural vision can be described structurally as four living creatures supporting the firmament or vault of the sky; on the firmament rests a throne, and on the throne, carried to and fro by the living creatues in co-ordinated movement, sits a divine being. The burning coals in the midst of the living creatures (v. 13) have no functional purpose in this vision, but they will have such a function in the similar vision described in chapter 10, and they have been inserted here in anticipation of that. Each of the four creatures has four faces, so that he can move in any direction without turning. Griffins and sphinxes and other mythical creatures in which different parts of different animals and birds and of man were combined were common in the art of the Ancient Near East, and it is hard to say whether the four faces of each of the creatures here, those of a man, a lion, an ox, and an eagle, have any particular significance or not. When the creatures supporting the firmament with the divine figure enthroned upon it move, they do so by the motive force of the wind or spirit. "Wind" and "spirit" are the same word in Hebrew, and when we use either of those English words to translate it, we lose the Hebrew word's pregnant ambivalence. The motive force is, on the one hand, the stormy wind of v. 4, but on the other hand the word for "wind" can also designate the breath which is the vital force of animals and human beings, and in the Book of Ezekiel, as elsewhere, it can, and does connote the impetus towards movement which comes from will or emotion, human or divine—"Spirit," if we will.

The description of the four creatures is given in vv. 5-14. The expansion in vv. 15-21 engenders some confusion, because it introduces wheels, one to go with each creature, designed, like the creatures with their four faces apiece, for changing direction without turning. Here again, we cut through the confusion when we realize that not everything in the present description comes from the same imaginative mind. Vv. 5-14 seem to be older than vv. 15-21. While the older section with its original imagery remains in our book, the picture is altered in the newer section. Some of the descriptive phrases of vv. 5-14 are borrowed for use in vv. 15-21 with alterations, so that the spirit as moving force is removed from the creatures (v. 12) to the wheels (vv. 20-21). While in v. 12 it is the creatures which move in any direction without having to turn, in vv. 17, 20 that is said of the wheels. In vv. 5-14 the creatures move only in the air, but in the expansion of the description in vv. 15-21 the wheels rest at times on earth and their rising is co-ordinated with a newly introduced rising of the creatures from the earth (vv. 19, 21).

The really important element in the vision is the divine being on the throne (vv. 26-28). His having "a likeness as it were of a human form" is designed to exclude from his appearance bestiary elements like those of the supporting creatures, but the human form is not emphasized, and the description moves on into the mythical details which serve to emphasize the divine in what Ezekiel saw. At the end comes the climax: what Ezekiel saw was the glory of the Lord. This glory is not an abstract quality of God. As often in the Old Testament, but particularly in Ezekiel and in the priestly component of the Pentateuch, the divine glory is a form, luminous but normally veiled from the eyes of mortals, through which God appears without being seen directly. In the priestly texts of the Pentateuch, the glory is found only in the tabernacle in the desert, the predecessor of the Temple in Jerusalem. Here it is unexpectedly visible to

Ezekiel in pagan Babylonia. The spatial context of God's glory in this vision is not the sacred space of the Temple but the vast sweep of the created world. Through the glory, God makes himself personally and intensely present to Ezekiel in the Exile, and in that awesome presence Ezekiel falls reverently upon his face.

GOD GIVES EZEKIEL HIS COMMISSION TO BE A PROPHET
2:1-3:15

2 And he said to me, "Son of man, stand upon your feet, and I will speak with you." ²And when he spoke to me the Spirit entered into me and set me upon my feet; and I heard him speaking to me. ³And he said to me, "Son of man, I send you to the people of Israel, to a nation of rebels, who have rebelled against me; they and their fathers have transgressed against me to this very day. ⁴The people also are impudent and stubborn: I send you to them; and you shall say to them, 'Thus says the Lord God.' ⁵And whether they hear or refuse to hear (for they are a rebellious house) they will know that there has been a prophet among them. ⁶And you, son of man, be not afraid of them, nor be afraid of their words, though briers and thorns are with you and you sit upon scorpions; be not afraid of their words, nor be dismayed at their looks, for they are a rebellious house. ⁷And you shall speak my words to them, whether they hear or refuse to hear; for they are a rebellious house.

⁸"But you, son of man, hear what I say to you; be not rebellious like that rebellious house; open your mouth, and eat what I give you." ⁹And when I looked, behold, a hand was stretched out to me, and lo, a written scroll was in it; ¹⁰and he spread it before me; and it had writing on the front and on the back, and there were written on it words of lamentation and mourning and woe.

3 And he said to me, "Son of man, eat what is offered to you; eat this scroll, and go, speak to the house of Israel." ²So I opened my mouth, and he gave me the scroll to eat.

³And he said to me, "Son of man, eat this scroll that I give you and fill your stomach with it." Then I ate it; and it was in my mouth as sweet as honey.

⁴And he said to me, "Son of man, go, get you to the house of Israel, and speak with my words to them. ⁵For you are not sent to a people of foreign speech and a hard language, but to the house of Israel — ⁶not to many peoples of foreign speech and a hard language, whose words you cannot understand. Surely, if I sent you to such, they would listen to you. ⁷But the house of Israel will not listen to you; for they are not willing to listen to me; because all the house of Israel are of a hard forehead and of a stubborn heart. ⁸Behold, I have made your face hard against their faces, and your forehead hard against their foreheads. ⁹Like adamant harder than flint have I made your forehead; fear them not, nor be dismayed at their looks, for they are a rebellious house." ¹⁰Moreover he said to me, "Son of man, all my words that I shall speak to you receive in your heart, and hear with your ears. ¹¹And go, get you to the exiles, to your people, and say to them, 'Thus says the Lord GOD'; whether they hear or refuse to hear."

¹²Then the Spirit lifted me up, and as the glory of the LORD arose from its place, I heard behind me the sound of a great earthquake; ¹³it was the sound of the wings of the living creatures as they touched one another, and the sound of the wheels beside them, that sounded like a great earthquake. ¹⁴The Spirit lifted me up and took me away, and I went in bitterness in the heat of my spirit, the hand of the LORD being strong upon me; ¹⁵and I came to the exiles at Tel-abib, who dwelt by the river Chebar. And I sat there overwhelmed among them seven days.

Now that the scene has been set by the preceding vision, the account of the momentous turn in Ezekiel's life continues with the report of God's commission to him to be a prophet, a commission given in words and in symbolic action. It is God who speaks and God who is the agent in the symbolic action, but Ezekiel's reverent discretion keeps him from saying so directly: the divine address is introduced as one heard from "the voice of one speaking" (1:28), and the symbolic action is one done by "a hand stretched out"(2:9). The multivalent ambiguity of the single Hebrew word which means "wind" and "breath" and "spirit," noticed in the preceding vision, needs to be taken into account here in the commission scene too. In 3:12, 14, where the visionary elements come again to the fore, it is primarily the wind rather than spirit which lifts Ezekiel up and carries him away, and yet it is the wind acting as God's servant. In the latter part of 3:14, though, Ezekiel uses the same Hebrew word to designate his own vital force or "spirit." In 2:2 the spirit enters Ezekiel from without and is thus some vital force acting as an instrument of God. Whether the Hebrew word in a given case is the numinously activated wind or something better translated as "spirit," it is in any case something invisible and intangible; Ezekiel was aware not only that he was seeing God in the form of his glory and hearing the divinely spoken words, but also that numinous forces were taking hold of him inwardly and outwardly.

What is essential in Ezekiel's prophetic commission is given in 2:3-7. Ezekiel, as a true prophet, must be, and now is, sent by God. When he speaks as a prophet, he is delivering not a message of his own but God's message. Consequently, his prophetic oracles throughout the book will be introduced with "Thus says the Lord God"(2:4), an Ancient Near Eastern messenger's introductory formula, adopted for prophetic use with God named as the person from whom the message comes. It is to "Israel," or, as in 3:4 and very often in the book, to all the "house of Israel," that Ezekiel is sent, not particularly to Judah, the political kingdom of which Jehoiachin and Zedekiah were kings. This subtlety broadens the scope of Ezekiel's mission. He is sent not only to those actually living in Judah but also to those members of God's people rooted in the former northern kingdom suppressed by Assyria 130 years earlier, and to those recently exiled in Babylonia. A certain chronological or historical broadening of the judgements which Ezekiel will proclaim is also announced here, when God denounces the transgressions not only of Ezekiel's own contemporaries but also of their fathers (2:3). Ezekiel will deliver oracles carrying judgement of wickedness back historically to the founding of Jerusalem (chapter 16), or even to the time of the exodus from Egypt (chapters 20 and 23). Finally, Ezekiel is told not to be afraid of the hostile reception he is likely to get (2:6-7). A similar exhortation was given to Jeremiah at the moment of his prophetic commissioning (Jer 1:8). Jeremiah was personally given to sentiments of fear and discouragement. Ezekiel, a relatively unsentimental person, hard in his approach (3:8-9), was less given to such sentiments, but a divine exhortation to fearlessness is aptly used in the commission of any true prophet. Unlike false prophets, he will have communications to make which well ensconced persons will not want to hear, as the story of the prophet Micaiah, the son of Imlah, in 1 Kgs 22:5-28 shows. Whether any prophet, saying what he has to say, is heard or not is irrelevant to his mission. Ezekiel is told here that a prophet's success or failure is a matter of other people's point of view, not of God's.

In 2:8-3:3 we have a rite of symbolic conferment, somewhat like the *traditio instrumentorum* in an ordination ritual or the handing over of the keys of office to a new incumbent. As a prophet, Ezekiel will deal with God's words, typically words of judgement, and so it is a scroll bearing such words that the divine hand gives to him. By eating the scroll he vitally assimilates the divine words and makes them part of himself. The results of the words of judgement will be, for the house of Israel, "lamentation and mourning and woe," but for Ezekiel, a sense of the sweetness of honey. This entails an implicit contrast of the obedience of the prophet with the rebelliousness of the house of Israel, on the basis of their respective reactions when the word of God becomes reality for them.

From 3:4 onward, the thought begins to move towards the particular situation of those members of the house of Israel who are in exile. Yet another contrast, in 3:4-7, sets the general unreceptiveness of the exiled Judeans towards the words of their own God against the paradoxical receptiveness of the heathen peoples among whom the exiles live. In 3:11 it becomes clear at last that Ezekiel is to deliver divine messages to his fellow exiles directly, although the burden of the messages will affect the whole house of Israel, both in exile and in the homeland. The history of Israel, distant and recent, has left its mark on the fate of the exiles, and it is evident, both from Ezekiel and from Jeremiah, that contemporary events in Jerusalem are matters of burning interest to the Judeans exiled in Babylonia.

In 3:12-15 the call-narrative closes as it opened, with a visionary experience in which the glory of God is swept out of sight and Ezekiel returns, as it were, to reality. Despite the retouchings and the extensions made to the text as our canonical Book of Ezekiel was taking shape, the call-narrative constitutes a unity easy enough to interpret as it is. With its combination of supernatural vision and divine speech, it shows an irruption of God into the banalities of Ezekiel's ordinary existence among the exiles in and around Tel-abib. Ezekiel becomes a seer of heavenly things, entrusted with God's word. He becomes a sign, and a bearer of messages of judgement, for repentance, but also for stating God's position on some of the vicissitudes of human history, whether the hearers hear or refuse to hear.

EZEKIEL'S CALL TO BE A WATCHMAN
3:16-21

[16]And at the end of seven days, the word of the LORD came to me: [17]"Son of man, I have made you a watchman for the house of Israel; whenever you hear a word from my mouth, you shall give them warning from me. [18]If I say to the wicked, 'You shall surely die,' and you give him no warning, nor speak to warn the wicked from his wicked way, in order to save his life, that wicked man shall die in his iniquity; but his blood I will require at your hand. [19]But if you warn the wicked, and he does not turn from his wickedness, or from his wicked way, he shall die in his iniquity; but you will have saved your life. [20]Again, if a righteous man turns from his righteousness and com-

mits iniquity, and I lay a stumbling block before him, he shall die; because you have not warned him, he shall die for his sin, and his righteous deeds which he has done shall not be remembered; but his blood I will require at your hand. [21]Nevertheless if you warn the righteous man not to sin, and he does not sin, he shall surely live, because he took warning; and you will have saved your life."

In this short passage we have an account of Ezekiel's further call to be a watchman to warn the house of Israel. The passage is drawn largely from chapter 33 and placed here as a supplement to the account of Ezekiel's more fundamental call to be a prophet. Vv. 17-19 are taken verbatim from 33:7-9, with some very minor alterations. Vv. 20-21 are based on the principles stated in 33:18 and in 18:24, 26. Peculiar to the passage here, although a related thought is found at 14:9, is God's statement that he himself places a stumbling block before a righteous man, who stumbles and must die. The sense of this is that, since God is the lord of all history, even when a good person turns to evil through his own choice the situation in which he makes that choice is not outside God's pervasive governance of all events. God puts the block there. Whether the righteous person stumbles or not is up to him. The responsibility of his fellowmen enters the picture too, and so Ezekiel himself is warned that he will have to account to God for any failure to carry out his commission to be a watchman and to warn.

AN INTERLUDE
3:22-27

[22]And the hand of the LORD was there upon me; and he said to me, "Arise, go forth into the plain, and there I will speak with you." [23]So I arose and went forth into the plain; and lo, the glory of the LORD stood there, like the glory which I had seen by the river Chebar; and I fell on my face. [24]But the Spirit entered into me, and set me upon my feet; and he spoke with me and said to me, "Go, shut yourself within your house. [25]And you, O son of man, behold, cords will be placed upon you, and you shall be

bound with them, so that you cannot go out among the people; [26]and I will make your tongue cleave to the roof of your mouth, so that you shall be dumb and unable to reprove them; for they are a rebellious house. [27]But when I speak with you, I will open your mouth, and you shall say to them, 'Thus says the Lord GOD'; he that will hear, let him hear; and he that will refuse to hear, let him refuse; for they are a rebellious house.

Like the section immediately preceding, on Ezekiel's call to be a watchman, this interlude is drawn from elements elsewhere in the book. Unlike the section immediately preceding, it is difficult to see why this section was put together and inserted here. The only original detail is the statement in v. 22 that Ezekiel was told to go forth into the Babylonian plain to hear God's words and to see God's glory. Otherwise, the elements of v. 22 are drawn from 1:3 (the hand of the Lord taking hold) and 2:1, those of vv. 23-24 from 1:28 and 2:2, while v. 25 points forward to Ezekiel's being bound in 4:8, and vv. 26-27 announce his being struck dumb in 24:27 and then having his mouth opened again for speaking in 33:21-22. All the elements in this passage have to do with personal experiences of the prophet.

A SET OF SYMBOLIC ACTIONS
4:1-5:4

4 "And you, O son of man, take a brick and lay it before you, and portray upon it a city, even Jerusalem; [2]and put siegeworks against it, and build a siege wall against it, and cast up a mound against it; set camps also against it, and plant battering rams against it round about. [3]And take an iron plate, and place it as an iron wall between you and the city; and set your face toward it, and let it be in a state of siege, and press the siege against it. This is a sign for the house of Israel.

[4]"Then lie upon your left side, and I will lay the punishment of the house of Israel upon you; for the number of the days that you lie upon it, you shall bear their punish-

ment. [5]For I assign to you a number of days, three hundred and ninety days, equal to the number of the years of their punishment; so long shall you bear the punishment of the house of Israel. [6]And when you have completed these, you shall lie down a second time, but on your right side, and bear the punishment of the house of Judah; forty days I assign you, a day for each year. [7]And you shall set your face toward the siege of Jerusalem, with your arm bared; and you shall prophesy against the city. [8]And behold, I will put cords upon you, so that you cannot turn from one side to the other, till you have completed the days of your siege.

[9]"And you, take wheat and barley, beans and lentils, millet and spelt, and put them into a single vessel, and make bread of them. During the number of days that you lie upon your side, three hundred and ninety days, you shall eat it. [10]And the food which you eat shall be by weight, twenty shekels a day; once a day you shall eat it. [11]And water you shall drink by measure, the sixth part of a hin; once a day you shall drink. [12]And you shall eat it as a barley cake, baking it in their sight on human dung." [13]And the LORD said, "Thus shall the people of Israel eat their bread unclean, among the nations whither I will drive them." [14]Then I said, "Ah Lord GOD! behold, I have never defiled myself; from my youth up till now I have never eaten what died of itself or was torn by beasts, nor has foul flesh come into my mouth." [15]Then he said to me, "See, I will let you have cow's dung instead of human dung, on which you may prepare your bread." [16]Moreover he said to me, "Son of man, behold, I will break the staff of bread in Jerusalem; they shall eat bread by weight and with fearfulness; and they shall drink water by measure and in dismay. [17]I will do this that they may lack bread and water, and look at one another in dismay and waste away under their punishment.

5 "And you, O son of man, take a sharp sword; use it as a barber's razor and pass it over your head and your beard; then take balances for weighing, and divide the hair. [2]A third part you shall burn in the fire in the midst of

the city, when the days of the siege are completed; and a third part you shall take and strike with the sword round about the city; and a third part you shall scatter to the wind, and I will unsheathe the sword after them. ³And you shall take from these a small number, and bind them in the skirts of your robe. ⁴And of these again you shall take some, and cast them into the fire, and burn them in the fire; from there a fire will come forth into all the house of Israel.

In this section of the book we find a series of symbolic actions or emblematic pantomimes which Ezekiel is to perform, by divine command, before the eyes of his neighbors. The actions symbolize various aspects of the coming fate of the Judeans and the burden of their guilt. Symbolic actions are entirely appropriate for a prophet, because a divine message can be communicated by signs as well as by words. The symbolic actions are efficacious signs, just as the words of the prophetic oracles are efficacious words. What they announce will come to pass; what they state is true. The signs are efficacious because they are prescribed by God, just as verbal oracles are prescribed by him, and the Lord who prescribes is the Lord who disposes the historical events to which the words or the symbolic actions point. Both the words and the signs express what the divine will has determined for the future, how the divine mind judges the present or the past. Although signs often need verbal interpretation if they are to be fully understood, they are more effective than words in the impact with which they drive their message home to those to whom they are given. In the passage which we have here in Ezekiel, the command to perform the actions is narrated, with some divine verbal interpretation, but the actual performance of the actions is not described, and so we do not get the reactions of the exilic spectators watching the performances.

The first of the symbolic actions (4:1-3) symbolizes the coming siege of Jerusalem. The emblematic object is one of those clay bricks used for building in Babylonia, and on it Ezekiel is to inscribe the sketch of a city, with siege instruments either inscribed on the brick or modeled and set around the brick. In v. 3, the basic action is supplemented: the emblematic instrument is an iron plate symbolizing hardness and hostile separation, and Ezekiel is instructed to represent the besiegers. The city is named: it is Jerusalem. The unnamed besiegers are, of course, Babylonian soldiers.

The second action (4:4-8) is less clear-cut, but in any case it symbolizes the burden of guilt weighing upon Ezekiel's people. While in the Book of Ezekiel generally the "house of Israel" designates the chosen people as a whole (so, implicitly, even when Judeans are directly intended), a distinction is made here between the house of Israel (v. 5), in the limited sense of the former northern kingdom whose independence was suppressed when the Assyrians took its capital, Samaria, in 722, and the house of Judah (v. 6), the southern kingdom whose imminent fate will be sealed when the Babylonians take its capital, Jerusalem, in 586. This, like some other problematic elements in the present text, is probably the result of a somewhat careless expansion of an original text in which Judah, called the "house of Israel," was alone intended. Ezekiel, in the present text, is to act the part of the house of Israel as he lies on his left side, and of the house of Judah as he lies on his right side. The length of years of guilt or punishment of the two regions surely has some historical significance, but its identification remains problematic because in the transmission of the expanded text, the number of years of punishment for Israel has become uncertain. In vv. 7-8 the point seems to change slightly: geographically the horizon is narrowed from the two ancient kingdoms to the city of Jerusalem, and chronologically the long years of guilt or punishment are narrowed to the short period of Jerusalem's siege. The prophet is to utter oracles against the city, with his arm bared (v. 7), but if he is bound with cords he can hardly bare his arm. There is no point in quibbling about logical problems of this sort, however. Vv. 7-8 may be logically inattentive expansions of an original instruction which is that of vv. 4-6. When we compare this entire second action (vv. 4-8) with the first, third, and fourth, we notice that its symbolic expressiveness is weak in comparison. Was this second action really meant for Ezekiel's exilic neighbors to behold, or was it a sign for the prophet himself, which he could talk about without acting it out in front of others?

The third action (4:9-17) symbolizes the misery of the people as the Babylonian siege cuts off their supplies of food and water. Ezekiel is to act the part of one of those living in the besieged city. For this, vv. 9-11, plus the verbal interpretation in vv. 16-17, suffice. The last part of v. 9 has been added in order to link this to the second action prescribed in vv. 4-8. Vv. 12-15 introduce a noticeably different set of concerns which confuse the symbolism. We clarify the issue in our own minds when we realize that in vv. 12-15 the essential point is no longer the lack of food but rather uncleanness affecting its preparation, and that the place is shifted (v. 13) from the besieged Jerusalem to the land of exile to which survivors of the siege will be driven. Furthermore, vv. 12-15 center on Ezekiel himself as one suffering directly, rather than as one symbolizing the sufferings of those in Jerusalem. As a man with a priestly background in Jerusalem, Ezekiel had an intensified horror of foods unclean according to the Law (v. 14). The pathos in vv. 12-15 is thus concentrated in the priestly prophet's own sensibilities. The original symbolic action seems to be that described in vv. 9-11 and interpreted in vv. 16-17.

The fourth action (5:1-4) symbolizes the different fates to be suffered by the inhabitants of Jerusalem as the siege of their city reaches its end and the Babylonian forces mete out punishment. The emblematic instruments are the warrior's sword and the scales of justice, and Ezekiel acts the part of destiny. Some of the inhabitants of Jerusalem will perish within the city, some will perish by the sword around the city walls (perhaps as active fighters in the failure of their final defense), and some will be scattered to the wind in flight or in forced exile. Some of the latter will be preserved, but of these some will perish on a later occasion.

THE SYMBOLIC ACTIONS INTERPRETED
5:5-17

[5]Thus says the Lord GOD: This is Jerusalem; I have set her in the center of the nations, with countries round about her. [6]And she has wickedly rebelled against my ordinances more than the nations, and against my statutes more than the countries round about her, by rejecting my ordinances and not walking in my statutes. [7]Therefore thus says the Lord GOD: Because you are more turbulent than the nations that are round about you, and have not walked in my statutes or kept my ordinances but have acted according to the ordinances of the nations that are round about you; [8]therefore thus says the Lord GOD: Behold, I, even I, am against you; and I will execute judgments in the midst of you in the sight of the nations. [9]And because of all your abominations I will do with you what I have never yet done, and the like of which I will never do again. [10]Therefore fathers shall eat their sons in the midst of you, and sons shall eat their fathers; and I will execute judgments on you, and any of you who survive I will scatter to all the winds. [11]Wherefore, as I live, says the Lord GOD, surely, because you have defiled my sanctuary with all your detestable things and with all your abominations, therefore I will cut you down; my eye will not spare, and I will have no pity. [12]A third part of you shall die of pestilence and be consumed with famine in the midst of you; a third part shall fall by the sword round about you; and a third part I will scatter to all the winds and will unsheathe the sword after them.

[13]"Thus shall my anger spend itself, and I will vent my fury upon them and satisfy myself; and they shall know that I, the LORD, have spoken in my jealousy, when I spend my fury upon them. [14]Moreover I will make you a desolation and an object of reproach among the nations round about you and in the sight of all that pass by. [15]You shall be a reproach and a taunt, a warning and a horror, to the nations round about you, when I execute judgments on you in anger and fury, and with furious chas-

tisement — I, the LORD, have spoken — [16]when I loose against you my deadly arrows of famine, arrows for destruction, which I will loose to destroy you, and when I bring more and more famine upon you, and break your staff of bread. [17]I will send famine and wild beasts against you, and they will rob you of your children; pestilence and blood shall pass through you; and I will bring the sword upon you. I, the LORD, have spoken."

The general interpretation of the symbolic actions for which divine instructions were given in 4:1-5:4 is now given in the form of a divine speech. Not every detail in the instructions for the symbolic actions is explained, since many details in the actions themselves speak too clearly to require explanation. The interpretation goes beyond the clear sense of the actions, as new details of the horror which the inhabitants of Jerusalem will soon experience are added, and reasons for the wrath of God and his judgement are expressed. At the very outset it is made perfectly clear that the original symbolic actions are aimed at Jerusalem. Through this speech Jerusalem's special place in God's dealings with the world is evident. Jerusalem is in this respect the center of the world (v. 5), and all the nations round about look to her (vv. 8, 14-15). Her people have received special ordinances and statutes because, unlike the people of other nations, they have been favored by God's choice of them as his own servants. As particular servants, they have to observe the regulations which a master makes for the members of his household. Their disregard of those laws turns God's particular favor into a particularly intense wrath.

This could be said of all the house of Israel, not only of Jerusalem, but in the Near Eastern way of looking at nationalism, a nation's capital stands for the entire nation. Furthermore, in Jerusalem itself stands the Temple, God's own house with God's own specific regulations for religious service. There, that special infidelity to God which is expressed in religious and sacral ways is naturally most evident and most flagrant (v. 11). The people persuade

themselves that they will be all right simply because they
have God's house in their midst (Jer 7:1-15). It is in fact
because they are not responding to that privilege by behaving as the privilege requires, that God's judgement lies all the
more heavily upon them. By the coming destruction of their
city they will know that God is indeed their God, but that he
is a jealous God (v. 13) who does not readily tolerate the
infidelity which his own servants show when they fail to
carry out the special expectations he has of them, deciding
instead to conform to the fashions of those people around
them who are not engaged in the service of God (v. 7).

ORACLES AGAINST THE MOUNTAINS OF ISRAEL
6:1-14

6 The word of the LORD came to me: [2]"Son of man,
set your face toward the mountains of Israel, and prophesy against them, [3]and say, You mountains of Israel,
hear the word of the Lord GOD! Thus says the Lord
GOD to the mountains and the hills, to the ravines and
the valleys: Behold, I, even I, will bring a sword upon you,
and I will destroy your high places. [4]Your altars shall
become desolate, and your incense altars shall be broken;
and I will cast down your slain before your idols. [5]And I
will lay the dead bodies of the people of Israel before their
idols; and I will scatter your bones round about your
altars. [6]Wherever you dwell your cities shall be waste and
your high places ruined, so that your altars will be waste
and ruined, your idols broken and destroyed, your
incense altars cut down, and your works wiped out. [7]And
the slain shall fall in the midst of you, and you shall know
that I am the LORD.

[8]"Yet I will leave some of you alive. When you have
among the nations some who escape the sword, and when
you are scattered through the countries, [9]then those of
you who escape will remember me among the nations
where they are carried captive, when I have broken their
wanton heart which has departed from me, and blinded
their eyes which turn wantonly after their idols; and they

will be loathsome in their own sight for the evils which they have committed, for all their abominations. [10]And they shall know that I am the LORD; I have not said in vain that I would do this evil to them."

[11]Thus says the Lord GOD: "Clap your hands, and stamp your foot, and say, Alas! because of all the evil abominations of the house of Israel; for they shall fall by the sword, by famine, and by pestilence. [12]He that is far off shall die of pestilence; and he that is near shall fall by the sword; and he that is left and is preserved shall die of famine. Thus I will spend my fury upon them. [13]And you shall know that I am the LORD, when their slain lie among their idols round about their altars, upon every high hill, on all the mountain tops, under every green tree, and under every leafy oak, wherever they offered pleasing odor to all their idols. [14]And I will stretch out my hand against them, and make the land desolate and waste, throughout all their habitations, from the wilderness to Riblah. Then they will know that I am the LORD.

While the symbolic actions of 4:1-5:4 and their interpretation in 5:5-17 were aimed at the city of Jerusalem, the pronouncements of judgement here are aimed at the rural districts outside the city, throughout the territorial homeland. The speeches are addressed to the mountains of Israel. The mountains are a characteristic feature of the landscape, but they are addressed as a part standing for the whole, which includes the hills and ravines and valleys (v. 3), in the territory extending from the wilderness between Judah and Egypt on the south all the way northward to Riblah in what is today that part of Syria which lies just north of Lebanon (v. 14). As the discourse moves along, however, the identity of those addressed fluctuates. At times, the mountains are specifically in focus to the tacit exclusion of the valleys, because it was on the mountains that the type of rural worship incurring God's wrath was being practiced. At other times yet — from the latter part of v. 5 through v. 7, and in vv. 8-10 — the people who live in the countryside seem to be addressed, but much that is said there could also be addressed to the mountains personified. Vv. 11-14 are about the people of Palestine, but these verses seem to be addressed to Ezekiel's hearers in Babylonia.

In this fluctuation of focus between landscape and people there is more than mere literary fancy. The cosmic and the social were far less separate in the minds of ancient peoples than they are in minds accustomed to our modern Western European kinds of logical distinction. The earth was something mysteriously animated, and human beings felt a certain solidarity with the earth as well as with other living creatures. Human behavior was felt to have its effects on the behavior of the earth. The behavior of Adam, after all, led to God's cursing the ground, which thereafter met mankind with thorns and thistles, and co-operated with human beings only at the cost of human labor and toil (Gen 3:17-19). After the Deluge, in which the ground and living creatures suffered drastically because of mankind's *hybris*, God resolved to exempt the ground and the beasts and the birds from the future penalties which human beings would continue to incur (Gen 8:21-22). In Ezek 6:1-14, the condemned sanctuaries and altars and idols are the people's, but because they are set upon mountains and hills and in groves they are also the landscape's, and upon the landscape the avenging sword will fall. In v. 5 the bones and the altars, and in v. 7 the slain, are those of the people, but they are also the bones and altars lying on the mountains, and the slain fallen in the midst of the mountains. It is impossible to say whether those phrases are addressed to the mountains or to the people of Palestine, for mountains and people are not clearly distinct in the oracular focus of vv. 5b-7.

In vv. 3-7 the execution of judgement on rural Palestine is pronounced because of the kind of worship typical of the rural sanctuaries. The Canaanite approach to religion had never been eradicated out there in the countryside, and besides, by Ezekiel's time, the Temple in Jerusalem had been declared the only place where Yahweh could rightly receive altar sacrifice and regular liturgical worship. Idols were retained in the mountains of Israel, and the very nature of Canaanite religious sentiment and expression was inadequate for what Yahweh required. The old Canaanite religion was attractive because in its practice, human sensation was riotously indulged. People could worship Baal and his fellow divinities, male and female, and have a good time doing so. The worship of Yahweh entailed such things as sacrifice and the use of incense too, but it was austere in comparison, and Yahweh imposed upon his worshipers a system of ethical requirements which were the expression of his own will for their social relations and their relations with him. The failure of the rural population to accept this wholeheartedly has led to God's condemnation. The cultic places out on the land will share in the punishment dealt out by God when they are profaned with the consummate ritual impurity rising from contact with dead bodies. Vv. 11-14 portray the slaughter which will lead to this.

Inserted into this section is a short passage (vv. 8-10) whose tone is clearly different. It announces the survival of a remnant of the rural population. The drastic events which the members of this remnant manage to survive will lead them, at last, to some insight and to a change of heart. The language of the Hebrew text expresses their erstwhile infidelity in terms of sexual infidelity rooted in their inner being and of lustful gazing toward other gods. Exile will contribute to their change of heart, for in exile, nostalgia will bring them to "remember" their own God, who cannot be worshiped liturgically in a land of exile, but who is theirs, nevertheless, no matter where they may be. The remembrance of God will lead to the shattering of their unfaithful cast of mind and to their conversion. Once they are converted, they will see the loathesomeness of their previous infidelity to their own God. As the Lord of history disposes the course of human events and follows the lives of persons who have drifted away from him, he may determine events which pull some of those persons away from their moorings in routine, habit, accustomed surroundings, so that they may be open to a sense of emptiness and of nostalgia in which they will remember God as they, individually or collectively, knew him in more faithful days; they may then act upon that memory to make it once again a reality. That is why God has decided to bring about the conversion of a remnant from the mountains of Israel.

PROCLAMATION OF THE END
7:1-27

7 The word of the LORD came to me: [2]"And you, O son of man, thus says the Lord GOD to the land of Israel: An end! The end has come upon the four corners of the land. [3]Now the end is upon you, and I will let loose my anger upon you, and will judge you according to your ways; and I will punish you for all your abominations. [4]And my eye will not spare you, nor will I have pity; but I will punish you for your ways, while your abominations are in your midst. Then you will know that I am the LORD.

[5]"Thus says the Lord GOD: Disaster after disaster! Behold, it comes. [6]An end has come, the end has come...

[10]"Behold, the day! Behold, it comes! Your doom has come, injustice has blossomed, pride has budded. [11]Violence has grown up into a rod of wickedness; none of them shall remain, nor their abundance, nor their wealth; neither shall there be pre-eminence among them. [12]The time has come, the day draws near. Let not the buyer rejoice, nor the seller mourn, for wrath is upon all their multitude. [13]For the seller shall not return to what he has sold, while they live. For wrath is upon all their multitude; it shall not turn back; and because of his iniquity, none can maintain his life.

[14]"They have blown the trumpet and made all ready; but none goes to battle, for my wrath is upon all their multitude. [15]The sword is without, pestilence and famine are within; he that is in the field dies by the sword; and him that is in the city famine and pestilence devour. [16]And if any survivors escape, they will be on the mountains, like doves of the valleys, all of them moaning, every one over his iniquity. [17]All hands are feeble, and all knees weak as water. [18]They gird themselves with sackcloth, and horror covers them; shame is upon all faces, and baldness on all their heads. [19]They cast their silver into

the streets, and their gold is like an unclean thing; their silver and gold are not able to deliver them in the day of the wrath of the LORD; they cannot satisfy their hunger or fill their stomachs with it. For it was the stumbling block of their iniquity. [20]Their beautiful ornament they used for vainglory, and they made their abominable images and their detestable things of it; therefore I will make it an unclean thing to them. [21]And I will give it into the hands of foreigners for a prey, and to the wicked of the earth for a spoil; and they shall profane it. [22]I will turn my face from them, that they may profane my precious place; robbers shall enter and profane it, [23]and make a desolation.

"Because the land is full of bloody crimes and the city is full of violence, [24]I will bring the worst of the nations to take possession of their houses; I will put an end to their proud night, and their holy places shall be profaned. [25]When anguish comes, they will seek peace, but there shall be none. [26]Disaster comes upon disaster, rumor follows rumor; they seek a vision from the prophet, but the law perishes from the priest, and counsel from the elders. [27]The king mourns, the prince is wrapped in despair, and the hands of the people of the land are palsied by terror. According to their way I will do to them, and according to their own judgments I will judge them; and they shall know that I am the LORD."

The cataclysmic end is announced in two oracles, one brief, the other long. The first, vv. 2-4, is addressed to the "land of Israel." The Hebrew word for "land" in that phrase is not one meaning "nation"; it is the word which designates the ground which is tilled, which is built upon, on which one walks. As in the address to the mountains of Israel in the preceding chapter, the symbiosis between human beings and the land on which they live is felt to be intense enough for the ground itself to bear guilt and to incur divine wrath together with the people who live in close contact with that ground. "Abominations" in Ezekiel seem generally to be cultic wrongs; when the ground is accused of them here that may contain an allusion to the practices of a natural religion with a fertility cult (cf. 6:13). The imminent end announced to the ground on which Israel lives is placed on a wider horizon, however, in which the political and social cataclysm is seen to envelope the entire inhabited world serving as the stage of history, for "the end has come upon the four corners of the land" (v. 2); in that phrase the Hebrew word translated "land" is not the one for "ground" but the one which can be used to designate the earth as a whole, and its four corners are the earth's uttermost extremities. In this short oracle the pronoun "you" is singular in Hebrew, addressed to Israel's vital soil, until the concluding sentence, "then you will know that I am the Lord," in which "you" is plural, addressed to human hearers. The lesson to be learned from God's dire intervention in history would be lost on the ground, but it is there for human hearers to hear, if they have ears to do so.

In the second of these two oracles, vv. 5-27, the end is described with forceful imagery. The Hebrew text has suffered much in transmission here. In a few places the text defies understanding, and the translator must simply do his or her best. Fortunately, the Greek version was made at a time when things had not gone quite so far, and at many points it helps us see what has happened to the text. The section from v. 6 (after the opening phrase) to v. 9 is a reworking of vv. 2-4 with vv. 3-4 repeated almost word for word. We have omitted this badly placed alternate section from the translation above, for economy of printed space.

The power of the description does not need to be pointed out. All that gives assurance to people in their daily life, and which they naturally expect to give them assurance in times of crisis, will fail them. Commercial enterprise (vv. 12-13), the power of wealth (v. 19), military force (v. 14), reassuring words from prophets, words about right and wrong from priests, sage guidance from society's leaders (v. 26) are of no avail when God has had enough. The presence of God's house in their midst will make no difference. God will simply remove his presence ("turn my face from them") and let his house be plundered along with the houses of everyone else (vv. 22-24). This oracle reminds us vaguely of descriptions of the end of this aeon composed in times closer to New Testament times. It contains nothing which pins it expressly to the historical moment which Judah faced in Ezekiel's early prophetical years. By that very fact it is easily applicable to other moments in history in which a people's proud might provokes God to impose upon it an end which neither power nor skill nor the external presence of religion will avert.

THE TEMPLE VISION, I: CULTIC SINS
8:1-18

8 In the sixth year, in the sixth month, on the fifth day of the month, as I sat in my house, with the elders of Judah sitting before me, the hand of the Lord GOD fell there upon me. [2]Then I beheld, and lo, a form that had the appearance of a man; below what appeared to be his loins it was fire, and above his loins it was like the appearance of brightness, like gleaming bronze. [3]He put forth the form of a hand, and took me by a lock of my head; and the Spirit lifted me up between earth and heaven, and brought me in visions of God to Jerusalem, to the entrance of the gateway of the inner court that faces north, where was the seat of the image of jealousy, which provokes to jealousy. [4]And behold, the glory of the God of Israel was there, like the vision that I saw in the plain.

[5]Then he said to me, "Son of man, lift up your eyes now in the direction of the north." So I lifted up my eyes toward the north, and behold, north of the altar gate, in the entrance, was this image of jealousy. [6]And he said to me, "Son of man, do you see what they are doing, the great abominations that the house of Israel are committing here, to drive me far from my sanctuary? But you will see still greater abominations."

[7]And he brought me to the door of the court; and when I looked, behold, there was a hole in the wall. [8]Then said he to me, "Son of man, dig in the wall"; and when I dug in the wall, lo, there was a door. [9]And he said to me, "Go in,

and see the vile abominations that they are committing here." [10]So I went in and saw; and there, portrayed upon the wall round about, were all kinds of creeping things, and loathsome beasts, and all the idols of the house of Israel. [11]And before them stood seventy men of the elders of the house of Israel, with Ja-azaniah the son of Shaphan standing among them. Each had his censer in his hand, and the smoke of the cloud of incense went up. [12]Then he said to me, "Son of man, have you seen what the elders of the house of Israel are doing in the dark, every man in his room of pictures? For they say, 'The LORD does not see us, the LORD has forsaken the land.'" [13]He said also to me, "You will see still greater abominations which they commit."

[14]Then he brought me to the entrance of the north gate of the house of the LORD; and behold, there sat women weeping for Tammuz. [15]Then he said to me, "Have you seen this, O son of man? You will see still greater abominations than these."

[16]And he brought me into the inner court of the house of the LORD; and behold, at the door of the temple of the LORD, between the porch and the altar, were about twenty-five men, with their backs to the temple of the LORD, and their faces toward the east, worshiping the sun toward the east. [17]Then he said to me, "Have you seen this, O son of man? Is it too slight a thing for the house of Judah to commit the abominations which they commit here, that they should fill the land with violence, and provoke me further to anger? Lo, they put the branch to their nose. [18]Therefore I will deal in wrath; my eye will not spare, nor will I have pity; and though they cry in my ears with a loud voice, I will not hear them."

At the beginning of chapter 8 Ezekiel is spirited off in vision to Jerusalem, and everything that follows is an account of what he saw there, with divine comments, until at the end of chapter 11 he is spirited back to Babylonia and the vision ends.

Some authors in our own century believe that Ezekiel's

visionary transportation from Babylonia to Jerusalem and back is quite misleading. They hold that Ezekiel was living in Jerusalem until around the time of the city's destruction in 586, and that it was only after that tragic moment that he joined the exiles in Babylonia. We follow the majority of scholars in rejecting this view and the arguments on which it is based. Ezekiel's words addressed specifically to Jerusalem (12:10-11; 16:2) or to those living in Judah (6:2; 7:2; 21:2; 22:2-3) before 586 do not require his being physically present to his addressees any more than do his oracles addressed to Ammon, to Tyre and its prince, to Egypt and its Pharaoh in chapters 25-32. Nor can it really be claimed that the visions of wickedness in Jerusalem, or the symbolic actions and the oracles of condemnation and woe aimed at Jerusalem and Judah, would have no salutary point for the exiles in Babylonia.

Before 586 the exiles hoped to go home soon and resume the life they had known there, unreformed. No profound conversion of the exiles themselves could be expected until they realized that the wickedness of the inhabitants of Jerusalem and Judah, with whom the exiles identified themselves in solidarity, was so great that God, despite his promises to their ancestors, had decided to deliver his (and their) holy city to punitive destruction. We accept Ezekiel's description of scenes in and around Jerusalem as the description of vision experienced in Babylonia, with realistic details drawn from his own memory of the topography of Jerusalem and its environs before his deportation to Babylonia in 597.

The date of the vision, transposed into our own system of dating, is 17 September 592. God, acting through a visionary form like that of a man (cf. 1:27) and through the agency of the wind or spirit, removes Ezekiel to the Temple area in Jerusalem. There, in four successive scenes described in chapter 8, he shows Ezekiel four types of cultic abomination being perpetrated by citizens of Jerusalem. There is movement from scene to scene. In order to make sense of the stages of movement, we have to see two courts: 1) an inner court of the house of the Lord (vv. 14, 16), by which is the Temple building itself (the house), opening onto the west

side of the court, with the great altar of sacrifice out in the
open air of the court, east of the building's entrance porch
(v. 16); 2) an outer court separated from the inner court by a
wall pierced by gateways on three sides, and itself separated
from the city and countryside beyond by another, outer,
wall pierced similarly by gateways. (See at the end of this
commentary the plan showing the arrangement of the Temple compound in Ezek 40:5-42:20, with the courts disposed
as they are in the vision of chapter 8.) We see Ezekiel
beginning his tour of abominations at the north gate in the
wall separating the outer court from the countryside
beyond. To do this we must remove from the text of v. 3 the
word "inner," which badly confuses the picture in the
Hebrew text; there is good reason for our removing that
word, for it presents a grammatical problem in the Hebrew
text, and it was still entirely absent from the Hebrew text
when the Greek version was made. With "inner" removed
from v. 3, the court in question can revert to its being the
outer one.

In the first scene (vv. 3-6) Ezekiel is shown a shrine just
outside the outer north gate, in the area to the north outside
the Temple compound. Opinions differ both on the precise
arrangement of the shrine and on the identity of the divinity
who "is jealousy and provokes to jealousy." In any case, the
very position of the shrine is an affront to Yahweh. Anyone
approaching Yahweh's Temple from the north would have
to pass by the shrine in which the competing heathen god's
or goddess' image is set up. Yahweh will not tolerate such
public affront, and his reaction is announced: he will depart
from the Temple.

In the second scene (vv. 7-13) Ezekiel is taken on into the
passageway of that same northern outer gate. It will help to
know that gates in major Ancient Near Eastern walls, like
the walls of a city, were more than mere openings cut
through the wall. They were often architectonic complexes
flanked by small rooms which could be used as guard-rooms
by defenders of the gates. Ezekiel penetrates in vision to
such a chamber flanking the passageway within the gate,
and there he sees the elders of the city rendering worship to

images of animals. The citizens of Jerusalem not only worship false gods: they worship false gods represented in the forms of beasts. Worse yet, the abomination in this scene is perpetrated by the elders, the leading figures in the city's society. In v. 12 God tells Ezekiel what the leaders say, and it amounts to a rationalizing justification of their behavior: Yahweh, they say, has gone away and does not see. In this may lie a petty justification of their turning to other gods. Yahweh, they feel, does not pay attention to them any more as he should, but other gods care about them, and so to those gods they will turn. Though they are leaders in society, their religious sentiment is infantile. For Yahweh, their rationalizing and their petty religious alienation do not bear weight. He has not abandoned them, but he has decided that he will abandon them.

In the third scene (vv. 14-15) Ezekiel is taken across the outer court to the northern gate leading from the outer court into the inner court, or court of the house of the Lord. There, probably just outside the gate (since he does not enter the inner court until the next scene), he sees women weeping for the dead Tammuz. Tammuz was an ancient divinity who had become a Mesopotamian god of vegetation, dying when vegetation dried up in the summer heat but rising to new life when the fields turned green again. By Ezekiel's time his cult had spread to the Eastern Mediterranean coastal areas. The women practicing it in the house of Yahweh have obviously convinced themselves that their fashionable imported cult will be tolerated by Israel's own God. They are wrong.

In the fourth scene (vv. 16-18) Ezekiel is led on into the inner court, so that he can see the men in the space between the Temple building, or house, and the altar which is located to the east of the house in the open air of the court. The men are worshiping the sun, but the reason for the scene's being the climax in the series of cultic abominations shown to the prophet lies in the position adopted for this abomination. The sacred space right between Yahweh's house and his altar of sacrifice is defiled by men turning their backs on Yahweh in his house and turning their worshiping faces toward the sun. It is not known what the expression "to put a branch (?) to the nose" means. The scene, and the visionary tour of cultic abominations, closes with God's determination to vent his fury on Jerusalem.

THE TEMPLE VISION, 2:
THE EXECUTION OF JUDGEMENT
9:1-10:17

9 Then he cried in my ears with a loud voice, saying, "Draw near, you executioners of the city, each with his destroying weapon in his hand." ²And lo, six men came from the direction of the upper gate, which faces north, every man with his weapon for slaughter in his hand, and with them was a man clothed in linen, with a writing case at his side. And they went in and stood beside the bronze altar.

³Now the glory of the God of Israel had gone up from the cherubim on which it rested to the threshold of the house; and he called to the man clothed in linen, who had the writing case at his side. ⁴And the LORD said to him, "Go through the city, through Jerusalem, and put a mark upon the foreheads of the men who sigh and groan over all the abominations that are committed in it." ⁵And to the others he said in my hearing, "Pass through the city after him, and smite; your eye shall not spare, and you shall show no pity; ⁶slay old men outright, young men and maidens, little children and women, but touch no one upon whom is the mark. And begin at my sanctuary." So they began with the elders who were before the house. ⁷Then he said to them, "Defile the house, and fill the courts with the slain. Go forth." So they went forth, and smote in the city. ⁸And while they were smiting, and I was left alone, I fell upon my face, and cried, "Ah Lord GOD! wilt thou destroy all that remains of Israel in the outpouring of thy wrath upon Jerusalem?"

⁹Then he said to me, "The guilt of the house of Israel and Judah is exceedingly great; the land is full of blood, and the city full of injustice; for they say, 'The LORD has forsaken the land, and the LORD does not see.' ¹⁰As for

me, my eye will not spare, nor will I have pity, but I will requite their deeds upon their heads."

[11] And lo, the man clothed in linen, with the writing case at his side, brought back word, saying, "I have done as thou didst command me."

10 Then I looked, and behold, on the firmament that was over the heads of the cherubim there appeared above them something like a sapphire, in form resembling a throne. [2] And he said to the man clothed in linen, "Go in among the whirling wheels underneath the cherubim; fill your hands with burning coals from between the cherubim, and scatter them over the city."

And he went in before my eyes. [3] Now the cherubim were standing on the south side of the house, when the man went in; and a cloud filled the inner court. [4] And the glory of the LORD went up from the cherubim to the threshold of the house; and the house was filled with the cloud, and the court was full of the brightness of the glory of the LORD. [5] And the sound of the wings of the cherubim was heard as far as the outer court, like the voice of God Almighty when he speaks.

[6] And when he commanded the man clothed in linen, "Take fire from between the whirling wheels, from between the cherubim," he went in and stood beside a wheel. [7] And a cherub stretched forth his hand from between the cherubim to the fire that was between the cherubim, and took some of it, and put it into the hands of the man clothed in linen, who took it and went out. [8] The cherubim appeared to have the form of a human hand under their wings... [14] And every one had four faces: the first face was the face of the cherub, and the second face was the face of a man, and the third the face of a lion, and the fourth the face of an eagle...

Now that the cultic abominations which are the main reasons for God's wrath have been shown to Ezekiel, the approaching execution of God's judgement is revealed to him. Seven otherworldly figures — six of them, the divinely sent executioners, and the seventh, God's scribal emissary

—approach from the northern gate between the inner and outer courts which is the gate of 8:14, called the "upper" gate here because the level of the inner court was higher than that of the outer court, and the inner gate leading up into it was accordingly higher than the gate leading into the outer court from the world outside. Those who are pained by the abominations committed in Jerusalem are to be marked by the scribal emissary, so that the avenging executioners may spare them, but the fearsome six executioners set out to do their lethal work on the rest of the populace, beginning with the slaughter of the sun-worshipers in the inner court in front of the Temple building (8:16), then passing on through the courtyards of the Temple compound and on out into the city. There is no asylum in the Temple, because God has been offended directly by acts of worship of other gods in the holy place which is his.

When an entire people elicits God's wrath, his anger is directed at the people as a whole, and the catastrophes he brings upon their land will affect all together, despite the survival of a remnant. In his response to Ezekiel's anguished cry, God seems to say that no one will be spared (9:8-10), but the return of the scribal emissary (9:11) from his marking tour through the city (9:4) reminds us that some people have in fact been marked for sparing. As soon as the linen-clad emissary has returned, he receives a command to take burning coals from between the cherubim and scatter them over the city (10:2). What is the significance of this?

In order to attempt an answer, we have to note that in chapter 10 Ezekiel's narrative description of his vision has been reworked in a rather radical way. The original description of the vision must have mentioned the two olivewood cherubim standing in the innermost room of Solomon's Temple as attendants to God's presence, manifested occasionally, as it is here, in cloud and in glory (1 Kgs 6:23-28; 8:6-11). In Ezek 10 as we now have it, however, these stationary cherubim supporting the divine glory stationary in the sanctuary have become mobile by identification with the four living beings, already described in chapter 1, who transport the divine glory and who have been introduced here because the divine glory itself, ready to move from the Temple building, first to the east gate of the inner court (10:18-19) and then on beyond the limits of the city (11:22-25), becomes mobile. Much of chapter 10 is devoted to a repetition of the description in chapter 1, with insistence on the identification of the beings as cherubim. (We have omitted most of this repeated description from the text above.) In the original account of the vision in chapter 10, the linen-clad emissary was told, perhaps, to go into the Temple building and take the burning coals from the altar of incense below and near the spreading wings of the stationary cherubim there (cf. 1 Kgs 6:22; 2 Chr 26:16). In that case, the apparent opposition between the rôle of the emissary in chapter 9, where he was entrusted not with slaughter but with sparing, and his role in chapter 10 may have been less sharp; the burning coals not only could destroy but could also purify, as did the burning coal brought from the altar of incense by the seraph in Isa 6:6-7. In the present form of Ezek 10 the result of the emissary's scattering the coals over the city is not depicted. Did the vision originally show God's wrath, symbolized by the burning coals from his holy altar, descending on wicked and just alike, destroying most, but painfully purifying those whom the emissary, on his prior mission into the city, had marked for sparing?

10:4, partly anticipated in 9:3, seems to be retained from the original form of the account. The cherubim there are still recognizable as the two stationary cherubim on which God's glory had for ages been enthroned in the innermost part of the Temple building. The substitution of the face of a cherub (10:14) for the face of an ox (1:10) among the four faces of living beings was effected, of course, when the four transporting beings of chapter 1 were introduced here and made into mobile glory-bearing cherubim.

THE TEMPLE VISION, 3:
JERUSALEMITES AND EXILES
10:18-11:25

¹⁸Then the glory of the LORD went forth from the threshold of the house, and stood over the cherubim. ¹⁹And the cherubim lifted up their wings and mounted up from the earth in my sight as they went forth, with the wheels beside them; and they stood at the door of the east gate of the house of the LORD; and the glory of the God of Israel was over them.

11 The spirit lifted me up, and brought me to the east gate of the house of the LORD, which faces east. And behold, at the door of the gateway there were twenty-five men; and I saw among them Ja-azaniah the son of Azzur, and Pelatiah the son of Benaiah, princes of the people. ²And he said to me, "Son of man, these are the men who devise iniquity and who give wicked counsel in this city; ³who say, 'The time is not near to build houses; this city is the caldron, and we are the flesh.' ⁴Therefore prophesy against them, prophesy, O son of man."

⁵And the Spirit of the LORD fell upon me, and he said to me, "Say, Thus says the LORD: So you think, O house of Israel; for I know the things that come into your mind. ⁶You have multiplied your slain in this city, and have filled its streets with the slain. ⁷Therefore thus says the Lord GOD: Your slain whom you have laid in the midst of it, they are the flesh, and this city is the caldron; but you shall be brought forth out of the midst of it. ⁸You have feared the sword; and I will bring the sword upon you, says the Lord GOD. ⁹And I will bring you forth out of the midst of it, and give you into the hands of foreigners, and execute judgments upon you. ¹⁰You shall fall by the sword; I will judge you at the border of Israel; and you shall know that I am the LORD. ¹¹This city shall not be your caldron, nor shall you be the flesh in the midst of it; I will judge you at the border of Israel; ¹²and you shall know that I am the LORD; for you have not walked in my statutes, nor executed my ordinances, but have acted

according to the ordinances of the nations that are round about you."

13And it came to pass, while I was prophesying, that Pelatiah the son of Benaiah died. Then I fell down upon my face, and cried with a loud voice, and said, "Ah Lord GOD! wilt thou make a full end of the remnant of Israel?"

14And the word of the LORD came to me: 15"Son of man, your brethren, even your brethren, your fellow exiles, the whole house of Israel, all of them, are those of whom the inhabitants of Jerusalem have said, 'They have gone far from the LORD; to us this land is given for a possession.' 16Therefore say, 'Thus says the Lord GOD: Though I removed them far off among the nations, and though I scattered them among the countries, yet I have been a sanctuary to them for a while in the countries where they have gone.' 17Therefore say, 'Thus says the Lord GOD: I will gather you from the peoples, and assemble you out of the countries where you have been scattered, and I will give you the land of Israel.' 18And when they come there, they will remove from it all its detestable things and all its abominations. 19And I will give them one heart, and put a new spirit within them; I will take the stony heart out of their flesh and give them a heart of flesh, 20that they may walk in my statutes and keep my ordinances and obey them; and they shall be my people, and I will be their God. 21But as for those whose heart goes after their detestable things and their abominations, I will requite their deeds upon their own heads, says the Lord GOD."

22Then the cherubim lifted up their wings, with the wheels beside them; and the glory of the God of Israel was over them. 23And the glory of the LORD went up from the midst of the city, and stood upon the mountain which is on the east side of the city. 24And the Spirit lifted me up and brought me in the vision by the Spirit of God into Chaldea, to the exiles. Then the vision that I had seen went up from me. 25And I told the exiles all the things that the LORD had showed me.

In the second stage of God's departure from the Temple, the glory borne by the cherubim moves from the threshold of the Temple building to the east gate of the Temple's inner court, where it pauses (10:18-19). Ezekiel is carried over to that inner east gate too; there he is shown some of the most important men in Jerusalem meeting in one of the chambers of the gate house (11:1). In time-reference, the vision returns from the future to the present. The coming execution of divine judgement which Ezekiel saw in chapters 9 and 10 has not yet happened, and he is again being shown scenes of contemporary life in Jerusalem, as he was in chapter 8. From the leading persons of the city, wise planning might be expected; they give foolish and wicked counsel instead. Against two notions held by these men Ezekiel receives two oracles.

According to the first notion, all the inhabitants of Jerusalem are flesh to be cooked in the pot, in the sense that all will perish like meat, in the city holding them like a pot, as the Babylonian army applies the fire of siege and devastation. (This at least seems to be the idea, but the words of the men quoted in 11:3 present exegetical problems.) In the oracle contradicting this opinion (11:5-12), the leading figures are told that the citizens in general will indeed perish like flesh cooked in a pot, but that the leaders themselves will be taken out of the city alive and sent to the borders of Israel to be put to death there. The fulfillment of that threat through the measures taken by the Babylonians after the capture of Jerusalem in 586 is recounted in 2 Kgs 25:20-21. The slaying of the citizens is here attributed not to the Babylonians but to the wicked leaders of the capital of Judah itself. It is their political folly which will lead to the Babylonians' intervention in the first place. Moreover, the influential leaders are the "house of Israel" *par excellence* (11:5), and they set the tone for the wickedness of all.

According to the second notion held by the leading figures of Jerusalem, they are God's chosen ones to whom he has given the land, and the exiles are far from him, both in spatial distance from Jerusalem where God's house is and in moral distance from his loving concern (11:15). In the oracle contradicting this (11:14-21), we discover God's actual preference for the exiles over those left in Jerusalem after 597, and we find an affirmation of hope for a future which will lie in their distant hands. Against the accepted theological tenet of God's earthly presence fixed exclusively and immutably in the Temple of Jerusalem, so reassuring for the Jerusalemites, God declares that he assures his presence to his exiles well enough, without benefit of man-made sanctuary. Against the smug ideology of the established representatives of Jerusalemite "right thinking," sure that they will retain God's favor no matter what they do, simply because they live where they do, God reveals that it is not in them but in the exiles that he is determined to affect a change of heart by which they will do his will, so that they will be genuinely worthy to possess the land again. Those whose power depends on God's favor to their society can not count on retaining that favor simply because it was once freely bestowed. Without a continuing effort on their part to conform to his will, he may replace them with others better disposed to be his stewards in this world.

In 11:22-25 the glory moves on eastward out of the city and comes to rest over the Mount of Olives. God has abandoned his Temple and his city, because of the wickedness of the inhabitants. He has demonstrated his sovereign freedom and removed the very foundation of the inhabitants' presumptuous confidence in his abiding presence, by just moving out. Ezekiel is transported back to Babylonia, and his Temple vision comes to its close.

THE APPROACHING DISASTER, IN PANTOMIMES AND SAYINGS
12:1-28

12 The word of the LORD came to me: ²"Son of man, you dwell in the midst of a rebellious house, who have eyes to see, but see not, who have ears to hear, but hear not; ³for they are a rebellious house. Therefore, son of man, prepare for yourself an exile's baggage, and go into exile by day in their sight; you shall go like an exile from your place to another place in their sight. Perhaps they will understand, though they are a rebellious house. ⁴You shall bring out your baggage by day in their sight, as baggage for exile; and you shall go forth yourself at evening in their sight, as men do who must go into exile. ⁵Dig through the wall in their sight, and go out through it. ⁶In their sight you shall lift the baggage upon your shoulder, and carry it out in the dark; you shall cover your face, that you may not see the land; for I have made you a sign for the house of Israel."

⁷And I did as I was commanded. I brought out my baggage by day, as baggage for exile, and in the evening I dug through the wall with my own hands; I went forth in the dark, carrying my outfit upon my shoulder in their sight.

⁸In the morning the word of the LORD came to me: ⁹"Son of man, has not the house of Israel, the rebellious house, said to you, 'What are you doing?' ¹⁰Say to them, 'Thus says the Lord GOD: This oracle concerns the prince in Jerusalem and all the house of Israel who are in it. ¹¹Say, 'I am a sign for you: as I have done, so shall it be done to them; they shall go into exile, into captivity.' ¹²And the prince who is among them shall lift his baggage upon his shoulder in the dark, and shall go forth; he shall dig through the wall and go out through it; he shall cover his face, that he may not see the land with his eyes. ¹³And I will spread my net over him, and he shall be taken in my snare, and I will bring him to Babylon in the land of the Chaldeans, yet he shall not see it; and he shall die there. ¹⁴And I will scatter toward every wind all who are round about him, his helpers and all his troops; and I will unsheathe the sword after them. ¹⁵And they shall know that I am the LORD, when I disperse them among the nations and scatter them through the countries. ¹⁶But I will let a few of them escape from the sword, from famine and pestilence, that they may confess all their abominations among the nations where they go, and may know that I am the LORD."

¹⁷Moreover the word of the LORD came to me: ¹⁸"Son

of man, eat your bread with quaking, and drink water with trembling and with fearfulness; [19]and say of the people of the land, Thus says the Lord GOD concerning the inhabitants of Jerusalem in the land of Israel: they shall eat their bread with fearfulness, and drink water in dismay, because their land will be stripped of all it contains, on account of the violence of all those who dwell in it. [20]And the inhabited cities shall be laid waste, and the land shall become a desolation; and you shall know that I am the LORD."

[21]And the word of the LORD came to me: [22]"Son of man, what is this proverb that you have about the land of Israel, saying, 'The days grow long, and every vision comes to nought'? [23]Tell them therefore, 'Thus says the Lord GOD: I will put an end to this proverb, and they shall no more use it as a proverb in Israel.' But say to them, The days are at hand, and the fulfilment of every vision. [24]For there shall be no more any false vision or flattering divination within the house of Israel. [25]But I the LORD will speak the word which I will speak, and it will be performed. It will no longer be delayed, but in your days, O rebellious house, I will speak the word and perform it, says the Lord GOD."

[26]Again the word of the LORD came to me: [27]"Son of man, behold, they of the house of Israel say, 'The vision that he sees is for many days hence, and he prophesies of times far off.' [28]Therefore say to them, Thus says the Lord GOD: None of my words will be delayed any longer, but the word which I speak will be performed, says the Lord GOD."

In this chapter there are four distinct oracles on the approaching disaster in Judah. The point of departure for each of the oracles is either a symbolic action which God interprets in the oracle or a saying which God has heard and which he contradicts in the oracle.

The first of these units, vv. 1-16, begins with a symbolic action which is a full pantomime, to be performed by the prophet according to directions given by God. The panto-

mime and its interpretation are intended for   Ezekiel's
Judean neighbors in Babylonia, who here are considered
just as bad as their fellow members of the house of Israel
living in the Judean homeland. In the pantomime, Ezekiel is
to represent an exile, throwing a few belongings together
and slipping out of his city. His execution of the instructions
is narrated in v. 7, and in the following verses the interpret-
ing oracle which he is to give to his neighbors is provided.
The point in the pantomime is that the exiles already
deported in 597 need not have high hopes of a speedy end to
the exilic chapter of Judah's history, for still more exiles will
soon be deported from Judah. At an early stage of this unit's
existence both the pantomime and its interpretation in the
oracle were extended with allusions to the particular fate of
King Zedekiah, who escaped Jerusalem when the Babylonians entered the city in 586 but was captured, blinded, and
sent off to Babylonia without his sight (2 Kgs 25:4-7; Jer
39:4-7; 52:7-11). The allusions to the fate of Zedekiah and
his companions are found in vv. 10, 12-14, and their preparation in the instructions for the pantomime can be seen in
the prophet's instructions to cover his face so that he may
not see the land (v. 6) — a symbol of Zedekiah's journey in
blindness. The oracle in the text as it now stands is closed
with a reason for God's letting some of his people escape the
mayhem in Judah and pass on into exile. Unlike the remnant provided for in 9:4, this remnant is made up of people
no better morally than those who perish in the siege and its
aftermath. Their role, by God's providence, will be that of
spreading among the nations of the earth a knowledge of
what God does when his own people are faithless to him.

In vv. 17-20, the symbolic action is too simple to be a fully
developed pantomime. The point to be made lies in Ezekiel's quaking and trembling. In the oracle this is interpreted
as a sign of the fear and anxiety which the people of Jerusalem will experience as the Babylonian army invests their
city. The mention of bread and water in the initial instructions for the action also furnishes an opportunity in the
oracle for remarks on the coming famine and desolation in
Judah.

The point of departure in the third unit, vv. 21-25, is not an action but a saying current among the exiles: time goes by, and the things which prophets have seen and announced do not come to pass. In other words, you can not take a prophet's words as infallible words, whether his words inspire hope or distress. In the oracle God contradicts this. What he reveals to a prophet will soon become reality. False prophets and false diviners serve up what people want to hear, and when things do not turn out that way people are disappointed. God gives to his prophets messages which people do not want to hear, and the people tend to think, wishfully, that with time he will forget about what he once announced. God says that he will not forget, and that not much more time is going to go by before his announcements come to pass.

In the final unit too, vv. 26-28, the point of departure is a saying, and it too is contradicted in the oracle. Unlike the saying in the preceding unit, this one is not a general denial of prophetic reliability. It is not even about prophecy in general. It is the expression of a specific reaction to Ezekiel's prophecies, and it admits that his prophecies will come to pass. The people whose thinking the saying represents have persuaded themselves, however, that the prophecies will not come to pass for a long time. They have thus persuaded themselves that they have time in which to continue as they are, without conversion of life. This is another instance of wishful thinking, and in the oracle God unmasks it as such.

FALSE PROPHETS AND PROPHETESSES
13:1-23

13 The word of the LORD came to me: ²"Son of man, prophesy against the prophets of Israel, prophesy and say to those who prophesy out of their own minds: 'Hear the word of the LORD!' ³Thus says the Lord GOD, Woe to the foolish prophets who follow their own spirit, and have seen nothing! ⁴Your prophets have been like foxes among ruins, O Israel. ⁵You have not gone up into the breaches, or built up a wall for the house of Israel, that it might stand in battle in the day of the LORD. [6]They have spoken falsehood and divined a lie; they say, 'Says the LORD,' when the LORD has not sent them, and yet they expect him to fulfil their word. [7]Have you not seen a delusive vision, and uttered a lying divination, whenever you have said, 'Says the LORD,' although I have not spoken?"

[8]Therefore thus says the Lord GOD: "Because you have uttered delusions and seen lies, therefore behold, I am against you, says the Lord GOD. [9]My hand will be against the prophets who see delusive visions and who give lying divinations; they shall not be in the council of my people, nor be enrolled in the register of the house of Israel, nor shall they enter the land of Israel; and you shall know that I am the Lord GOD. [10]Because, yea, because they have misled my people, saying, 'Peace,' when there is no peace; and because, when the people build a wall, these prophets daub it with whitewash; [11]say to those who daub it with whitewash that it shall fall! There will be a deluge of rain, great hailstones will fall, and a stormy wind break out; [12]and when the wall falls, will it not be said to you, 'Where is the daubing with which you daubed it?' [13]Therefore thus says the Lord GOD: I will make a stormy wind break out in my wrath; and there shall be a deluge of rain in my anger, and great hailstones in wrath to destroy it. [14]And I will break down the wall that you have daubed with whitewash, and bring it down to the ground, so that its foundation will be laid bare; when it falls, you shall perish in the midst of it; and you shall know that I am the LORD. [15]Thus will I spend my wrath upon the wall, and upon those who have daubed it with whitewash; and I will say to you, The wall is no more, nor those who daubed it, [16]the prophets of Israel who prophesied concerning Jerusalem and saw visions of peace for her, when there was no peace, says the Lord God.

[17]"And you, son of man, set your face against the daughters of your people, who prophesy out of their own minds; prophesy against them [18]and say, Thus says the Lord GOD: Woe to the women who sew magic bands

upon all wrists, and make veils for the heads of persons of every stature, in the hunt for souls! Will you hunt down souls belonging to my people, and keep other souls alive for your profit? [19]You have profaned me among my people for handfuls of barley and for pieces of bread, putting to death persons who should not die and keeping alive persons who should not live, by your lies to my people, who listen to lies.

[20]"Wherefore thus says the Lord GOD: Behold, I am against your magic bands with which you hunt the souls, and I will tear them from your arms; and I will let the souls that you hunt go free like birds. [21]Your veils also I will tear off, and deliver my people out of your hand, and they shall be no more in your hand as prey; and you shall know that I am the LORD. [22]Because you have disheartened the righteous falsely , although I have not disheartened him, and you have encouraged the wicked, that he should not turn from his wicked way to save his life; [23]therefore you shall no more see delusive visions nor practice divination; I will deliver my people out of your hand. Then you will know that I am the LORD."

Chapter 13 contains a double oracle against false prophets (vv. 2-9 and 10-16) followed by a double oracle against false prophetesses (vv. 17-21 and 22-23).

In the first of these double oracles the problem of false prophets who deceive others by telling them what they want to hear is addressed. The problem, dealt with in several places in the Old Testament (1 Kgs 22:5-28; Isa 30:10-11; Jer 14:13-16; 23:9-39; Mic 3:5-12), has been grazed already in Ezek 12:24, and it is developed more fully here. The oracle is addressed more immediately to false prophets in exile (cf. v. 9), but it is aimed at all false prophets in the house of Israel, no matter where they may be. They are characteristically men posing as prophets who, as the first part of the oracle says, speak from the figments of their minds or spirits, not from what God has told them, and who, as the second part of the oracle says, mislead people by telling them things which make them feel comfortable, even when they need to be corrected. They announce peace when the people should be preparing for war, and like men who conveniently cover a shoddily built wall with gleaming whitewash, they make things look good which urgently need improvement. Unlike the true prophet, who works hard to defend his society, even exposing himself to danger by manning figurative breaches in times of attack (v. 5), the false prophet has an irresponsible preference for staying out of trouble. In the first part of this double oracle the divinely announced penalty affects the false prophets only; it amounts to their exclusion from the ranks of God's truly elect (v. 9). The penalty announced in the second part affects not only the false prophets but also all those who, because they put their trust in the pleasant words of false prophets, fail to do what needs to be done to keep their society's figurative walls from crumbling when adversity strikes (vv. 11-16).

The double oracle on false prophetesses which occupies the rest of the chapter from v. 17 onward exposes us to facets of Israelite life of which we know too little. There are allusions here to magical practices which the inspired writer obviously had no interest in describing in detail, and comparative material from the Ancient Near East is also too sparse to enable us to judge whether the practices alluded to here were typically Mesopotamian practices adopted during the Exile or Palestinian practices which the exiles brought with themselves. We encounter prophetesses rarely in the Old Testament. The present context should not lead us to think that Israelite prophetesses were necessarily false or evil. Moses' sister Miriam is called a prophetess once in Exod 15:20, and so are Deborah in Judg 4:4 and Isaiah's wife in Isa 8:3; in each of those passages "prophetess" is an epithet of honor, but in none of them is it evident what it meant. Closer to Ezekiel's time, we find good and honorable prophetesses who deliver true messages from God to important persons: Huldah in the latter part of the seventh century (2 Kgs 22:14-20) and Noadiah in the fifth (Neh 6:14). We must add immediately that the word translated "prophetess" here in Ezek 13 is not the feminine form of the Hebrew word for "prophet" but one which means something like "(a woman) who goes around behaving like a prophet." What these women actually did is fascinating but obscure. What did they do with "bands" and "veils" (presuming that the obscure Hebrew words mean that), and just how did they "hunt down" some souls and "keep other souls alive"? We do not know. In this double oracle's first part (vv. 17-21) some things, at least, are clear: 1) these women practiced some kind of magic or divination or fortune-telling; 2) by their pronouncements they seriously harmed some clients unfairly and did some kind of good turn to other clients undeservedly; 3) they did so for gain; 4) they did so by posing as agents of Yahweh. Point 2 is clarified a bit in the oracle's second part (vv. 22-23): like the false prophets against whom the preceding double oracle is aimed, they have failed to say appropriately hard words to those who needed warning or correction, and furthermore they have failed to give words of encouragement to those who were disheartened. The man or woman who is God's agent is guilty of neither of those failures. God's solution, in both parts of the oracle (vv. 20-21, 23) lies in delivering his people from such women, but it is not clear how he intends to do so. Perhaps by letting the victims see that the prophecies do not come true, that the evaluations of personal situations are wrong. God knows how things are, and he disposes events. The women going around behaving like prophets, with all their magical trappings and their fortune-telling devices, have received no knowledge from him, and he will somehow show their pronouncements to be wrong. The depths of human existence, expressed in the great antithesis of life and death (vv. 18-19) cannot be fathomed by charlatans claiming some communication of knowledge which can only be God's. God loves his people too much to let them be victimized by such persons in the long run.

THE ELDERS OF ISRAEL RECEIVE A SURPRISE
14:1-11

14 Then came certain of the elders of Israel to me, and sat before me, [2]And the word of the LORD came to me:

[3]"Son of man, these men have taken their idols into their hearts, and set the stumbling block of their iniquity before their faces; should I let myself be inquired of at all by them? [4]Therefore speak to them, and say to them, Thus says the Lord GOD: Any man of the house of Israel who takes his idols into his heart and sets the stumbling block of his iniquity before his face, and yet comes to the prophet, I the LORD will answer him myself because of the multitude of his idols, [5]that I may lay hold of the hearts of the house of Israel, who are all estranged from me through their idols.

[6]"Therefore say to the house of Israel, Thus says the Lord GOD: Repent and turn away from your idols; and turn away your faces from all your abominations. [7]For any one of the house of Israel, or of the strangers that sojourn in Israel, who separates himself from me, taking his idols into his heart and putting the stumbling block of his iniquity before his face, and yet comes to a prophet to inquire for himself of me, I the LORD will answer him myself; [8]and I will set my face against that man, I will make him a sign and a byword and cut him off from the midst of my people; and you shall know that I am the LORD. [9]And if the prophet be deceived and speak a word, I, the LORD, have deceived that prophet, and I will stretch out my hand against him, and will destroy him from the midst of my people Israel. [10]And they shall bear their punishment — the punishment of the prophet and the punishment of the inquirer shall be alike — [11]that the house of Isrel may go no more astray from me, nor defile themselves any more with all their transgressions, but that they may be my people and I may be their God, says the Lord GOD."

In 8:1 the elders who came to Ezekiel's house were called the elders of Judah. That was a statement of fact. They were elders from Judah, exiled in Babylonia, and since they had no real significance in 8:1-11:25 there was no reason to call them anything else. Here in 14:1 they are called elders of Israel, and that is a signal to us that in this passage they stand as typical representatives of all God's people, the house of Israel. The occasion is their coming to the prophet Ezekiel to seek a divine answer to some unspecified question which they have on their minds, perhaps a question about how something will turn out, whether something will happen or not, what course of action they should take. It was perfectly normal to have recourse to a prophet for this sort of thing, so that the prophet might procure a word of answer from God. The problem with these elders is that in matters of religious practice they do not conform entirely to that exclusive and disciplined worship of Yahweh, their own God, which is required by Yahweh himself, whom they have come to consult. In this respect they represent the whole house of Israel everywhere. God gives them an oracle through his prophet, but instead of its being a response to their question, it is an oracle of judgement with threat of punishment.

In this oracle of judgement, however, there are some peculiarities not normally found in that type of oracle. For one thing, formal elements with which casuistic law was framed in the Pentateuch — "If, or when, someone does such-and-such, then he will be punished in such-and-such a way," or "Whoever does such-and-such will be punished in such-and-such a way" — turn up here in vv. 4, 7, 9. Formulas which in Israel's sacral law express excommunication or separation from the Israelite community of worship — "He shall be cut off," "I will set my face against him," "He shall bear his guilt" — are found here in vv. 8-10. The elders of Israel receive a divine communication whose framework is an oracle of judgement of the sort one would receive from a prophet, but whose content is largely Israelite *torah* in its original sense of a response to a question of cultic right and wrong, of what was correct for a worshiper of Yahweh, the sort of declaratory response which one would normally receive not from a prophet but from a priest. As God's intermediary in pronouncing this oracle, Ezekiel shows both priestly and prophetic traits. God, interrogated about some unspecified course of secular action, responds instead to an unasked question about the superstition and the illicit cultic practices of the elders and all the house of Israel. In his answer to the question which was not asked, he declares the superstition and the religious practices to fall within the category of cultic wrong, unacceptable for a worshiper of Yahweh, and he adds an announcement that the penalty for that is excommunication from normal relations with God (hence God's refusal to answer the question which the elders really asked, v. 3). If a prophet violates that ban by giving a prophetic response to such people, he himself incurs the excommunication (v. 9).

Another peculiarity in an oracle of judgement like this is the invitation to repent (vv. 5-6), addressed to all Israel. In this, the significance of the elders as "elders of Israel" becomes clear. Their unacceptable religious practices are characteristic of all Israel, and all the house of Israel is excommunicated, "estranged" (v. 5) from God on the same grounds. The excommunication is a medicinal penalty, intended to favor the offenders' conversion. God wants all offending Israel to be converted to him and to be related to him as his people to their God (v. 11). The elders sought a divine answer. As models of the house of Israel they have received instead a call to repentance which all Israel should heed.

WHO WILL ESCAPE GOD'S PUNISHMENT?
14:12-23

> [12]And the word of the LORD came to me: [13]"Son of man, when a land sins against me by acting faithlessly, and I stretch out my hand against it, and break its staff of bread and send famine upon it, and cut off from it man and beast, [14]even if these three men, Noah, Daniel, and Job, were in it, they would deliver but their own lives by their righteousness, says the Lord GOD. [15]If I cause wild beasts to pass through the land, and they ravage it, and it be made desolate, so that no man may pass through because of the beasts; [16]even if these three men were in it, as I live, says the Lord GOD, they would deliver neither

sons nor daughters; they alone would be delivered, but the land would be desolate. . .

[21]"For thus says the Lord GOD: How much more when I send upon Jerusalem my four sore acts of judgment, sword, famine, evil beasts, and pestilence, to cut off from it man and beast! [22]Yet, if there should be left in it any survivors to lead out sons and daughters, when they come forth to you, and you see their ways and their doings, you will be consoled for the evil that I have brought upon Jerusalem, for all that I have brought upon it. [23]They will console you, when you see their ways and their doings; and you shall know that I have not done without cause all that I have done in it, says the Lord GOD."

As in the preceding section, so too here, in vv. 12-20 we find certain formal characteristics of sacral law cast in casuistic form. If a given case arises, then a given consequence is to follow. In vv. 12-20 a general principle is stated: if an entire society is unfaithful to God, that entire society will perish in divine punishment. There is provision for exception from the punishment in the case of anyone whose personal righteousness in relation to God constitutes an outstanding exception to the society's general infidelity, but even if there are such exceptional persons the exception from the general punishment will be limited exclusively to them. The point of this is that God's justice is rigorously even-handed. Those who really do not deserve punishment will not receive it, but no one will escape punishment simply because he or she happens to have good connections with someone who is on good terms with the judge. The exception made for the eminently righteous will not even benefit their close relatives. This reflects a line harder than that taken by God on the eve of his destruction of Sodom and Gomorrah, which he would have spared, at Abraham's request, if he had found ten righteous people in them (Gen 18:23-33). Similar to our present passage in several details, including the hard line divinely taken, is Jer 15:1-4, in which God says that his heart would not turn toward his people just then, even if Moses and Samuel were there to intercede for them. The men mentioned by name here in Ezekiel are chosen as examples of persons spared because of their righteousness, which also enabled them to save some others from the destructive effects of God's wrath. As such an example, Noah was known to Ezekiel's hearers and readers from the story of the Deluge in Gen 6:5-9:17, and Job was already known as a man tried and found steadfast in his own righteousness who got back more than he had lost, and who was also enabled to deliver his partners in dialogue from the effects of God's displeasure (Job 42). Ezekiel is too early for the Daniel named here to be the figure known to us in the Book of Daniel. In Ugaritic literature there was a wise and righteous ruler named Danel (the form of the name used in the Hebrew text of Ezekiel also), but the story of Danel which is supposed here as known to Ezekiel's Judean contemporaries escapes us.

In vv. 21-23 the general principle enunciated in the immediately preceding verses is applied to the specific case of Jerusalem's inhabitants, but an inconsistency enters. While in the general principle the escape of any but the eminently righteous from the punitive destruction was rigorously excluded, in the specific application it is stated that some of the inhabitants of Jerusalem will in fact escape the destruction of 586 and will join the exiles who are already in Babylonia. The reason for the inconsistency is not given in the text, but it is easily inferred. The oracle is meant for the exiles already in Babylonia. When the new group of exiles arrives there after the destruction of Jerusalem, those there before them will have the opportunity to see for themselves what kind of people the inhabitants of Jerusalem were at the time of the destruction, what their attitudes were towards God's law. When the earlier exiles have seen that, they will understand better how well justified God was in allowing the destruction of Jerusalem, and they will thus "be consoled" (v. 23). Law is law, and God's justice is, in principle, rigid. That is the point of the more legalistic section in vv. 12-20. In vv. 21-23, however, less legal in literary form and in purpose, God's freedom to make exceptions to his own legal pronouncements comes forward. In the particular case envisaged, his exercising that freedom by letting some of Jerusalem's inhabitants escape and head for Babylonia will give the Judeans exiled earlier the chance to learn how right his justice was in the particular case of Jerusalem's destruction.

THE PARABLE OF THE VINE WOOD
15:1-8

15 And the word of the LORD came to me: ²"Son of man, how does the wood of the vine surpass any wood, the vine branch which is among the trees of the forest? ³Is wood taken from it to make anything? Do men take a peg from it to hang any vessel on? ⁴Lo, it is given to the fire for fuel; when the fire has consumed both ends of it, and the middle of it is charred, is it useful for anything? ⁵Behold, when it was whole, it was used for nothing; how much less, when the fire has consumed it and it is charred, can it ever be used for anything! ⁶Therefore thus says the Lord GOD: Like the wood of the vine among the trees of the forest, which I have given to the fire for fuel, so will I give up the inhabitants of Jerusalem. ⁷And I will set my face against them; though they escape from the fire, the fire shall yet consume them; and you will know that I am the LORD, when I set my face against them. ⁸And I will make the land desolate, because they have acted faithlessly, says the Lord GOD."

In this brief chapter, we have an oracle of judgement consisting of a parable (vv. 2-5) and its interpretation (vv. 6-8). In the parable, the essential element is the intrinsic uselessness of the wood of the vine, which becomes still more useless when it has been partially burnt before being pulled out of a fire. In the interpretation, the parable is applied to the inhabitants of Jerusalem. Uselessness, the main point of the parable, is not, however, the main point made in the interpretation. The interpretation is centered on historical events. The inhabitants of Jerusalem are likened to a piece of vine wood which still exists after partial damage (sustained when the Babylonians took the city in 597) but which will be totally destroyed (when the Babylonians destroy the city in 586). The uselessness of the vine wood in the parable implicitly underlies the faithlessness of the inhabitants, given in the interpretation as the motive for their destruction (v. 8). Because they are faithless, they are useless. Ezekiel's hearers might think of Judah and Jerusalem as a vine, beautiful and fine, with its seasonal leaves and fruit, but in this oracle the beautiful part of the vine is totally ignored, as though nothing were left of the vine but what is permanent: the wood. The people of Jerusalem are thus taken in their perduring characteristics. They may like to think of their seasonally fine moments, but they are perduringly unfaithful, and God has no more use for them.

JERUSALEM THE UNGRATEFUL HARLOT
16:1-63

16 Again the word of the LORD came to me: ²"Son of man, make known to Jerusalem her abominations, ³and say, Thus says the Lord GOD to Jerusalem: Your origin and your birth are of the land of the Canaanites; your father was an Amorite, and your mother a Hittite. ⁴And as for your birth, on the day you were born your navel string was not cut, nor were you washed with water to cleanse you, nor rubbed with salt, nor swathed with bands. ⁵No eye pitied you, to do any of these things to you out of compassion for you; but you were cast out on the open field, for you were abhorred, on the day that you were born.

⁶"And when I passed by you, and saw you weltering in your blood, I said to you in your blood, 'Live, ⁷and grow up like a plant of the field.' And you grew up and became tall and arrived at full maidenhood; your breasts were formed, and your hair had grown; yet you were naked and bare.

⁸"When I passed by you again and looked upon you, behold, you were at the age for love; and I spread my skirt over you, and covered your nakedness: yea, I plighted my

troth to you and entered into a covenant with you, says the Lord GOD, and you became mine. [9]Then I bathed you with water and washed off your blood from you, and anointed you with oil. [10]I clothed you also with embroidered cloth and shod you with leather, I swathed you in fine linen and covered you with silk. [11]And I decked you with ornaments, and put bracelets on your arms, and a chain on your neck. [12]And I put a ring on your nose, and earrings in your ears, and a beautiful crown upon your head. [13]Thus you were decked with gold and silver; and your raiment was of fine linen, and silk, and embroidered cloth; you ate fine flour and honey and oil. You grew exceedingly beautiful, and came to regal estate. [14]And your renown went forth among the nations because of your beauty, for it was perfect through the splendor which I had bestowed upon you, says the Lord GOD.

[15]"But you trusted in your beauty, and played the harlot because of your renown, and lavished your harlotries on any passer-by. [16]You took some of your garments, and made for yourself gaily decked shrines, and on them played the harlot; the like has never been, nor ever shall be. [17]You also took your fair jewels of my gold and of my silver, which I had given you, and made for yourself images of men, and with them played the harlot; [18]and you took your embroidered garments to cover them, and set my oil and my incense before them. [19]Also my bread which I gave you — I fed you with fine flour and oil and honey — you set before them for a pleasing odor, says the Lord GOD. [20]And you took your sons and your daughters, whom you had borne to me, and these you sacrificed to them to be devoured. Were your harlotries so small a matter [21]that you slaughtered my children and delivered them up as an offering by fire to them? [22]And in all your abominations and your harlotries you did not remember the days of your youth, when you were naked and bare, weltering in your blood. . . .

[35]"Wherefore, O harlot, hear the word of the LORD: [36]Thus says the Lord GOD, Because your shame was laid bare and your nakedness uncovered in your harlotries

with your lovers, and because of all your idols, and because of the blood of your children that you gave to them, [37]therefore, behold, I will gather all your lovers, with whom you took pleasure, all those you loved and all those you loathed; I will gather them against you from every side, and will uncover your nakedness to them, that they may see all your nakedness. ...

[44]Behold, every one who uses proverbs will use this proverb about you, 'Like mother, like daughter.' [45]You are the daughter of your mother, who loathed her husband and her children; and you are the sister of your sisters, who loathed their husbands and their children. Your mother was a Hittite and your father an Amorite. [46]And your elder sister is Samaria, who lived with her daughters to the north of you; and your younger sister, who lived to the south of you, is Sodom with her daughters. [47]Yet you were not content to walk in their ways, or do according to their abominations; within a very little time you were more corrupt than they in all your ways. [48]As I live, says the Lord GOD, your sister Sodom and her daughters have not done as you and your daughters have done. ...

[59]"Yea, thus says the Lord GOD: I will deal with you as you have done, who have despised the oath in breaking the covenant, [60]yet I will remember my covenant with you in the days of your youth and I will establish with you an everlasting covenant. [61]Then you will remember your ways, and be ashamed when I take your sisters, both your elder and your younger, and give them to you as daughters, but not on account of the covenant with you. [62]I will establish my covenant with you, and you shall know that I am the LORD, [63]that you may remember and be confounded, and never open your mouth again because of your shame, when I forgive you all that you have done, says the Lord GOD."

This oracle consists mainly of a lengthy accusation couched in allegorical terms. Various points of accusation in the original form of the oracle have been stretched out by added details, and the end of the oracle has been extended by a supplement in which the original point of view is partially modified. God speaks for himself in the first person, and Jerusalem is personified as a woman who, in the original oracle, clearly represents all Israel. The allegorical components of the oracle have historical references. The mutual relations between God and his people are reviewed as they have been, and as they are in Ezekiel's day. Not all details have allegorical significance. Many of them, in the original form of the oracle especially, are simply colorful imaginative details which enhance the description of Israel's stages of development; their function is poetic and evocative. For brevity's sake we have omitted passages in this somewhat overloaded text which do not seem to have been part of the oracle's original form and whose omission does not remove essential parts of the entire oracle's message. The allegory proceeds by periods, as Israel's historical development, depicted as the development of a girl who is the object of God's loving care, is sketched. Other prophets have been inspired to use powerful metaphors of love and infidelity between man and woman in expressing relations between God and his people (Jer 2:1; 3:6-12; Hos 1-3), and Ezekiel will do so again in chapter 23. This oracle is more than an allegory, however. It is an oracle of judgement whose first part, as is regularly the case in an oracle of judgement, shows the reasons found in the behavior of the guilty person or persons for the condemnation and punishment declared in the second part. The allegorical sketch of Israel's development in the first part of this oracle begins with God's favors to early Israel shown in such a way that a more mature Israel's faithlessness to God appears all the more despicable, and hence all the more worthy of God's anger.

The first period portrayed is the period of Israel's origins (vv. 3-7). The pejorative reminder that the Israelites were originally indistinguishable from their Canaanite neighbors prepares the accusation of typically Canaanite religious abominations hurled in vv. 15-22. The hearers of the oracle can grasp the insinuation: once a Canaanite always a

Canaanite. Although the Hittites in the second millennium
B.C. were a well defined ethnic group established in Asia
Minor, and the Amorites a poorly defined group of West
Semites, they stand here as no more than vaguely remembered immigrant components of a Palestine still ethnically
mixed when Israel appeared on the scene. The description
emphasizes nascent Israel's helplessness, as a people which
would not have survived had not God looked upon it with
pity and decreed its life and growth.

The second period is the period which began when Israel
was coming of age as a nation ready to receive the cultural
and economic adornment which God provided in his continuing love (vv. 8-14). He entered into a covenant with
Israel. The marriage covenant in the allegory is a symbol of
the historical covenant between God and Israel mediated
through Moses.

This happy picture of God's love yields to a violently
contrasted picture of his loved one's failure to requite his
love, in the accusations against the house of Israel which
follow in vv. 15-52. Israel as a nation and a people remained
spiritually and humanly immature, narcissistic in her confidence in her own glory, ungrateful to God for his favors, and
chronically ready to turn to other gods instead of remaining
faithful to her own God. The use of the metaphor of prosti-
tution to express infidelity to Yahweh through cultic
recourse to other gods is a commonplace in the Old Testament. In a Canaanite context the metaphor drew much of its
sharpness from the fact that the word *baal*, used almost
generically to designate any Canaanite male divinity, was
also a word of respect used by a woman to refer to her
husband.

With v. 44 a slight shift of focus takes place. Jerusalem
stands less clearly for all the house of Israel and begins to be
addressed as a city, the capital of Judah, whose other cities
are her "daughters." Two other "mother" cities, "sisters" of
Jerusalem, are introduced: Samaria, capital of the former
northern Israelite kingdom, and Sodom, once the chief city
of the region around the southern end of the Dead Sea.
Their introduction makes possible a comparison of Jeru-

salem and the cities of Judah, as they are on the eve of their coming destruction, with Samaria and Sodom and their daughter cities, as they were before God punished them with destruction. As is so often the case with people who think of their society as one enjoying special divine favor, the Judeans, whether still in Judah or exiled in Babylonia, liked to think of their own Judah as a nation which was better than any other. Judah's capital was Jerusalem, David's city, the city of Zion in which was Yahweh's earthly dwelling place, a city which had survived, while Samaria and Sodom with their "daughters" had long before perished because of their inhabitants' wickedness. The Judeans are faced here with the shocking statement that Jerusalem and Judah are worse in God's eyes than Samaria and the former northern kingdom, worse even than Sodom and Gomorrah. *Noblesse oblige*; God's election of a particular society obliges that society to rise to a higher level of moral response, and if it fails to do so he will end by rejecting it with particular vehemence. Thus, Jerusalem, who stands for all of Judah, will be destroyed because she has broken her covenant with God and turned away from him to pursue other lovers.

This conclusion leads immediately, though, to a final word of hope for the future (vv. 59-63). Despite Jerusalem's faithlessness, God, her real lover, is faithful in contrast, and he will remember his original covenant with her. He will establish it anew. Future generations of the people of Jerusalem, for their part, will remember their ancestors' infidelity to that covenant. They will be less presumptuous and less insolent, and God will not hold against them the evil of their forbears. The news that the sins of ancestors will not be held against their descendants will be developed in chapter 18. As an extra favor, just as unmerited as was God's original decree that Jerusalem, the helpless Canaanite infant, should live, God will even subject to Jerusalem the former territories centered on Samaria and Sodom, to the north and south of Judah (v. 61). All depends on God's grace and God's faithfulness, not on the merits or the attractiveness of his people.

THE CEDAR, THE VINE, AND THE EAGLES
17:1-24

17 The word of the LORD came to me: [2]"Son of man, propound a riddle, and speak an allegory to the house of Israel; [3]say, Thus says the Lord God: A great eagle with great wings and long pinions, rich in plumage of many colors, came to Lebanon and took the top of the cedar; [4]he broke off the topmost of its young twigs and carried it to a land of trade, and set it in a city of merchants. [5]Then he took of the seed of the land and planted it in fertile soil; he placed it beside abundant waters. He set it like a willow twig, [6]and it sprouted and became a low spreading vine, and its branches turned toward him, and its roots remained where it stood. So it became a vine, and brought forth branches and put forth foliage.

[7]"But there was another great eagle with great wings and much plumage; and behold, this vine bent its roots toward him, and shot forth its branches toward him that he might water it. From the bed where it was planted [8]he transplanted it to good soil by abundant waters, that it might bring forth branches, and bear fruit, and become a noble vine. [9]Say, Thus says the Lord God: Will it thrive? Will he not pull up its roots and cut off its branches, so that all its fresh sprouting leaves wither? It will not take a strong arm or many people to pull it from its roots. [10]Behold, when it is transplanted, will it thrive? Will it not utterly wither when the east wind strikes it — wither away on the bed where it grew?"

[11]Then the word of the LORD came to me: [12]"Say now to the rebellious house, Do you not know what these things mean? Tell them, Behold, the king of Babylon came to Jerusalem, and took her king and her princes and brought them to him to Babylon. [13]And he took one of the seed royal and made a covenant with him, putting him under oath. (The chief men of the land he had taken away, [14]that the kingdom might be humble and not lift itself up, and that by keeping his covenant it might stand.) [15]But he rebelled against him by sending ambassadors to

Egypt, that they might give him horses and a large army. Will he succeed? Can a man escape who does such things? Can he break the covenant and yet escape? [16]As I live, says the Lord GOD, surely in the place where the king dwells who made him king, whose oath he despised, and whose covenant with him he broke, in Babylon he shall die. [17]Pharaoh with his mighty army and great company will not help him in war, when mounds are cast up and siege walls built to cut off many lives. [18]Because he despised the oath and broke the covenant, because he gave his hand and yet did all these things, he shall not escape. [19]Therefore thus says the Lord GOD: As I live, surely my oath which he despised and my covenant which he broke, I will requite upon his head. [20]I will spread my net over him, and he shall be taken in my snare, and I will bring him to Babylon and enter into judgment with him there for the treason he has committed against me. [21]And all the pick of his troops shall fall by the sword, and the survivors shall be scattered to every wind; and you shall know that I, the LORD, have spoken."

[22]Thus says the Lord GOD: "I myself will take a sprig from the lofty top of the cedar, and will set it out; I will break off from the topmost of its young twigs a tender one, and I myself will plant it upon a high and lofty mountain; [23]on the mountain height of Israel will I plant it, that it may bring forth boughs and bear fruit, and become a noble cedar; and under it will dwell all kinds of beasts; in the shade of its branches birds of every sort will nest. [24]And all the trees of the field shall know that I the LORD bring low the high tree, and make high the low tree, dry up the green tree, and make the dry tree flourish. I the LORD have spoken, and I will do it."

In vv. 3-10 there is an allegorical fable, phrased as an extended question, so that it thus becomes a sort of riddle. In vv. 11-21 the allegorical fable is interpreted. The interpretation points to a contemporary political situation whose delineation becomes the motive section of an oracle of judgement (vv. 11-15a), followed by the condemnation of the political behavior and the decree of its punishment (vv. 15b-21).

Since the allegorical references in the fable are less immediately evident to us today than they were when the oracle was composed, it may be helpful if we clarify them here. The eagle of vv. 3-6 is the Babylonian king, Nebuchadrezzar (Nebuchadnezzar) II, while the other eagle, introduced in v. 7 is the contemporary Egyptian ruler, Psammetichus II. The topmost branch of the lofty cedar, broken off by the first eagle and carried to a land of trade, where it was set in a city of merchants, is King Jehoiachin of Judah, the freshest scion of the house of David, removed from his throne in Jerusalem in 597 and taken to Babylonia, where he was given residence in the city of Babylon itself. It was in Lebanon that the great Near Eastern cedars grew, but the mention of Lebanon in this context does not seem to have any allegorical significance or historical reference. The seed of the land well planted so that it became a vine, less lofty than the cedar but flourishing nevertheless, which turned toward the first eagle (vv. 5-6) is Zedekiah, the Judean kinsman of Jehoiachin whom Nebuchadrezzar set up to rule in Jerusalem from 597 onward, a king of less real stature than Jehoiachin but a king well placed, able to turn to Nebuchadrezzar for continuing support. Zedekiah has made the foolish mistake of turning away from Nebuchadrezzar to Psammetichus for support. For this mistake Zedekiah will perish when the Babylonian army, in the military operation to be completed in 586, strikes him like the withering wind from the eastern desert (vv. 7-10). In the allegorical fable Zedekiah's political folly becomes clearer when we attach the end of v. 7 to what precedes rather than to what follows, reading that the vine shot forth its branches toward the second eagle from the bed where it was planted, and when at the beginning of v. 8 we read "It was planted" with the Hébrew text instead of "he transplanted it" with the English version printed above. V. 8 thus refers to the state of the vine as it was before its mistake, and it ought logically to come before v. 7. It probably entered the text here by early editorial inadvertence, and our reading gains if we pass from v. 7 immediately to v. 9.

This is one of the most pointedly political oracles in the Book of Ezekiel. The idea is that Zedekiah's position as vassal king, less than his predecessor Jehoiachin in independence and stature, was like that of the vine less splendid than the cedar but flourishing nevertheless. Zedekiah's position has been that of a ruler who was indeed a vassal but who had all the space and favor he needed, thanks to the political alliance established with him by his suzerain, Nebuchadrezzar. The power of Egypt cannot match that of Babylonia, and to turn rebelliously from Babylonia to Egypt in the hope of coming off better somehow is political folly. Besides, it entails a violation of a covenant oath, which in the Ancient Near East was customarily taken with each of the two contracting parties calling upon his god or gods as guarantors. Zedekiah, in making his part of the alliance with Nebuchadrezzar, swore in the name of Yahweh. By breaking that alliance he has violated his oath. For all this, he will perish. Zedekiah made his disastrous mistake because he was unduly concerned with matters of political ambition. Morality and fidelity to religious obligation are more important and since Babylonian hegemony does not necessarily stand in the way of that, Zedekiah and the Judeans should not have upset the arrangement with Babylonia. They could have taken advantage of it and gone about living their lives in righteousness. Instead, they yielded to the enticements of political and diplomatic manoeuvring, which is always more exciting, but sometimes unwise, and in this case it entailed the breaking of a fealty sworn in God's name.

To the end of the oracle, in vv. 22-24, a promise of a brighter future is appended. Zedekiah, the vine, has no part in this future. Another king will be plucked off from the lofty cedar which is the royal line of David and will be planted on the mountain height of the promised land. He will introduce a reign in which all nature will be at peace in a sort of restored paradisiac existence. A final political note is thus sounded, but it actually raises the question of the ultimate efficacy of worldly politics. In all ages, God casts down the mighty and exalts the lowly. It is he who casts down Jehoiachin and Zedekiah, and that is an assurance of his exalting the Davidic king of the future.

THE RESPONSIBILITY OF THE INDIVIDUAL
18:1-32

18 The word of the LORD came to me again: [2]"What do you mean by repeating this proverb concerning the land of Israel, 'The fathers have eaten sour grapes, and the children's teeth are set on edge'? [3]As I live, says the Lord GOD, this proverb shall no more be used by you in Israel. [4]Behold, all souls are mine; the soul of the father as well as the soul of the son is mine: the soul that sins shall die.

[5]"If a man is righteous and does what is lawful and right — [6]if he does not eat upon the mountains or lift up his eyes to the idols of the house of Israel, does not defile his neighbor's wife or approach a woman in her time of impurity, [7]does not oppress any one, but restores to the debtor his pledge, commits no robbery, gives his bread to the hungry and covers the naked with a garment, [8]does not lend at interest or take any increase, withholds his hand from iniquity, executes true justice between man and man, [9]walks in my statutes, and is careful to observe my ordinances — he is righteous, he shall surely live, says the Lord GOD.

[10]"If he begets a son who is a robber, a shedder of blood, [11]who does none of these duties, but eats upon the mountains, defiles his neighbor's wife, [12]oppresses the poor and needy, commits robbery, does not restore the pledge, lifts up his eyes to the idols, commits abomination, [13]lends at interest, and takes increase; shall he then live? He shall not live. He has done all these abominable things; he shall surely die; his blood shall be upon himself.

[14]"But if this man begets a son who sees all the sins which his father has done, and fears, and does not do

likewise, [15]who does not eat upon the mountains or lift up his eyes to the idols of the house of Israel, does not defile his neighbor's wife, [16]does not wrong any one, exacts no pledge, commits no robbery, but gives his bread to the hungry and covers the naked with a garment, [17]withholds his hand from iniquity, takes no interest or increase, observes my ordinances, and walks in my statutes; he shall not die for his father's iniquity; he shall surely live. [18]As for his father, because he practiced extortion, robbed his brother, and did what is not good among his people, behold, he shall die for his iniquity.

[19]"Yet you say, 'Why should not the son suffer for the iniquity of the father?' When the son has done what is lawful and right, and has been careful to observe all my statutes, he shall surely live. [20]The soul that sins shall die. The son shall not suffer for the iniquity of the father, nor the father suffer for the iniquity of the son; the righteousness of the righteous shall be upon himself, and the wickedness of the wicked shall be upon himself.

[21]"But if a wicked man turns away from all his sins which he has committed and keeps all my statutes and does what is lawful and right, he shall surely live; he shall not die. [22]None of the transgressions which he has committed shall be remembered against him; for the righteousness which he has done he shall live. [23]Have I any pleasure in the death of the wicked, says the Lord GOD, and not rather that he should turn from his way and live? [24]But when a righteous man turns away from his righteousness and commits iniquity and does the same abominable things that the wicked man does, shall he live? None of the righteous deeds which he has done shall be remembered; for the treachery of which he is guilty and the sin he has committed, he shall die.

[25]"Yet you say, 'The way of the Lord is not just.' Hear now, O house of Israel: Is my way not just? Is it not your ways that are not just? [26]When a righteous man turns away from his righteousness and commits iniquity, he shall die for it; for the iniquity which he has committed he shall die. [27]Again, when a wicked man turns away from

the wickedness he has committed and does what is lawful and right, he shall save his life. [28]Because he considered and turned away from all the transgressions which he had committed, he shall surely live, he shall not die. [29]Yet the house of Israel says, 'The way of the Lord is not just.' O house of Israel, are my ways not just? Is it not your ways that are not just?

[30]"Therefore I judge you, O house of Israel, every one according to his ways, says the Lord GOD. Repent and turn from all your transgressions, lest iniquity be your ruin. [31]Cast away from you all the transgressions which you have committed against me, and get yourselves a new heart and a new spirit! Why will you die, O house of Israel? [32]For I have no pleasure in the death of any one, says the Lord GOD; so turn, and live."

Despite v. 30, this oracle as a whole is not an oracle of judgement. It has some of the characteristics of an authoritative lecture on norms of life which might be delivered to an audience inclined to debate and discussion (see vv. 19, 25, 29, which, together with the citation and its contradiction in vv. 2-4, add to the "lecture" an element reminiscent of a scholastic disputation. The formal elements of casuistic law, which we have already noted in chapter 14, turn up again in this chapter: "When" or "if" a given act of commission or omission has been posited, then a stated legal consequence follows. Here the stated legal consequence is one of guilt or lack thereof, and the behavioral acts mentioned in vv. 5-18 are examples of acts regulated by Israel's sacral law. They are matters of behavior which a priest, as guardian and interpreter of sacral law, might be called upon to adjudicate when there was a question of someone's "righteousness" (see vv. 5, 9), of his or her fitness for entering the sphere of the holy. Pss 15(14) and 24(23):3-4, priestly declarations of moral criteria for entering a holy place, are similar to Ezek 18:5-18 in this respect. What we have here is a sort of lecture on sacral law delivered by God, the sacral lawgiver himself, leading to a hortatory conclusion.

A legitimate interpreter of law can introduce new interpretations. So too, and with even greater authority, can the lawgiver. God, the lawgiver, does not alter here the sacral law which he has given to Israel. He restates that law. What he does alter here is a traditional idea of the application of the sanctions attached to the infringement of that law. That idea is expressed in the proverb quoted in v. 2 as well as in Jer 31:29: "The fathers have eaten sour grapes, and the children's teeth are set on edge." The sense of the proverb is that when a father, or one generation, has sinned by breaking God's law, the son, or following generations, share the guilt of their ancestors and may have to pay the penalty attached to that guilt.

The Judeans of Ezekiel's and Jeremiah's time found it convenient to apply this principle to the historical situation in which they found themselves, with so much going so terribly wrong. They might recognize their miseries as the result of divine punishment, but the principle expressed in the proverb enabled them to find the cause of the punishment in the sins of their ancestors rather than in their own sins. The principle was rooted in an ancient view of group solidarity in which the individual's own identity was absorbed into the identity of his family, clan, people, or nation as a group having a personality of its own. In that ancient way of perceiving reality, individuation was loose and fluid, but so was the limiting category of time. The identity and solidarity of the group was not limited to that of its members who were contemporary with one another; it included all members of the group in all generations. Adam in Gen 2:4b—3:24 is not just an individual person who lived at a limited moment at the beginning of human history. He is Everyman, and both his action and his penalty are those of the entire human race. Ezekiel's contemporaries were abusing this ancient sense of group solidarity by ignoring the reality of their own contribution, as individual sinners, to their nation's sinning, while recognizing in their own historical suffering the divinely afflicted penalty for their nation's sins. Because this enabled them to deny their own blameworthiness, the penalty being inflicted upon them was not likely to lead them to their own moral conversion. They

could blame other people, who lived earlier. To rectify this,
God gives this oracular lecture in which he makes two very
important points: 1) the individual person is directly responsible for his or her own actions, so that punishment for those
actions will be inflicted on no one else, and 2) anyone can
have a change of heart or conversion from good to evil or
from evil to good.

In general, Ezekiel faces a situation in which the corruption of society, ethically and religiously, is an issue. Here,
however, he delivers an oracle on righteousness and
unrighteousness, and that is a matter of the individual person within society. The observance or non-observance of
God's statutes and ordinances (vv. 9, 19-20) is a powerful
factor in the identity of any religious group, in its survival
even, when it has to struggle to retain its religious identity
against the pressures of an immense majority belonging to
another religious system; so it is with the Judean exiles in
Babylonia, just as with Christians in Muslim lands today or
Jews in the diaspora, but here in Ezek 18 that is not the issue.
The issue here is the individual's getting it right or wrong
with God. No matter what happens to society as a whole, the
individual can turn from life to death, or from death to life.
The life and death in question are not physical but spiritual,
a life and death which amount to participation in God's
effective favor or lack thereof.

The structure of the oracle is clear-cut. After the topic has
been set up by the quotation of the proverb and by God's
claim to be master of the destinies of each individual person
in vv. 2-4, the series of behavioral examples expressed as
cases is set forth in vv. 5-18, in which vv. 5-9 serve as a
description of a man who observes sacral law and thus will
live, vv. 10-13 as a description of a wicked son who will not
live, and vv. 14-18 as a description of a righteous son who
will live while his wicked father will die. In vv. 19-20 an
objection to what precedes is set up, only to be thrown out of
court, and the principle of individual responsibility is enunciated. The second main point of the lecture-oracle then
follows. In vv. 21-24, phrased in casuistic manner, the real
possibility of conversion is stated, and in vv. 25-29 an objec-

tion to this second point is raised, only to be rejected by repetition of the casuistic presentation, in more summary form. The second objection is that God is not "even-handed" (the sense of the Hebrew word translated "just" in the English version above). This objection is no longer a matter of sons suffering penalties for their fathers' deeds. It is a criticism of God's way of dealing, more generally . In answer to this objection God points to the people's own lack of even-handedness: it is they who first shift their ethical behavior, and God merely shifts with their changes of heart. If the wicked person becomes righteous, he or she will not be punished.

In vv. 30-32 the oracle moves from lecture to exhortation. God calls the members of the house of Israel to that conversion on whose possibility he has just insisted. Not only were the people blaming their ancestors for their own misfortunes: they were sinking into a mood of hopelessness, letting themselves think that God was unfair, and that they could do nothing. God insists that he is fair, that he wants no one's death and everyone's life. For that, the only requirement is that the individual person be righteous by following the sacral law which God has already given to Israel. That may call for inner conversion, for "a new heart and a new spirit" which, here, the people must make for themselves, while in 11:19-20 and 36:26 it is God who will give them a new heart and a new spirit. In those other passages, it is God's initiative which is stressed. Here, the initiative of the believer is stressed, because the context here is one of repentance and of personal responsibility. Initiative is required on both sides.

THE KINGS OF JUDAH REIGN NO LONGER
19:1-14

19 And you, take up a lamentation for the princes of Israel, [2]and say:
What a lioness was your mother among lions!
She couched in the midst of young lions,
    rearing her whelps.

³And she brought up one of her whelps;
  he became a young lion,
and he learned to catch prey;
  he devoured men.
⁴The nations sounded an alarm against him;
  he was taken in their pit:
and they brought him with hooks
  to the land of Egypt.
⁵When she saw that she was baffled,
  that her hope was lost,
she took another of her whelps
  and made him a young lion.
⁶He prowled among the lions;
  he became a young lion,
and he learned to catch prey;
  he devoured men.
⁷And he ravaged their strongholds,
  and laid waste their cities;
and the land was appalled and all who were in it
  at the sound of his roaring.
⁸Then the nations set against him
  snares on every side;
they spread their net over him;
  he was taken in their pit.
⁹With hooks they put him in a cage,
  and brought him to the king of Babylon;
they brought him into custody,
  that his voice should no more be heard
    upon the mountains of Israel.

¹⁰Your mother was like a vine in a vineyard
  transplanted by the water,
fruitful and full of branches
  by reason of abundant water.
¹¹Its strongest stem became
  a ruler's scepter;
it towered aloft
  among the thick boughs;
it was seen in its height
  with the mass of its branches.

¹²But the vine was plucked up in fury,
    cast down to the ground;
the east wind dried it up;
    its fruit was stripped off,
its strong stem was withered;
    the fire consumed it.
¹³Now it is transplanted in the wilderness,
    in a dry and thirsty land.
¹⁴And fire has gone out from its stem,
    has consumed its branches and fruit,
so that there remains in it no strong stem,
    no scepter for a ruler.

This is a lamentation, and has become a lamentation.

We are told in vv. 2 and 14 that this is a lamentation. That is confirmed by the sentiments expressed (most clearly at the end of v. 9) and by the meter of the Hebrew text. The change of allegorical metaphor from that of the lioness and her whelps in vv. 2-9 to that of the vine and its parts in vv. 10-14 marks the division of the lamentation into two sections, related but distinct. In vv. 2-9, the lion is Judah, and her two whelps are two of Judah's kings, taken into exile in Ezekiel's generation. The first king (vv. 1-4) is Jehoahaz, taken to Egypt by the Pharaoh Necho in 609 after a very short reign (2 Kgs 23:31-34), but who is the second king (vv. 5-9), taken off to Babylon? Both Jehoiachin (in 597) and Zedekiah (in 586) were dethroned and sent to exile in Babylon. Since Jehoiachin, throughout the Book of Ezekiel, seems to be accorded a legitimacy not given to Zedekiah, we may perhaps suspect that the second king here is Jehoiachin. In any case, the statements made in vv. 4a, 6-7 about what the two kings did before they were taken captive do not fit any particular events in what we know of the reigns of Jehoahaz or Jehoiachin or Zedekiah; they must be expressions of what a valiant king ideally does. The real point of vv. 2-9 is that the Judean kings who are still alive are no longer able to do anything for their nation. The nation cannot place in them its hope for deliverance. Despite all the divine promises to the house of David, the latest kings of

that house have been reduced definitively to complete royal
impotence. God's freedom to dispose history at this particular moment is not limited by his long-term promises. The
members of the house of Israel cannot appeal to those divine
promises and expect their kings to get them out of their
present situation.

In vv. 10-14, the vine is Judah, and its stems are Judah's
kings. In the Hebrew text, stems, rulers, and scepters are
plural at the beginning of v. 11: "Its strongest stems became
rulers' scepters," while the rest of v. 11 speaks of a single
stem. At the beginning of v. 14, too, there is a single stem
from which fire went out to the rest of the vine, and this
seems to be an allusion to Zedekiah, whose rebellion against
the king of Babylonia was responsible for the events leading
to the disaster of 586. That disaster is described metaphori-
cally in v. 12, and Judah's condition afterward is traced in v.
13, which apparently refers to movement into exile, but
which may refer more abstractly to a situation resulting
from the removal of God's blessings from Judah, in contrast
with the blessed situation described in v. 10. The allusion to
Zedekiah in v. 14 comes illogically there, for Zedekiah's
rebellion preceded the events and the condition metaphori-
cally described in vv. 12-13. Perhaps an original form of the
section which is now vv. 10-14 mentioned the plural stems,
rulers, and scepters, without specific reference to Zedekiah;
the main point of that original form of vv. 10-14 would then
be the same as that of vv. 2-9, carried further. Not only are
the two exiled kings unable to help Judah: Judah is now
reduced to such impotence that she can no longer produce
any ruler, and the worst has already happened. With the
subsequent introduction of the allusions to the single stem,
Zedekiah, from whom the disastrous fire spread to the
entire vine (v. 14), a note of irony is added: it is that ruler's
royal folly which has destroyed all effective possibility of
royal aid. It is not only for the end of the two kings' rule but
for the end of kingship itself in Judah that the lamentation is
raised. From that quarter the house of Israel cannot expect
any help.

THE HOUSE OF ISRAEL'S SINFUL HISTORY
20:1-31

20 In the seventh year, in the fifth month, on the tenth day of the month, certain of the elders of Israel came to inquire of the LORD, and sat before me. ²And the word of the LORD came to me: ³"Son of man, speak to the elders of Israel, and say to them, Thus says the Lord GOD, Is it to inquire of me that you come? As I live, says the Lord GOD, I will not be inquired of by you. ⁴Will you judge them, son of man, will you judge them? Then let them know the abominations of their fathers, ⁵and say to them, Thus says the Lord GOD: On the day when I chose Israel, I swore to the seed of the house of Jacob, making myself known to them in the land of Egypt, I swore to them, saying, I am the LORD your God. ⁶On that day I swore to them that I would bring them out of the land of Egypt into a land that I had searched out for them, a land flowing with milk and honey, the most glorious of all lands. ⁷And I said to them, Cast away the detestable things your eyes feast on, every one of you, and do not defile yourselves with the idols of Egypt; I am the LORD your God. ⁸But they rebelled against me and would not listen to me; they did not every man cast away the detestable things their eyes feasted on, nor did they forsake the idols of Egypt.

"Then I thought I would pour out my wrath upon them and spend my anger against them in the midst of the land of Egypt. ⁹But I acted for the sake of my name, that it should not be profaned in the sight of the nations among whom they dwelt, in whose sight I made myself known to them in bringing them out of the land of Egypt. ¹⁰So I led them out of the land of Egypt and brought them into the wilderness. ¹¹I gave them my statutes and showed them my ordinances, by whose observance man shall live. ¹²Moreover I gave them my sabbaths, as a sign between me and them, that they might know that I the LORD sanctify them. ¹³But the house of Israel rebelled against me in the wilderness; they did not walk in my statutes but rejected my ordinances, by whose observance man shall live; and my sabbaths they greatly profaned.

"Then I thought I would pour out my wrath upon them in the wilderness, to make a full end of them. [14]But I acted for the sake of my name, that it should not be profaned in the sight of the nations, in whose sight I had brought them out. [15]Moreover I swore to them in the wilderness that I would not bring them into the land which I had given them, a land flowing with milk and honey, the most glorious of all lands, [16]because they rejected my ordinances and did not walk in my statutes, and profaned my sabbaths; for their heart went after their idols. [17]Nevertheless my eye spared them, and I did not destroy them or make a full end of them in the wilderness.

[18]"And I said to their children in the wilderness, Do not walk in the statutes of your fathers, nor observe their ordinances, nor defile yourselves with their idols. [19]I the LORD am your God; walk in my statutes, and be careful to observe my ordinances, [20]and hallow my sabbaths that they may be a sign between me and you, that you may know that I the LORD am your God. [21]But the children rebelled against me; they did not walk in my statutes, and were not careful to observe my ordinances, by whose observance man shall live; they profaned my sabbaths.

"Then I thought I would pour out my wrath upon them and spend my anger against them in the wilderness. [22]But I withheld my hand, and acted for the sake of my name, that it should not be profaned in the sight of the nations, in whose sight I had brought them out. [23]Moreover I swore to them in the wilderness that I would scatter them among the nations and disperse them through the countries, [24]because they had not executed my ordinances, but had rejected my statutes and profaned my sabbaths, and their eyes were set on their fathers' idols. [25]Moreover I gave them statutes that were not good and ordinances by which they could not have life; [26]and I defiled them through their very gifts in making them offer by fire all their first-born, that I might horrify them; I did it that they might know that I am the LORD.

[27]"Therefore, son of man, speak to the house of Israel and say to them, Thus says the Lord GOD: In this again your fathers blasphemed me, by dealing treacherously with me. [28]For when I had brought them into the land which I swore to give them, then wherever they saw any high hill or any leafy tree, there they offered their sacrifices and presented the provocation of their offering; there they sent up their soothing odors, and there they poured out their drink offerings. [29](I said to them, What is the high place to which you go? So its name is called Bamah to this day.) [30]Wherefore say to the house of Israel, Thus says the Lord GOD: Will you defile yourselves after the manner of your fathers and go astray after their detestable things? [31]When you offer your gifts and sacrifice your sons by fire, you defile yourselves with all your idols to this day. And shall I be inquired of by you, O house of Israel? As I live, says the Lord GOD, I will not be inquired of by you.

The date in v. 1 corresponds to 14 August 591. At that time Hezekiah was still being a good vassal king in Jerusalem, and Judeans both at home and in exile could understandably hope for some improvement in their political situation. As in 14:1-11, some Judean elders who are Ezekiel's neighbors in exile have come to seek an oracular pronouncement from God through Ezekiel. We are not told what they came to ask God about. They may have come with questions about their immediate historical destiny, or about the possibility of some sort of political deliverance in the near future. Instead of an answer, they receive an oracular pronouncement in which God refuses to respond to their own questions, for reasons which constitute an unsought oracle of judgement. The negative judgement is made on grounds of faithlessness to the stipulations of the covenant which God has made with his people by oath. The infidelity is the house of Israel's, not only in Ezekiel's own time but from the very beginning of the special relation established between Israel and Yahweh. In other prophetical books —one thinks of Hosea, Isaiah, and Ezekiel's own contemporary, Jeremiah — Israel's history appears as one with a good beginning followed by progressive degeneration, but here Israel's whole history is seen as one of rebellion against Yahweh, right from the beginning in Egypt. The entire history of the people of God's special favor is reduced to a history of religious infidelity.

The review of that history is centered on its early stages: in Egypt (vv. 5-9), in the desert during the first generation (vv. 10-17), in the desert or wilderness during the next generation (vv. 18-26). In the account of each of these stages there is a pattern: 1) God's requirements communicated to the people during that period (in Egypt: rejection of false gods, v. 7; in both of the wilderness stages: observance of the laws which are the stipulations of the covenant and of the sabbaths which are a sign of the covenant, vv. 11-12, 18-20); 2) the rebellion of the people which meant the failure to observe those requirements (in Egypt, v. 8; in the first wilderness stage, v. 13; in the second, v. 21); 3) God's initial intention to punish the rebellion, withdrawn afterwards by his decision to spare the people (vv. 8-9, 13-14, 21-22); this is followed, not in Egypt but in the two wilderness stages, by 4) a new divine determination to inflict on the people a specific penalty. The penalty determined for the first generation in the wilderness (their failure to enter the promised land, vv. 15-17) was carried out then. The penalty determined for the people while they were in their second wilderness stage (their dispersion in foreign lands, vv. 23-24) was a long-term penalty whose execution stretched over the intervening centuries and was actually being experienced by Ezekiel's own contemporaries. The Judeans of Ezekiel's time, in other words, were still in the second wilderness stage, or were again in that stage, despite the entry of their ancestors into the promised land long before. (It will be helpful to remember this later, when we come to 20:34-38.)

Vv. 27-29 seem rather clearly not to belong to the original form of the oracle. They break the schematic pattern we have just noted, and the reason for their addition is not hard to see: the historical review in the original form of the oracle stopped in the wilderness, and some inspired person felt the need to add something on the stage of history which opened when the Israelites settled in the promised land. The original form of the oracle reaches its climax in vv. 30-31: those exiles who receive the oracle, and all the house of Israel in their generation, are guilty of the same cultic offenses against their own God of which their ancestors in the wilderness were guilty. From that, God draws the practical conclusion that he will not respond to the request of the contemporary elders for an oracular answer to their questions (itself a cultic procedure).

There are in addition conclusions of principle which the Judean elders in exile can draw for themselves from the oracle. In the mind of God's people, their history was of great importance. It was a history of God's saving acts. Ezekiel's neighbors could easily think that since God had delivered them so often before, he might deliver them from their present plight. Perhaps the questions which the neighboring elders wanted to put to him through Ezekiel had to do precisely with that: was something political going to happen in their favor or not? From the oracular communication which they did not ask for but which they have received, they can conclude that God is not likely to send them political deliverance. They are in principle still in the rebellious condition of their ancestors in the wilderness, and the penalty for that is the dispersion among the nations which is indeed their lot. The house of Israel, as a society on the stage of history, shares in the iniquity of its forefathers, and as a society it suffers the general penalty. That does not necessarily contradict what is said in chapter 18 about the individual in society, punished for his or her own sins and no one else's, with the real possibility of his or her own conversion. This oracle in chapter 20 deals with the social responsibility of the entire people. It is with Israel as a people that God made a covenant, and the people as a whole is responsible for fidelity thereto.

God's statements about giving the people laws and observances which they could not keep (vv. 25-26) often cause the reader difficulty, as does the analogous statement in 14:9. We need only to remember that the word of God is not necessarily to be taken in a rigidly literal sense, and that it is not coolly and logically formulated dogmatic proposition. In these verses there is exaggeration for effect. The laws and observances which the people failed to keep were, after all, given to them by God. Though God may literally say here that he deliberately set the people up for sinning, his intent is that of claiming to be the master and director of all that happens in the history of human actions and events, even of those actions which amount to free decisions to rebel against him.

ISRAEL'S RETURN FROM THE WILDERNESS 20:32-44

³²"What is in your mind shall never happen — the thought, 'Let us be like the nations, like the tribes of the countries, and worship wood and stone.'

³³"As I live, says the Lord GOD, surely with a mighty hand and an outstretched arm, and with wrath poured out, I will be king over you. ³⁴I will bring you out from the peoples and gather you out of the countries where you are scattered, with a mighty hand and an outstretched arm, and with wrath poured out; ³⁵and I will bring you into the wilderness of the peoples, and there I will enter into judgment with you face to face. ³⁶As I entered into judgment with your fathers in the wilderness of the land of Egypt, so I will enter into judgment with you, says the Lord GOD. ³⁷I will make you pass under the rod and I will let you go in by number. ³⁸I will purge out the rebels from among you, and those who transgress against me; I will bring them out of the land where they sojourn, but they shall not enter the land of Israel. Then you will know that I am the LORD.

³⁹"As for you, O house of Israel, thus says the Lord GOD: Go serve every one of you his idols, now and hereafter, if you will not listen to me; but my holy name you shall no more profane with your gifts and your idols.

⁴⁰"For on my holy mountain, the mountain height of Israel, says the Lord GOD, there all the house of Israel,

all of them, shall serve me in the land; there I will accept them, and there I will require your contributions and the choicest of your gifts, with all your sacred offerings. [41]As a pleasing odor I will accept you, when I bring you out from the peoples, and gather you out of the countries where you have been scattered; and I will manifest my holiness among you in the sight of the nations. [42]And you shall know that I am the LORD, when I bring you into the land of Israel, the country which I swore to give to your fathers. [43]And there you shall remember your ways and all the doings with which you have polluted yourselves; and you shall loathe yourselves for all the evils that you have committed. [44]And you shall know that I am the LORD, when I deal with you for my name's sake, not according to your evil ways, nor according to your corrupt doings, O house of Israel, says the Lord GOD."

The oracle given to the elders of Judah in the preceding section (20:1-31) is complete in itself, but the present section, added later by Ezekiel or by someone following in his prophetic footsteps, is closely linked to it, for some of the preceding section's basic ideas are picked up and carried further here. With this extension, we have another example of an oracle of salvation or deliverance added to, and completing, an oracle of judgement. Like the oracle in chapter 18, it begins with a current saying of the people, quoted in v. 32, which is then contradicted and corrected in what follows. The gist of the current saying is that the house of Israel will fade away and become a pagan nation like all the rest. The Israelites are resigned to the end of their cultural, political, and religious identity. The reasons for that pessimistic attitude are reasons which can be drawn from implications of the preceding oracle in 20:1-31: no political deliverance seems to be forthcoming, and the curse of dispersion (v. 23) is currently being fulfilled, without any indication given that it is going to cease. In the extension here, those pessimistic conclusions are partially dissipated. Although there will be no deliverance through the intervention of a Judean king, God will be his people's king (v. 33).

Although the divine penalty of dispersion is being inflicted, there will be a return from exile (v. 34), but only after individual rebels against the requirements of God's covenant have been sifted from those who, as individuals, are faithful to those requirements (vv. 35-38).

God made his original decision to scatter Israel among the nations when Israel, after the exodus from Egypt, had reached the second generation in the wilderness; in the original form of the oracle in 20:1-31 (i.e. without the later addition of vv. 27-29), Israel has in principle never moved beyond that rebellious stage in the wilderness and so Israel, because of the divine penalty attached to that stage, has never effectively entered the land promised to the Israelites if they were faithful. Now, however, there will be, as it were, a new exodus and a new passage out into the wilderness. Israel will be brought from dispersion in exile into the wilderness again, so that a new trial can take place (vv. 34-38). When in this new trial the individual Israelites rebelling in action against the covenant with God have been sifted out, those individually faithful to that covenant will move on into their promised land, to constitute a people worthy at last to receive the blessing flowing from the covenant, the blessing by which they receive the land. Vv. 39-44 show how they will be then, when they have definitively accomplished their progress from the wilderness into the promised land. They will abandon their worship of alien gods and worship Yahweh in ways which enable them to participate in his holiness (vv. 39-41). They will recognize their faithless past as a people, and they will deeply regret that past (v. 43). God's resolution to bring them out of Egypt into the promised land (20:5-6) will at last be accomplished (v. 42). As a result, the people will know that he deals with his elect as he sees fit, whether in punishment or in mercy (v. 44).

SOME SWORD ORACLES
20:45 — 21:32*

⁴⁵And the word of the LORD came to me: ⁴⁶"Son of man, set your face toward the south, preach against the south, and prophesy against the forest land in the Negeb; ⁴⁷say to the forest of the Negeb, Hear the word of the LORD: Thus says the Lord GOD, Behold, I will kindle a fire in you, and it shall devour every green tree in you and every dry tree; the blazing flame shall not be quenched, and all faces from south to north shall be scorched by it. ⁴⁸All flesh shall see that I the LORD have kindled it; it shall not be quenched." ⁴⁹Then I said, "Ah Lord GOD! they are saying of me, 'Is he not a maker of allegories?' "

21 The word of the LORD came to me: ²"Son of man, set your face toward Jerusalem and preach against the sanctuaries; prophesy against the land of Israel ³and say to the land of Israel, Thus says the LORD: Behold I am against you, and will draw forth my sword out of its sheath, and will cut off from you both righteous and wicked. ⁴Because I will cut off from you both righteous and wicked, therefore my sword shall go out of its sheath against all flesh from south to north; ⁵and all flesh shall know that I the LORD have drawn my sword out of its sheath; it shall not be sheathed again. ⁶Sigh therefore, son of man; sigh with breaking heart and bitter grief before their eyes. ⁷And when they say to you, 'Why do you sigh?' you shall say, 'Because of the tidings. When it comes, every heart will melt and all hands will be feeble, every spirit will faint and all knees will be weak as water. Behold, it comes and it will be fulfilled,' " says the Lord GOD.

⁸And the word of the LORD came to me: ⁹"Son of man, prophesy and say, Thus says the Lord, Say:

A sword, a sword is sharpened
    and also polished,

---

*The numberings of chapter and verse given here for this section are those followed in the Revised Standard Version. Some English versions follow another system, in which what is here 20:45-49 = 21:1-5 and what is here 21:1-32 = 21:6-37.

[10]sharpened for slaughter,
    polished to flash like lightning!
Or do we make mirth? You have despised the rod, my
son, with everything of wood. [11]So the sword is given to
be polished, that it may be handled; it is sharpened and
polished to be given into the hand of the slayer. [12]Cry and
wail, son of man, for it is against my people; it is against
all the princes of Israel; they are delivered over to the
sword with my people. Smite therefore upon your thigh.
[13]For it will not be a testing — what could it do if you
despise the rod?" says the Lord GOD.

[14]"Prophesy therefore, son of man; clap your hands
and let the sword come down twice, yea thrice, the sword
for those to be slain; it is the sword for the great slaughter,
which encompasses them, [15]that their hearts may melt,
and many fall at all their gates. I have given the glittering
sword; ah! it is made like lightning, it is polished for
slaughter. [16]Cut sharply to right and left where your edge
is directed. [17]I also will clap my hands, and I will satisfy
my fury; I the LORD have spoken."

[18]The word of the LORD came to me again: [19]"Son of
man, mark two ways for the sword of the king of Babylon
to come; both of them shall come forth from the same
land. And make a signpost, make it at the head of the way
to a city; [20]mark a way for the sword to come to Rabbah
of the Ammonites and to Judah and to Jerusalem the
fortified. [21]For the king of Babylon stands at the parting
of the way, at the head of the two ways, to use divination;
he shakes the arrows, he consults the teraphim, he looks
at the liver. [22]Into his right hand comes the lot for Jerusalem, to open the mouth with a cry, to lift up the voice with
shouting, to set battering rams against the gates, to cast
up mounds, to build siege towers. [23]But to them it will
seem like a false divination; they have sworn solemn
oaths; but he brings their guilt to remembrance, that they
may be captured.

[24]"Therefore thus says the Lord GOD: Because you
have made your guilt to be remembered, in that your
transgressions are uncovered, so that in all your doings

your sins appear — because you have come to remembrance, you shall be taken in them. [25]And you, O unhallowed wicked one, prince of Israel, whose day has come, the time of your final punishment, [26]thus says the Lord GOD: Remove the turban, and take off the crown; things shall not remain as they are; exalt that which is low, and abase that which is high. [27]A ruin, ruin, ruin I will make it; there shall not be even a trace of it until he comes whose right it is; and to him I will give it.

[28]"And you, son of man, prophesy, and say, Thus says the Lord GOD concerning the Ammonites, and concerning their reproach; say, A sword, a sword is drawn for the slaughter, it is polished to glitter and to flash like lightning— [29]while they see for you false visions, while they divine lies for you — to be laid on the necks of the unhallowed wicked, whose day has come, the time of their final punishment. [30]Return it to its sheath. In the place where you were created, in the land of your origin, I will judge you. [31]And I will pour out my indignation upon you; I will blow upon you with the fire of my wrath; and I will deliver you into the hands of brutal men, skilful to destroy. [32]You shall be fuel for the fire; your blood shall be in the midst of the land; you shall be no more remembered; for I the LORD have spoken."

Here we have three distinct oracles of judgement against Judah, with a fourth added against Ammon. A sword figures in all of them. All of them foretell imminent doom. The army of Nebuchadrezzar is on its way towards Judah and Ammon.

The first oracle (20:45-21:7) opens with a prophecy of destruction by fire in the "forest of the Negeb"; the fire will consume all the trees, both green and dry. This is intentionally too obscure for its reference to be grasped. That obscurity is the point made in 20:49, which leads to a clarifying interpretation made with a change of metaphors (21:1-5). The fire becomes a sword, the forest becomes Jerusalem, and all the trees, green and dry, become all the people, the righteous and the wicked. Since the Negeb, as a geographical district, lies entirely to the south not only of Jerusalem but also of Judah as a whole, the interpretation given in 21:1-5 makes it difficult to take the Hebrew word *negeb* in 20:46-47 in its territorial sense. It is probably used here, as it is elsewhere in Ezekiel, in its directional sense: "south." Although Jerusalem is actually west of Babylonia, it was until our own times approached necessarily from the north by anyone coming from Babylonia, because of the vast Syro-Arabian desert lying between Babylonia and the regions to its west and south. This first sword oracle is concluded in 21:6-7 with a command that Ezekiel perform an expressive action which, like the oracle in its first form (cf. 20:46-48), will elicit a reaction of incomprehension (as in 20:49), followed by the interpretation divinely provided. God's wrath against Jerusalem cannot now be avoided, and its effects will be dire.

The second oracle (21:8-17) is very difficult. The Hebrew text is corrupt, and the ancient versions are of little help. Some inconsistencies within the text suggest that it has also been retouched here and there. This oracle is a savage poem representing vividly a sword's destruction. In v. 16 the sword itself is addressed. Those who wield it are left unnamed, but they are, of course, the approaching Babylonians. It is God himself, though, who urges the sword on in its terrible movements (v. 17). This text, inspired and canonical, reminds us today of the reality of God's fury, which many of us like to forget by thinking that fury is something which does not befit God, and that divine fury has somehow ceased with the arrival of salvation in Christ. This oracle lets us see the reality of God's fury, which leads to just punishment of those societies which have gravely and habitually offended him. The earthly agents of punishment may quite well be unaware that they are God's instruments. Like the Babylonian soldiers, they may even be unbelievers.

The third oracle (21:18-27) has to do explicitly with the sword of the king of Babylon. It is actually the same sword as that of the preceding two oracles. This oracle begins with directions for another of Ezekiel's symbolic actions (vv.

19-20). The interpretation of the action follows (vv. 21-23): the Babylonian army is approaching from the north, but it is still too far away for one to know whether it will eventually head southwest towards Judah or southeast towards the land of the Ammonites with its capital, Rabbah. The Judeans, mindful of their divine election, their Davidic king, their Temple, may think that God will direct the pagan Babylonian horde towards Ammon, but their expectation will be confounded because of their collective guilt, and the siege of Jerusalem is soon to begin. Then oracular messages are given, to all the people of Judah (v. 24), and to the "prince," Zedekiah (vv. 25-27), who is not given the title "king" in Ezekiel.

V. 27 is difficult in the Hebrew text. Some have suspected in the latter part of v. 27 a parallel to an equally problematic phrase in Gen 49:10, "The scepter shall not depart from Judah...*until he comes* to whom it belongs, and to him shall be the obedience of the peoples." Yet this translation of Gen 49:10 is uncertain and the reference to a messiah of the line of David questionable. In Ezek 21:27 the words translated, "until he comes" may mean "while he is coming." The added phrase in RSV, "whose *right* it is," might be better translated in terms of "judgement" in the light of the Hebrew text of the latter part of 23:24. The person who comes is probably, but not certainly, Nebuchadrezzar, whom God has commissioned to execute judgement on Judah.

In any event, neither the people nor Zedekiah can rely on their divine election for deliverance from the sword of the king of Babylon. They have forfeited their right to God's protection.

Although the Babylonian army, according to vv. 20-23, will turn towards Judah instead of towards Ammon, a supplementary oracle against the Ammonites has been added in vv. 28-32. In this supplement addressed to the Ammonites, phrases from the preceding sword oracles against Judah are put together and reused.

FILTH AND DROSS
22:1-31

22 Moreover the word of the LORD came to me, saying, ²"And you, son of man, will you judge, will you judge the bloody city? Then declare to her all her abominable deeds. ³You shall say, Thus says the Lord GOD: A city that sheds blood in the midst of her, that her time may come, and that makes idols to defile herself! ⁴You have become guilty by the blood which you have shed, and defiled by the idols which you have made; and you have brought your day near, the appointed time of your years has come. Therefore I have made you a reproach to the nations, and a mocking to all the countries. ⁵Those who are near and those who are far from you will mock you, you infamous one, full of tumult.

⁶"Behold, the princes of Israel in you, every one according to his power, have been bent on shedding blood. ⁷Father and mother are treated with contempt in you; the sojourner suffers extortion in your midst; the fatherless and the widow are wronged in you. ⁸You have despised my holy things, and profaned my sabbaths. ⁹There are men in you who slander to shed blood, and men in you who eat upon the mountains; men commit lewdness in your midst. ¹⁰In you men uncover their fathers' nakedness; in you they humble women who are unclean in their impurity. ¹¹One commits abomination with his neighbor's wife; another lewdly defiles his daughter-in-law; another in you defiles his sister, his father's daughter. ¹²In you men take bribes to shed blood; you take interest and increase and make gain of your neighbors by extortion; and you have forgotten me, says the Lord GOD.

¹³"Behold, therefore, I strike my hands together at the dishonest gain which you have made, and at the blood which has been in the midst of you. ¹⁴Can your courage endure, or can your hands be strong, in the days that I shall deal with you? I the LORD have spoken, and I will do it. ¹⁵I will scatter you among the nations and disperse

you through the countries, and I will consume your filthiness out of you. [16]And I shall be profaned through you in the sight of the nations; and you shall know that I am the LORD."

[17]And the word of the LORD came to me: [18]"Son of man, the house of Israel has become dross to me; all of them, silver and bronze and tin and iron and lead in the furnace, have become dross. [19]Therefore thus says the Lord GOD: Because you have all become dross, therefore, behold, I will gather you into the midst of Jerusalem. [20]As men gather silver and bronze and iron and lead and tin into a furnace, to blow the fire upon it in order to melt it; so I will gather you in my anger and in my wrath, and I will put you in and melt you. [21]I will gather you and blow upon you with the fire of my wrath, and you shall be melted in the midst of it. [22]As silver is melted in a furnace, so you shall be melted in the midst of it; and you shall know that I the Lord have poured out my wrath upon you."

[23]And the word of the LORD came to me: [24]"Son of man, say to her, You are a land that is not cleansed, or rained upon in the day of indignation. [25]Her princes in the midst of her are like a roaring lion tearing the prey; they have devoured human lives; they have taken treasure and precious things; they have made many widows in the midst of her. [26]Her priests have done violence to my law and have profaned my holy things; they have made no distinction between the holy and the common, neither have they taught the difference between the unclean and the clean, and they have disregarded my sabbaths, so that I am profaned among them. [27]Her princes in the midst of her are like wolves tearing the prey, shedding blood, destroying lives to get dishonest gain. [28]And her prophets have daubed for them with whitewash, seeing false visions and divining lies for them, saying, 'Thus says the Lord GOD,' when the LORD has not spoken. [29]The people of the land have practiced extortion and committed robbery; they have oppressed the poor and needy, and

> have extorted from the sojourner without redress. [30]And
> I sought for a man among them who should build up the
> wall and stand in the breach before me for the land, that I
> should not destroy it; but I found none. [31]Therefore I
> have poured out my indignation upon them; I have con-
> sumed them with the fire of my wrath; their way have I
> requited upon their heads, says the Lord GOD."

In this section there are three distinct oracles having in
common their severe and total judgement on people and the
role which metaphorical or real uncleanness or trash plays
to some extent in all of them.

The first oracle (vv. 1-16) is directed against the city of
Jerusalem, a "bloody city" (v. 2). Unclean blood and the less
physical notion of defilement are unifying themes. The royal
family and the ordinary citizens shed blood directly, or
cause others to do so. Bloodshed for bribery is associated
with other crimes involving money (v. 12). The defilements
incurred by violation of sexual taboos and, more metaphor-
ically, by idolatry (itself often represented in the Old Testament as a form of harlotry with gods other than Yahweh)
are among the indictments here. Violation of the sexual
taboos, and all the other crimes mentioned, are among those
forbidden by the sacral law which God has given to Israel.
Their violation thus renders profane what should be holy by
extension of God's holiness. The oracle in the strict sense
ends with v. 12, but the concluding expansion which follows
remains close to the ideas of the oracle. If in v. 16 we accept
the English rendering of the Revised Standard Version
(printed above), which, with good critical reasons, follows
the ancient versions instead of the received Hebrew text,
then the defilement of what is holy has been carried over to
God himself: some of the filth of the people has externally
defiled God, the very center and source of all holiness. The
defilements of which rulers and people are guilty are not
accidental defilements incurred by thoughtless contact with
the unclean. They are fully deliberate defilements. God will
cleanse his holy people, now deeply defiled, by purifying
them as though by fire and by dispersing them among the

nations, even though this will allow the pagan nations to see the opprobrium inflicted on the God of Israel by the people of his holy city.

The second oracle (vv. 17-22) is directed against all the house of Israel, all Israelites everywhere. They are compared to dross, the metallic refuse left over in the process of refining silver. The crucible in which they are heated by the fire of God's anger is Jerusalem. The oracle might thus seem to be directed more particularly against the inhabitants of the capital city, and so it is, but again we might remember the fluidity of identity by which the capital city of a nation is to some extent identified with the entire nation in the Oriental mind. Among the people of the house of Israel there is no longer any silver. All belong to the category of dross, which is useless and is thrown away. In the case of the inhabitants of Jerusalem and all the house of Israel, the dross is not discarded and dumped until it has been subjected to a final violent heating. The tragedy lies in the fact that the house of Israel should contain God's silver, but it now contains none. God's disappointed anger is unmitigated.

The third oracle (vv. 23-31) is directed against the land —realistically the land of Judah, more idealistically all the land of Israel. The land suffers because of the behavior of its inhabitants. (On the symbiosis which the ancient Israelites felt between the land or ground and the people who lived on it, a symbiosis which allowed the people's guilt and punishment to flow over the land, see the commentary on 6:1-14.) God punishes the land by withholding rain from it, and, if we follow the Hebrew text of v. 24, this divine curse keeps the rain from washing away the uncleanness which is the land's because of the wickedness of its people. The influential classes of society are mentioned, with the sinful behavior characteristic of each. Rulers abuse their power by confiscating precious belongings and by taking measures which lead to the loss of citizens' lives. Priests, responsible for vigilant separation of the holy from the profane, the ritually clean from the ritually unclean, holy time like that of the sabbath from common time used for secular work, have neglected their responsibilities; they are thus responsible for violations of the holiness of God, the source of holiness. Prophets, who are supposed to communicate the mind of God, even when it is unpleasant and unwelcome, follow the easier course of telling people what they want to hear, even when it is false. The people of the land, i.e. the active members of those families who control the countryside, exploit and oppress, instead of protecting and helping. Not one exception has been found, and the universal wickedness in the land is requited with a punishment which affects the land itself in cosmic ways.

SAMARIA AND JERUSALEM, THE TWO HARLOTS 23:1-49

23 The word of the LORD came to me: [2]"Son of man, there were two women, the daughters of one mother; [3]they played the harlot in Egypt; they played the harlot in their youth; there their breasts were pressed and their virgin bosoms handled. [4]Oholah was the name of the elder and Oholibah the name of her sister. They became mine, and they bore sons and daughters. As for their names, Oholah is Samaria, and Oholibah is Jerusalem.

[5]"Oholah played the harlot while she was mine; and she doted on her lovers the Assyrians, [6]warriors clothed in purple, governors and commanders, all of them desirable young men, horsemen riding on horses. [7]She bestowed her harlotries upon them, the choicest men of Assyria all of them; and she defiled herself with all the idols of every one on whom she doted. [8]She did not give up her harlotry which she had practiced since her days in Egypt; for in her youth men had lain with her and handled her virgin bosom and poured out their lust upon her. [9]Therefore I delivered her into the hands of her lovers, into the hands of the Assyrians, upon whom she doted. [10]These uncovered her nakedness; they seized her sons and her daughters; and her they slew with the sword; and she became a byword among women, when judgment had been executed upon her.

[11]"Her sister Oholibah saw this, yet she was more

corrupt than she in her doting and in her harlotry, which was worse than that of her sister. [12]She doted upon the Assyrians, governors and commanders, warriors clothed in full armor, horsemen riding on horses, all of them desirable young men. [13]And I saw that she was defiled; they both took the same way. [14]But she carried her harlotry further; she saw men portrayed upon the wall, the images of the Chaldeans portrayed in vermilion, [15]girded with belts on their loins, with flowing turbans on their heads, all of them looking like officers, a picture of Babylonians whose native land was Chaldea. [16]When she saw them she doted upon them, and sent messengers to them in Chaldea. [17]And the Babylonians came to her into the bed of love, and they defiled her with their lust; and after she was polluted by them, she turned from them in disgust. [18]When she carried on her harlotry so openly and flaunted her nakedness, I turned in disgust from her, as I had turned from her sister. [19]Yet she increased her harlotry, remembering the days of her youth, when she played the harlot in the land of Egypt [20]and doted upon her paramours there, whose members were like those of asses, and whose issue was like that of horses. [21]Thus you longed for the lewdness of your youth, when the Egyptians handled your bosom and pressed your young breasts."

[22]Therefore, O Oholibah, thus says the Lord GOD: "Behold, I will rouse against you your lovers from whom you turned in disgust, and I will bring them against you from every side: [23]the Babylonians and all the Chaldeans, Pekod and Shoa and Koa, and all the Assyrians with them, desirable young men, governors and commanders all of them, officers and warriors, all of them riding on horses. [24]And they shall come against you from the north with chariots and wagons and a host of peoples; they shall set themselves against you on every side with buckler, shield, and helmet, and I will commit the judgment to them, and they shall judge you according to their judgements. [25]And I will direct my indignation against you, that they may deal with you in fury. They shall cut off

your nose and your ears, and your survivors shall fall by the sword. They shall seize your sons and your daughters, and your survivors shall be devoured by fire. [26]They shall also strip you of your clothes and take away your fine jewels. [27]Thus I will put an end to your lewdness and your harlotry brought from the land of Egypt; so that you shall not lift up your eyes to the Egyptians or remember them any more. [28]For thus says the Lord GOD: Behold, I will deliver you into the hands of those whom you hate, into the hands of those from whom you turned in disgust; [29]and they shall deal with you in hatred, and take away all the fruit of your labor, and leave you naked and bare, and the nakedness of your harlotry shall be uncovered. Your lewdness and your harlotry [30]have brought this upon you, because you played the harlot with the nations, and polluted yourself with their idols. [31]You have gone the way of your sister; therefore I will give her cup into your hand. [32]Thus says the Lord GOD:

"You shall drink your sister's cup
    which is deep and large;
you shall be laughed at and held in derision,
    for it contains much;
[33]you will be filled with drunkenness and sorrow.
A cup of horror and desolation,
    is the cup of your sister Samaria;
[34]you shall drink it and drain it out,
    and pluck out your hair,
    and tear your breasts;
for I have spoken, says the Lord GOD. [35]Therefore thus says the Lord GOD: Because you have forgotten me and cast me behind your back, therefore bear the consequences of your lewdness and harlotry." . . .

This chapter and chapter 16 are similar. Both are oracles of judgement on capital cities representing their respective nations. In both, the capital cities are personified as women, and their relations with foreign nations and the gods of those nations are represented allegorically as harlotry, matrimonial infidelity to a proper husband and master who

is Yahweh. In both, an original oracle has been supplemented and extended. While chapter 16 dealt with Jerusalem alone, there are two capital cities in chapter 23:
Samaria, capital of the former Israelite northern kingdom,
and Jerusalem, capital of Judah. The accusations proceed
by historical stages and they are made in allegorical fashion.
In this chapter, the allegorical imagery is thinner than it is in
chapter 16; political and cultural history lies nearer the
surface.

While in chapter 16 God's love and care for his chosen
people was included, the only divine attitude shown here is
anger in the face of the relations of the two allegorical sisters
with pagan nations and the gods. Both of the unfaithful
sisters, Oholah (Samaria with the northern kingdom) and
Oholibah (Jerusalem with Judah) share in the infidelity of
the first historical stage, in Egypt (v. 3), before the historical
division of Israel into two separate kingdoms was effected
after the death of Solomon in the latter part of the tenth
century. Mention of that early infidelity in Egypt is not
without significance. The occasion for this oracle was evidently Zedekiah's currying favor with Egypt in the hope of
receiving Egyptian aid and support, in his bid for independence from Babylonian suzerainty (v. 17 end, vv. 19-21, 27), a
rebellious bid which led the Babylonians to undertake the
punitive invasion of Judah which ended in the destruction
of Jerusalem in 586. In the oracle, the infidelity of the
chosen people in Egypt long ago, before the exodus,
becomes existentially significant because it is seen as a kind
of "original sin" of all Israel. Because all Israel at the dawn
of its history turned from Yahweh to the Egyptians and their
gods, the tendency to repeat that original infidelity runs
through the rest of Israel's history right down to Zedekiah's
reign, when tendency turns to action.

The accusations against the two sisters independently
follow. Oholah (Samaria) is accused of turning from Yahweh to the Assyrians and their gods, a sin for which Yahweh
brought about the end of the northern kingdom, consum-
mated when the Assyrians took Samaria in 722 (vv. 5-10).
More attention is given to Oholibah (Jerusalem, whose end

was drawing near when the oracle was given). Oholibah is accused of her dalliance with Assyria off and on in the eighth and seventh centuries, then with Babylonia much more recently, and finally, at the time of the oracle's delivery, with Egypt (vv. 11-21). Although it is not accurate to say that the native land of all the Babylonians was Chaldea near the head of the Persian Gulf (v. 15), Chaldeans and other ethnic Arameans were numerous in Babylonia by the time of Ezekiel and his fellow exiles, and the ruling dynasty in Babylon was itself of Chaldean origin. The impending punishment of Jerusalem is announced in frightening terms in vv. 22-27. Vengeance will be wrought by those Babylonians from whom fickle Jerusalem has turned towards Egypt, but the punishment will be a punishment of that political "original sin" which marks the history of the house of Israel: apostasy from political obedience to Yahweh's will and from exclusive worship of Yahweh, with Egypt as the dangerously treacherous lodestar.

With the new messenger formula of v. 28 (after the first such formula in v. 22), a section begins which supplements the basic oracle of vv. 1-27. In vv. 28-35 we find repetition of what we have already seen in the basic oracle, with minor alterations. The idea that turning towards pagan nations includes the infidelity of turning towards their gods is made explicit (v. 30). Jerusalem (Oholibah) has turned to Babylon, and then away from Babylon to Egypt, just as Samaria (Oholah) earlier turned to Assyria and then away from Assyria; Jerusalem will suffer the same fate as Samaria by being ravished by the very nation from which she turned away (vv. 31-34). The ravishing is ultimately God's doing, a punishment for forgetting God. To ignore God's political will and to practice the cult of foreign gods is indeed to forget God (v. 35). Fidelity to God is an absolute requirement. It comes before the expediencies of political alliances with pagan states. Vv. 36-49 (omitted from the text printed above) contain more supplementary material, but the material is not very well unified, the text is disturbed, and the inconsistencies are several; hence, we have made the decision not to consider those verses here.

THE BLOOD-STAINED POT
24:1-14

24 In the ninth year, in the tenth month, on the tenth day of the month, the word of the LORD came to me: [2]"Son of man, write down the name of this day, this very day. The king of Babylon has laid siege to Jerusalem this very day. [3]And utter an allegory to the rebellious house and say to them, Thus says the Lord GOD:

Set on the pot, set it on,
>   pour in water also;
[4]put in it the pieces of flesh,
>   all the good pieces, the thigh and the shoulder;
>   fill it with choice bones.
[5]Take the choicest one of the flock,
>   pile the logs under it;
> boil its pieces,
>   seethe also its bones in it.

[6]"Therefore thus says the Lord GOD: Woe to the bloody city, to the pot whose rust is in it, and whose rust has not gone out of it! Take out of it piece after piece, without making any choice. [7]For the blood she has shed is still in the midst of her; she put it on the bare rock, she did not pour it upon the ground to cover it with dust. [8]To rouse my wrath, to take vengeance, I have set on the bare rock the blood she has shed, that it may not be covered. [9]Therefore thus says the Lord GOD: Woe to the bloody city! I also will make the pile great. [10]Heap on the logs, kindle the fire, boil well the flesh, and empty out the broth, and let the bones be burned up. [11]Then set it empty upon the coals, that it may become hot, and its copper may burn, that its filthiness may be melted in it, its rust consumed. [12]In vain I have wearied myself; its thick rust does not go out of it by fire. [13]Its rust is your filthy lewdness. Because I would have cleansed you and you were not cleansed from your filthiness, you shall not be cleansed any more till I have satisfied my fury upon you. [14]I the LORD have spoken; it shall come to pass, I will do it; I will not go back, I will not spare, I will not repent;

according to your ways and your doings I will judge you,
says the Lord GOD."

The date given in v. 1 is the equivalent of our 15 January
588. The occasion is the beginning of the siege of Jerusalem
begun by Nebuchadrezzar's orders. On this fateful occasion
Ezekiel is given the present oracle. The oracle begins with an
"allegory" or parable (vv. 3-5) which shows some untypical
features. It takes the form not of a story or of a gnomic
saying but rather of a series of imperatives by which directions are given for preparing a pot or cauldron of broth and
cooking it. The allegorical references are obscure enough to
need an interpretation. An interpretation does follow in vv.
6-14, but as an interpretation this too is somewhat unusual.
It adds new allegorical details absent from the allegory of
vv. 3-5, the most significant of them being the rust symbolizing blood in vv. 6-8 (verses which may have been added
secondarily to expand the interpretation's original form).
The allegory itself is extended inside the interpretation, with
further instructions to the cook in vv. 10-11. In actual fact,
what the text of v. 3 calls an allegory or parable is a set of
instructions for a symbolic action not carried out, pointing
allegorically to realities which will come to pass, and the
interpretation which follows in vv. 6-14 is basically an oracle
of judgement and threat in which God announces meta-
phorically the punishment of the inhabitants of Jerusalem
in the misery of the siege and the horror of the city's ultimate
destruction.

The solution of most of the allegorical details is left to the
interpretative imagination of the hearers (but not every
detail has an allegorical function). The pot is Jerusalem. The
pieces of meat are the inhabitants, including the choicest
people of Judah. The rust is the blood whose sinful shedding
in the city has so defiled the city that it can be removed only
by the city's destruction. Behind vv. 7-8 is the idea that
blood cries to God for vengeance unless it has been covered
by soil (cf. Gen 4:10; 37:26; Job 16:18; Isa 26:21). The cook
who will accomplish that desperate and final cleansing after
cooking the flesh and pouring out all that is inside the pot is

the Babylonian army. It is God who gives the instructions ending with those for the violent treatment of the pot itself. Jerusalem, the pot, may be the city of God, but it is so deeply stained by the wickedness of its inhabitants that God must do violence to it in order to scour off the stain that cries to him for vengeance.

EZEKIEL GRIEVES BUT DOES NOT MOURN
24:15-27

[15]Also the word of the LORD came to me: [16]"Son of man, behold, I am about to take the delight of your eyes away from you at a stroke; yet you shall not mourn or weep nor shall your tears run down. [17]Sigh, but not aloud; make no mourning for the dead. Bind on your turban, and put your shoes on your feet; do not cover your lips, nor eat the bread of mourners." [18]So I spoke to the people in the morning, and at evening my wife died. And on the next morning I did as I was commanded.

[19]And the people said to me, "Will you not tell us what these things mean for us, that you are acting thus?" [20]Then I said to them, "The word of the LORD came to me: [21]"Say to the house of Israel, Thus says the Lord GOD: Behold, I will profane my sanctuary, the pride of your power, the delight of your eyes, and the desire of your soul; and your sons and your daughters whom you left behind shall fall by the sword. [22]And you shall do as I have done; you shall not cover your lips, nor eat the bread of mourners. [23]Your turbans shall be on your heads and your shoes on your feet; you shall not mourn or weep, but you shall pine away in your iniquities and groan to one another. [24]Thus shall Ezekiel be to you a sign; according to all that he has done you shall do. When this comes, then you will know that I am the Lord GOD.'

[25]"And you, son of man on the day when I take from them their stronghold, their joy and glory, the delight of their eyes and their heart's desire, and also their sons and daughters, [26]on that day a fugitive will come to you to

report to you the news. [27]On that day your mouth will be
opened to the fugitive, and you shall speak and be no
longer dumb. So you will be a sign to them; and they will
know that I am the LORD."

In vv. 15-24 we see again, as we saw in chapter 12, a
formal structure consisting of instructions for symbolic
actions (vv. 16-17), followed by a notice of their being
carried out by the prophet (v. 18), whose resulting behavior
is puzzling enough to elicit from its observers a question
about its significance (v. 19), which leads to the divinely
given interpretation (vv. 20-24). The statement at the beginning of v. 18 that Ezekiel spoke to the people in the morning,
before his wife actually died, anticipates what could not
happen until after she had died; that statement may have
been placed where it is out of editorial inadvertence.

God uses the sudden death of Ezekiel's beloved wife as an
event on which to base the components of the oracle. Ezekiel's divinely enjoined omission of the customary rites of
mourning constitutes the symbolic action, really an act of
omission of what was universally expected. The interpretation takes the death of Ezekiel's wife itself as a sort of
symbol of the dissolution of Jerusalem, and takes Ezekiel's
prescribed external reaction (the omission of all formal
mourning) as a symbol of what should be the external
reaction of the exilic hearers when they learn of Jerusalem's
fate. This is not all, however. Ezekiel's own natural grief,
which is not at all a matter of prescribed behavior, is given
symbolic value, too, as a symbol of the exiles' interior grief
over the loss of their Temple and of their loved ones. Ezekiel
as a person, with his very human emotions, thus becomes a
personal sign to his fellow exiles (v. 24). The fact that in the
divine message of vv. 21-24, in which God, quoted verbatim,
speaks in the first person, Ezekiel suddenly speaks in the
first person in vv. 22-23 has caused trouble for modern
readers with a critical eye. Perhaps the explanation of this
shift from God's words to the prophet's words and back
again to God's words in v. 24 is that we have a quotation
within a quotation, that the words of vv. 22-23 which Eze-

kiel is to speak in the first person were given to him verbatim as an integral part of the whole message of vv. 21-24 spoken by God; the words which Ezekiel is told to speak may originally have been introduced at the beginning of v. 22 by a divine command like "Say" which later fell out of the text. Precisely that construction (a quotation of words to be said by Ezekiel, introduced by "Say" in the words spoken by God) is found at 12:11 in the formally similar chapter 12.

After the violent expression of divine wrath in the preceding oracles, this oracle's quiet melancholy takes us by surprise. Ezekiel's austere grief seems to have elicited reserve and compassion on God's part. "Sigh," he says in v. 17, "but not aloud." That divine compassion is extended to the exiles, many of whose loved ones, left behind in Jerusalem, will perish when the city is destroyed. God no longer thunders angrily against the sinfulness of Jerusalem and of the house of Israel. He thinks rather of his Temple, the delight of his people's eyes (v. 21), as Ezekiel's wife was the delight of his eyes. God comprehends the grief of all, even though the wickedness of Jerusalem moves him to order the suspension of mourning for its punished inhabitants.

Vv. 25-27 have been introduced editorially to forge the first part of a link between this point in the book and 33:21-22, where historical allusion to the fate of Jerusalem again enters, after the long section which intervenes between those two points. The first part of the Book of Ezekiel is here concluded.

PART TWO

JUDGEMENT ON FOREIGN NATIONS

Between the first part of the book, containing mainly oracles of judgement on the house of Israel, and the third part, containing mainly oracles of deliverance for Israel, we have a collection of oracles against foreign nations — the Transjordanian states to the east of Judah, and Philistia to the west in chapter 25, the Phoenician city-states of Tyre and Sidon in chapters 26-28, and Egypt in chapters 29-32. The existence of this collection of oracles directed against foreign nations may seem curious, because Ezekiel, according to the call-narrative at the beginning of the book, was called to speak to the house of Israel in the Judean homeland and in the Babylonian Exile (3:4-11), not to the peoples of other nations. Each of the nations addressed in this part of the book has shown hostility towards the house of Israel, or has in one way or another constituted a danger for Judah. Several of these oracles are dated. This leads us to expect clear allusions to historical situations in particular moments, but in fact the guilt which these nations have incurred is, on the whole, vaguely expressed, and it can in some cases be taken as a guilt incurred by national behavior, or national attitudes, spread over several generations, or even several centuries. These oracles contain stereotyped, formulaic, condemnations and stereotyped threats which could refer to different nations at different times. The imagery of these oracles, picturesque rather than historical, at times even mythic, expresses the characteristics of the nations addressed, their cultural traits, their geographical features. There are caricatures here, and there is a level of poetic expression quite untypical of the rest of the Book of Ezekiel.

AGAINST THE EASTERN AND WESTERN NEIGHBORS
25:1-17

25 The word of the LORD came to me: 2"Son of man, set your face toward the Ammonites, and prophesy against them. 3Say to the Ammonites, Hear the word of the Lord GOD: Thus says the Lord GOD, because you said, 'Aha!' over my sanctuary when it was profaned, and over the land of Israel when it was made desolate, and over the house of Judah when it went into exile; 4therefore I am handing you over to the people of the East for a possession, and they shall set their encampments among you and make their dwellings in your midst; they shall eat your fruit, and they shall drink your milk. 5I will make Rabbah a pasture for camels and the cities of the Ammonites a fold for flocks. Then you will know that I am the LORD. 6For thus says the Lord GOD: Because you have clapped your hands and stamped your feet and rejoiced with all the malice within you against the land of Israel, 7therefore, behold, I have stretched out my hand against you, and will hand you over as spoil to the nations; and I will cut you off from the peoples and will make you perish out of the countries; I will destroy you. Then you will know that I am the LORD.

8"Thus says the Lord GOD: Because Moab said, Behold, the house of Judah is like all the other nations, 9therefore I will lay open the flank of Moab from the cities on its frontier, the glory of the country, Beth-jeshimoth, Baal-meon, and Kiriathaim. [10]I will give it along with the Ammonites to the people of the East as a possession, that it may be remembered no more among the nations, [11]and I will execute judgments upon Moab. Then they will know that I am the LORD.

[12]"Thus says the Lord GOD: Because Edom acted revengefully against the house of Judah and has grievously offended in taking vengeance upon them, [13]therefore thus says the Lord GOD, I will stretch out my hand against Edom, and cut off from it man and beast; and I will make it desolate; from Teman even to Dedan they shall fall by the sword. [14]And I will lay my vengeance upon Edom by the hand of my people Israel; and they shall do in Edom according to my anger and according to my wrath; and they shall know my vengeance, says the Lord GOD.

[15]"Thus says the Lord GOD: Because the Philistines acted revengefully and took vengeance with malice of heart to destroy in never-ending enmity; [16]therefore thus says the Lord GOD, Behold, I will stretch out my hand against the Philistines, and I will cut off the Cherethites, and destroy the rest of the seacoast. [17]I will execute great vengeance upon them with wrathful chastisements. Then they will know that I am the LORD, when I lay my vengeance upon them."

This chapter contains five short oracles — the first four against Judah's eastern neighbors across the Jordan and the Dead Sea, arranged in geographical order from north to south (the Ammonites, Moabites, and Edomites), and the fifth against her western neighbors along the Mediterranean coast of Palestine (the Philistine city-states). The first two oracles are both against Amon (vv. 3-5 and 6-7). All of these oracles have the same basic structure: an introductory "Thus says the Lord God" is followed by an accusation of behavior which is the reason for the divine displeasure, introduced by "because," and the oracle is completed by the announcement of the punishment which is to be inflicted on the nation, introduced by the word "therefore." These oracles are not dated, but one gathers from what is said in them that they were composed after the destruction of Jerusalem in 586.

Each of these small states is judged negatively because of its attitude towards its shamed and fallen neighbor, Judah. Ammon has mocked Judah in her misfortune (vv. 3, 6), and God's own sanctuary in Jerusalem has been an object of the Ammonites' mockery (v. 3). We begin to see why the attitudes of these neighboring nations is offensive to God. Their attitudes may have Judah as their object, but no matter how wicked the Judeans may have been, they have quite special ties with Yahweh, from whom the oracles come. The Moabites are accused of denying just such a special aspect of Judah's identity. Edom is guilty of directly hostile behavior towards Judah (v. 12; see 35:5), whose battles and defeats are, in a way, the battles and defeats of the divine warrior who is Judah's God. The Philistines are accused of a long-standing enmity reaching far back beyond recent events, an enmity expressed in acts of hostile revenge (v. 15). These acts of revenge may be recent ones, perpetrated in circumstances which were also those of the vengeful acts of the Edomites.

The threatened punishments are more concrete in their allusions, and more colorful in their imagery, than are the accusations of guilt. The cities of Ammon and Moab will be reduced to encampments and grazing lands used by bedouin, the "people of the East" (vv. 4, 10), from the nearby deserts and steppes. Because the offenses of the Edomites and of the Philistines have been acts of violence against Judah, their punishment will be equally violent. Their vengeance against God's people will be avenged by God (vv. 14, 17). Teman and Dedan (v. 13) were two southern Edomite cities in what is now northern Arabia. The Cherethites of v. 16 are, like all Philistines, people whose distant ancestors came to Palestine from the Aegean region; their name may be related etymologically to the name of the island of Crete. In each of these oracles the announcement of divine punishment is concluded with a solemn declaration that the foreign people will know that he who has

punished them is Yahweh, the Lord. Yahweh it is who
determines all historical happenings, but Yahweh is also the
particular god of a particular people. When other nations
abuse his people, they anger him. Yahweh avenges wrongs
done to his people, unfaithful to him though his own people
may themselves be.

THE DOWNFALL OF TYRE
26:1-21

26 In the eleventh year, on the first day of the month,
the word of the LORD came to me: [2]"Son of man,
because Tyre said concerning Jerusalem, 'Aha, the gate
of the peoples is broken, it has swung open to me; I shall
be replenished, now that she is laid waste,'[3]therefore thus
says the Lord GOD: Behold, I am against you, O Tyre,
and will bring up many nations against you, as the sea
brings up its waves. [4]They shall destroy the walls of Tyre,
and break down her towers; and I will scrape her soil
from her, and make her a bare rock. [5]She shall be in the
midst of the sea a place for the spreading of nets; for I
have spoken, says the Lord GOD; and she shall become a
spoil to the nations; [6]and her daughters on the mainland
shall be slain by the sword. Then they will know that I am
the LORD.

[7]"For thus says the Lord GOD: Behold, I will bring
upon Tyre from the north Nebuchadrezzar king of Babylon, king of kings, with horses and chariots, and with
horsemen and a host of many soldiers. [8]He will slay with
the sword your daughters on the mainland; he will set up
a siege wall against you, and throw up a mound against
you, and raise a roof of shields against you. [9]He will direct
the shock of his battering rams against your walls, and
with his axes he will break down your towers. [10]His
horses will be so many that their dust will cover you; your
walls will shake at the noise of the horsemen and wagons
and chariots, when he enters your gates as one enters a
city which has been breached. [11]With the hoofs of his

horses he will trample all your streets; he will slay your people with the sword; and your mighty pillars will fall to the ground. ¹²They will make a spoil of your riches and a prey of your merchandise; they will break down your walls and destroy your pleasant houses; your stones and timber and soil they will cast into the midst of the waters. ¹³And I will stop the music of your songs, and the sound of your lyres shall be heard no more. ¹⁴I will make you a bare rock; you shall be a place for the spreading of nets; you shall never be rebuilt; for I the LORD have spoken, says the Lord GOD.

¹⁵"Thus says the Lord GOD to Tyre: Will not the coastlands shake at the sound of your fall, when the wounded groan, when slaughter is made in the midst of you? ¹⁶Then all the princes of the sea will step down from their thrones, and remove their robes, and strip off their embroidered garments; they will clothe themselves with trembling; they will sit upon the ground and tremble every moment, and be appalled at you. ¹⁷And they will raise a lamentation over you, and say to you,

'How you have vanished from the seas,
     O city renowned,
that was mighty on the sea,
     you and your inhabitants,
who imposed your terror
     on all the mainland!
¹⁸Now the isles tremble
     on the day of your fall;
yea, the isles that are in the sea
     are dismayed at your passing.'

¹⁹"For thus says the Lord GOD: When I make you a city laid waste, like the cities that are not inhabited, when I bring up the deep over you, and the great waters cover you, ²⁰then I will thrust you down with those who descend into the Pit, to the people of old, and I will make you to dwell in the nether world, among primeval ruins, with those who go down to the Pit, so that you will not be inhabited or have a place in the land of the living. ²¹I will

bring you to a dreadful end, and you shall be no more;
though you be sought for, you will never be found again,
says the Lord GOD."

The small states against which the brief oracles of chapter
25 were addressed were relatively unimportant. They mer-
ited no more oracular attention than they received in the
preceding chapter. Most of the oracles against foreign
nations are directed against Tyre and against Egypt, two
important and strong states in the Eastern Mediterranean
world of Ezekiel's time. Egypt was a large nation with much
territory. Tyre was a small city-state centered on an island
just off the coast of what is today southern Lebanon, with a
restricted area on the mainland included in its national
territory. Its small size belied its power, however. The
mother-city's position on an island made it difficult for
attacking armies to seize, until Alexander the Great, in 332
B.C., built a narrow causeway from the mainland to the
island, over which his soldiers could approach the city
which he was besieging. The sand washed up against the
causeway through the centuries afterward has left modern
Tyre a city at the end of a narrow sandy peninsula. The base
of ancient Tyre's power and influence was the wealth it
gained from maritime shipping and commerce. What it
could not accomplish by military force it could often
accomplish by economic pressure or by financial
diplomacy.

The date of this first oracle against Tyre is the first day of
an unnamed month in the eleventh year of Jehoachin, i.e.
one of the twelve month-beginnings running from 23 April
587 to 15 March 586. A date no later than 15 March 586 for
this oracle runs into the difficulty of the oracle's mention of
the fall of Jerusalem as an accomplished fact (v. 2), if we
accept the summer of 586 as the time of Jerusalem's fall. The
form of the compound word for the number eleven in the
Hebrew text here is not the form of the word "eleven" found
in 30:20 and 31:1; we should perhaps presume that a single
Hebrew letter in the word "twelve" has fallen out of the
original text, to leave the word "eleven" of the present

Hebrew text. If so, then our oracle was originally dated in the twelfth year of Jehoachin, i.e. 586/85. Since the news of Jerusalem's fall did not reach the exiles until December of that year (33:21), the month, now missing in the text, must have been one of the last three months of that year, whose first days fell on 4 January, 3 February, and 3 March 585.

The sole point of accusation against Tyre in this oracle is Tyre's self-centered glee over the fate of the conquered and devastated Jerusalem (v. 2). In this respect, the accusation against Tyre is like that against Ammon in 25:3, but commercially minded Tyre has its own reasons for satisfaction with Jerusalem's misfortune. The somewhat cryptic words put in Tyre's mouth in v. 2 suggest that the island city rejoices in an increase of trade and profit, now that Jerusalem is out of the way as a competitor. To unfeeling mockery Tyre has added a crass and materialistic gratification of self-interest, when she might have had compassion on a neighboring capital which was down and out. Jerusalem, the neighboring capital, happens to be God's city, and Tyre's attitude towards it in its misfortune angers God. As a penalty, God announces Tyre's destruction in such a way that she will be reduced to a desolate rocky island, so thoroughly denuded of all traces of urban construction that fishermen can easily spread out their nets on her surface (vv. 3-5). As the fundamental oracle of judgement is concluded in v. 6, the announcement of the destruction of insular Tyre, the mother-city, is extended by inclusion of the towns on the mainland territory of Tyre ("her daughters").

The oracle of judgement (vv. 2-6) has been expanded by what follows in the rest of the chapter. Vv. 7-14 are a graphic description of the destruction of Tyre and her coastal daughter-cities by the army of Nebuchadrezzar. Except for the mention of Tyre's mainland daughters in v. 8 and the imagery of the rock on which nets will be spread in v. 14, the description is general enough to be used for a Babylonian siege and occupation of any city at any time in that political and cultural age. The Jewish historian Josephus, writing in the first century A.D., reported a statement by Philostrates that Nebuchadrezzar besieged Tyre for thirteen years. If this is accurate information, the long siege probably began after the fall of Jerusalem in 586, but by 570/69 Babylonian records show a Babylonian commissioner in Tyre alongside a native Tyrian king, and the Book of Ezekiel itself contains information dated 570 which indicates that the Babylonians got little for their trouble in besieging Tyre (29:17-18), which may not even have been sacked. From this we may perhaps conclude that the description of the coming siege and fall of Tyre in chapter 26 is an abstract, ideal description whose details are not necessarily tied to those of the actual historical outcome of the Babylonian siege.

In vv. 15-18 there is a highly poetic expression of reaction to the fall of Tyre felt by a personified coastland and personified isles, and by rulers of maritime places. It is addressed to Tyre personified. The maritime rulers perform rites of lamentation (v. 16), and they utter a formal lament in vv. 17-18. Tyre did not lament the death of Jerusalem, when it should have done so. Other states will lament the death of Tyre, knowing that in the vicissitudes of history they may soon share the same fate. Thoughts of death continue in vv. 19-21, but here the imagery shifts from funerary rites of the everyday world to mythically charged views of the nether world. There is also a shift from the waters of the Mediterranean, in which Tyre sits, to the mythic waters of chaos which covered the earth before life and order began (Gen 1:1). As the cosmic waters engulfed the whole world and snuffed out most of its life, as a divine punishment, in Gen 7:11-24, so do they here engulf Tyre. Like the human person in Jonah 2:1-9, the city sinks through the waves of the cosmic sea and passes into the Pit of the nether world, where dead persons — and dead cities — of all previous ages lie, without hope of return to the exciting world of human history.

TYRE FOUNDERS LIKE A SHIP IN THE SEA
27:1-36

27 The word of the LORD came to me: [2]"Now you, son of man, raise a lamentation over Tyre, [3]and say to Tyre, who dwells at the entrance to the sea, merchant of the

peoples on many coastlands, thus says the Lord GOD:
"O Tyre, you have said,
'I am perfect in beauty.'
4Your borders are in the heart of the seas;
your builders made perfect your beauty.
5They made all your planks
of fir trees from Senir;
they took a cedar from Lebanon
to make a mast for you.
6Of oaks of Bashan
they made your oars;
they made your deck of pines
from the coasts of Cyprus,
inlaid with ivory.
7Of fine embroidered linen from Egypt
was your sail,
serving as your ensign;
blue and purple from the coasts of Elishah
was your awning.
8The inhabitants of Sidon and Arvad
were your rowers;
skilled men of Zemer were in you,
they were your pilots.
9The elders of Gebal and her skilled men were in you,
caulking your seams;
all the ships of the sea with their mariners were in you,
to barter for your wares.

10"Persia and Lud and Put were in your army as your men of war; they hung the shield and helmet in you; they gave you splendor. 11The men of Arvad and Helech were upon your walls round about, and men of Gamad were in your towers; they hung their shields upon your walls round about; they made perfect your beauty.

12"Tarshish trafficked with you because of your great wealth of every kind; silver, iron, tin, and lead they exchanged for your wares. 13Javan, Tubal, and Meshech traded with you; they exchanged the persons of men and vessels of bronze for your merchandise. 14Beth-togarmah exchanged for your wares horses, war horses, and mules.

¹⁵The men of Rhodes traded with you; many coastlands were your own special market, they brought you in payment ivory tusks and ebony. ¹⁶Edom trafficked with you because of your abundant goods; they exchanged for your wares emeralds, purple, embroidered work, fine linen, coral, and agate. ¹⁷Judah and the land of Israel traded with you; they exchanged for your merchandise wheat, olives and early figs, honey, oil, and balm. ¹⁸Damascus trafficked with you for your abundant goods, because of your great wealth of every kind; wine of Helbon, and white wool, ¹⁹and wine from Uzal they exchanged for your wares; wrought iron, cassia, and calamus were bartered for your merchandise. ²⁰Dedan traded with you in saddlecloths for riding. ²¹Arabia and all the princes of Kedar were your favored dealers in lambs, rams, and goats; in these they trafficked with you. ²²The traders of Sheba and Raamah traded with you; they exchanged for your wares the best of all kinds of spices, and all precious stones, and gold. ²³Haran, Canneh, Eden, Asshur, and Chilmad traded with you. ²⁴These traded with you in choice garments, in clothes of blue and embroidered work, and in carpets of colored stuff, bound with cords and made secure; in these they traded with you. ²⁵The ships of Tarshish traveled for you with your merchandise.

"So you were filled and heavily laden
in the heart of the seas.
²⁶Your rowers have brought you out
into the high seas.
The east wind has wrecked you
in the heart of the seas.
²⁷Your riches, your wares, your merchandise,
your mariners and your pilots,
your caulkers, your dealers in merchandise,
and all your men of war who are in you,
with all your company
that is in your midst,
sink into the heart of the seas
on the day of your ruin.

²⁸At the sound of the cry of your pilots
   the countryside shakes,
²⁹and down from their ships
   come all that handle the oar.
The mariners and all the pilots of the sea
   stand on the shore
³⁰and wail aloud over you,
   and cry bitterly.
They cast dust on their heads
   and wallow in ashes;
³¹they make themselves bald for you,
   and gird themselves with sackcloth,
and they weep over you in bitterness of soul,
   with bitter mourning.
³²In their wailing they raise a lamentation for you,
   and lament over you:
'Who was ever destroyed like Tyre
   in the midst of the sea?
³³When your wares came from the seas,
   you satisfied many peoples;
with your abundant wealth and merchandise
   you enriched the kings of the earth.
³⁴Now you are wrecked by the seas,
   in the depths of the waters;
your merchandise and all your crew
   have sunk with you.
³⁵All the inhabitants of the coastlands
   are appalled at you;
and their kings are horribly afraid,
   their faces are convulsed.
³⁶The merchants among the peoples hiss at you;
   you have come to a dreadful end
   and shall be no more for ever.' "

In many ways chapter 27 is best understood as an extension of chapter 26. The only oracle of judgement passed so far on Tyre is that of 26:2-6. There is no new accusation of Tyre in chapter 27, apart from the one implicitly rising from her pride shown at the end of v. 3, and her fate is not again said to be a divine penalty. Her fate, though, is the subject of chapter 27. The entire chapter is a lament for her demise, after the previous lament in 26:17-18. We also find, in 27:25-34, the idea of Tyre's sinking through the waves, as in 26:19-20, but here the waves are no longer the waves of cosmic chaos: once again they are the waves of the Mediterranean Sea. In chapter 27, Tyre's demise is represented as that of a merchant ship, holding the city's wares, which has been wrecked and which sinks into the sea.

Our reading of the chapter may gain clarity if we notice two literary phenomena. For one thing, we have here a lament within a lament. Within the extensive words of lamentation given by God to Ezekiel which begin in v. 3 and end with v. 36 there is a description of rites of lamentation performed by the known world's mariners (vv. 30-36), and a part of this is a quoted lament uttered by the mariners in vv. 32b-36. It is this quoted lament which actually confirms the whole chapter as a lament, as far as formal expression goes, although the rhythmic pattern or meter of most of the Hebrew text gives its reader a signal that he or she is reading a Hebrew lament.

The other literary phenomenon which we ought to notice is the alternation between the metaphorical representation of Tyre as a ship and its non-metaphorical representation — from the last half of v. 9 through the first half of v. 25 — as a commercial city. (Mention of its borders in v. 4 implies its being a city, too, but there the text can be questioned.) In this "city" section, the meter of the Hebrew lament is also abandoned. The section interrupts the lament. The "city" section is a survey of the economic geography of the world then known to Mediterranean traders. Identification of some of the places mentioned in the "city" section remains uncertain, but in general the correlation of products with places is confirmed by other sources of historical geography. Persia and Edom, Judah and the former northern kingdom of Israel (designated by the name of its capital, Samaria), the city of Damascus too, we recognize easily. Dedan we have met in 25:13, and Kedar is the northern part of the Syro-Arabian desert, to the east of the Transjordani-

an states of Ammon, Moab, and Edom. Sheba and Raa-
mah are in southern Arabia. The Javan of v. 13 is
Greek-speaking Ionia, on the eastern shores of the Aegean
Sea. Tubal and Meshech and (Beth-) togarmah were in Asia
Minor. Tarshish was probably a trading colony in far-away
Spain, Lud may be Lydia in Asia Minor, and Put seems to
have been in what is today Libya.

We find no explicit religious "message" in this chapter,
and yet it comes to us in the form of a divine oracle. This can
remind us that the aesthetic pathos of a lament, and the
sheer delight of encyclopedic listing evident in the "city"
section, can nurture the religious side of our humanity if we
are open to that. God's dealing with us need not always be
reduced to explicitly and formally religious messages. Poetry and secular learning can be integrated into our contem-
plation of all reality, as we remain aware that it all speaks to
us ultimately of God.

THE PRINCE OF TYRE'S PRIDE AND FALL
28:1-19

28 The word of the LORD came to me: [2]"Son of man,
say to the prince of Tyre, Thus says the Lord GOD:
"Because your heart is proud;
    and you have said, 'I am a god,
I sit in the seat of the gods,
    in the heart of the seas,'
yet you are but a man, and no god,
    though you consider yourself as wise as a god—
[3]you are indeed wiser than Daniel;
    no secret is hidden from you;
[4]by your wisdom and your understanding
    you have gotten wealth for yourself,
and have gathered gold and silver
    into your treasuries;
[5]by your great wisdom in trade
    you have increased your wealth,
and your heart has become proud in your wealth—
[6]therefore thus says the Lord GOD:

"Because you consider yourself
as wise as a god,
[7]therefore, behold, I will bring strangers upon you,
the most terrible of the nations;
and they shall draw their swords against the
beauty of your wisdom
and defile your splendor.
[8]They shall thrust you down into the Pit,
and you shall die the death of the slain
in the heart of the seas.
[9]Will you still say, 'I am a god,'
in the presence of those who slay you,
though you are but a man, and no god,
in the hands of those who wound you?
[10]You shall die the death of the uncircumcised
by the hand of foreigners;
for I have spoken, says the Lord GOD."
[11]Moreover the word of the LORD came to me: [12]"Son
of man, raise a lamentation over the king of Tyre, and say
to him, Thus says the Lord GOD:
"You were the signet of perfection,
full of wisdom
and perfect in beauty.
[13]You were in Eden, the garden of God;
every precious stone was your covering,
carnelian, topaz, and jasper,
chrysolite, beryl, and onyx,
sapphire, carbuncle, and emerald;
and wrought in gold were your settings
and your engravings.
On the day that you were created
they were prepared.
[14]With an anointed guardian cherub I placed you;
you were on the holy mountain of God;
in the midst of the stones of fire you walked.
[15]You were blameless in your ways
from the day you were created,
till iniquity was found in you.
[16]In the abundance of your trade

you were filled with violence, and you sinned;
so I cast you as a profane thing from the mountain of God,
and the guardian cherub drove you out
    from the midst of the stones of fire.
[17]Your heart was proud because of your beauty;
    you corrupted your wisdom for the sake of
        your splendor.
I cast you to the ground;
    I exposed you before kings,
    to feast their eyes on you.
[18]By the multitude of your iniquities,
    in the unrighteousness of your trade
    you profaned your sanctuaries;
so I brought forth fire from the midst of you;
    it consumed you,
and I turned you to ashes upon the earth
    in the sight of all who saw you.
[19]All who know you among the peoples
    are appalled at you;
you have come to a dreadful end
    and shall be no more for ever."

An oracle of judgement in vv. 1-10 is followed by, and extended by, a section whose literary genre we shall have to examine more closely. Both sections are directed against the ruler of Tyre, its king. He does not appear with any traits which might mark him as a particular historical person. The ancient mind saw in a king such a total identification with his people that he incorporated all of the people's character, while his own good and evil qualities, all that he did and all that he suffered, were the qualities, the actions, and the sufferings of the entire society over which he ruled. In 28:1-19 the king of Tyre and his kingdom are not neatly distinguishable. The king of Tyre is his kingdom, and the kingdom is personified in its king.

In the oracle of judgement with which the chapter begins, the point of accusation made against the king is his pride (vv. 1-6). Tyre had reason to be proud of its splendor and its riches, of its successful commercial drive, all evoked in chapter 27, but here we see finally that Tyre's pride had exceeded the bounds of what is divinely tolerable in creatures. The Hebrew word conventionally translated "wisdom" names a mental quality including all sorts of practical skills, in craftsmanship, diplomacy, commerce and organization, in the art of living. We have encountered Daniel, the ancient paragon of wisdom, before, in 14:14. Tyre and its ruler, smug in their own wisdom, in their proven ability to do things well on a large scale, had forgotten their subordination to the supremely wise ruler of the universe, who accuses the earthly prince of Tyre, the incorporation of all that Tyre is, of thinking falsely that he is one of the gods (v. 2). Just as the first man and his wife, standing for Everyman and Everywoman in Gen 2:4b—3:24, became like one of the gods when they rose to a level of knowledge which was not to have been theirs, and had to suffer the divinely imposed consequences of their offensive usurpation of divine prerogative (Gen 3:22-24), so has the prince of Tyre's pride in his wisdom led him to see himself as one of the gods. That is an insolent attitude for which he will have to suffer divine punishment, announced in vv. 7-10. In 26:2, Tyre's guilt lay in its gloating reaction to the fall of Jerusalem, an attitude offensive to Yahweh as the national god of Israel. Now, in 28:2-6, Tyre's guilt lies in mental usurpation of divine prerogatives, an attitude offensive to Yahweh as lord of all creation. Yahweh will bring from another nation the soldiers who will put to death the king and kingdom of Tyre. Mortality, indeed, is the ultimate proof of a humanity that has not succeeded in usurping divinity (v. 9). That theme is a commonplace in Ancient Near Eastern accounts of humanity's origins, and it too appears in Gen 3:22: when the primeval man, who is Everyman, has already become like one of the gods by the knowledge which he has gained, he is banished from Eden "lest he put forth his hand and take also of the tree of life, and eat, and live for ever," like a god.

This oracle of judgement is expanded by the poem in vv. 11-19. In the text itself, this section is called a lamentation (v. 12), but a comparison with the lamentations in 26:17-18 and 27:3-36, and elsewhere in the Old Testament, will show that 28:11-19 departs significantly from the literary *genre* of the lamentation. It conforms to a lamentation's commemoration of the dead person's beauty or splendor or valorous deeds in life, but with v. 15 it moves suddenly to a harsh reminder of the king of Tyre's fall from proud splendor into the pervasive iniquity which has provoked God to bring him to perdition. This is quite untypical of a lamentation. It is God himself who utters the inexorable accusation of the Tyrian king, and it is God who has determined the punishment accordingly meted out to him, meted out to the entire nation whose iniquity and whose fate are indistinguishable from those of its king. In this respect, the poem resembles an oracle of judgement, in which an accusation of guilt is followed by the announcement of the punishment which the guilty person must suffer for his crime. Here, though, the punishment is not announced as one which is still to come but is narrated as one which has been inflicted already, and which can thus be commemorated in a lamentation. What we have here is an oracle of judgement expressed in the formal framework of a lamentation. This combination of the two literary *genres* makes it possible to contrast the guilt of the Tyrian king with his former splendor, to give to the description of his punishment the immediacy of that which has already happened, and to color the entire oracle with the tragic tones of lamentation. In vv. 1-10 the king of Tyre was accused of letting pride in his wisdom lead him to think himself divine. In vv. 11-19 some of that is picked up and restated, but the Tyrian king, who *is* Tyre, is also accused of violence and injustice flowing from all that commercial activity whose splendid results are at the root of much of Tyre's pride (vv. 16, 18).

We have already noted in the oracle of vv. 1-10 some similarity to the story of the fall of primeval man in Gen 2:4b—3:24. This similarity is greater still in vv. 11-19. The portrayal of the Tyrian king, blameless in the splendor of the day of his creation, falling subsequently from divine favor and ejected from the garden and mountain of God, is parallel to the portrayal of the first man and woman in paradise, their disobedience, fall, and ejection from paradise in Genesis. In both passages, the name of the garden is Eden. The guardian cherub of Ezek 28:14, 16 recalls the guardian cherubim of Gen 3:24. The cherub, the stones of fire, the mountain of God, the cataclysmic downfall, all give to Ezek 28:11-19 that mythic tone found in all ancient stories of the beginning of human history, of a primeval human being whose exploits, and the divine reactions to them, determine the fate of their entire race. Here, in vv. 11-19, such a story has clearly been drawn upon. The king of Tyre is presented as a primevally perfect man whose pride has led to his spectacular downfall through divine displeasure.

The metaphorical application of the mythic elements to the figure of the king of Tyre is broken in places with non-mythic elements drawn from the historical reputation of the Tyrian state — Tyre's trade, and the unrighteous dealing which has been a part of its trade. Tyre may once have been a state which enjoyed God's favor, but by its proud tendency to be godlike in glory it has violated God's holiness. The violation of holiness is symbolized perhaps by the Tyrian king's profanation of sanctuaries (v. 18). In consequence, God has rejected the king and his nation as a thing now profane (v. 16). Some ancient story about a primeval Everyman with traits of kingship and dominion has been applied to a primeval king of Tyre, standing for every Tyrian, all of Tyrian society. Tyre has been guilty both of proud *hybris* offending the rights of divinity and of sinful violence offending the rights of humanity. For both, God has brought about Tyre's ruin.

JUDGEMENT ON SIDON, HOPE FOR ISRAEL
28:20-26

> [20]The word of the LORD came to me: [21]"Son of man, set your face toward Sidon, and prophesy against her [22]and say, Thus says the Lord GOD:
> "Behold, I am against you, O Sidon,
>   and I will manifest my glory in the midst of you.
> And they shall know that I am the LORD
>   when I execute judgments in her,

and manifest my holiness in her;
23for I will send pestilence into her,
and blood into her streets;
and the slain shall fall in the midst of her,
by the sword that is against her on every side.
Then they will know that I am the LORD.

24"And for the house of Israel there shall be no more a brier to prick or a thorn to hurt them among all their neighbors who have treated them with contempt. Then they will know that I am the Lord GOD.

25"Thus says the Lord GOD: When I gather the house of Israel from the peoples among whom they are scattered, and manifest my holiness in them in the sight of the nations, then they shall dwell in their own land which I gave to my servant Jacob. 26And they shall dwell securely in it, and they shall build houses and plant vineyards. They shall dwell securely, when I execute judgments upon all their neighbors who have treated them with contempt. Then they will know that I am the LORD their God."

The word of judgement on Sidon in vv. 20-24 is made up of stereotyped phrases which could be uttered against any nation at any time. No reason is given for God's being against Sidon. The inclusion of this brief oracle against Sidon in this part of the book seems to have no purpose other than that of having a complete series of oracles against each and all of Judah's small West Semitic neighboring states, before the series of oracles against Egypt begins; the oracle against Sidon rounds off the series against the small neighbors. On the other hand, when we consider the anti-Sidonian oracle in connection with v. 24, we see that the words against Sidon constitute a kind of summary of the general reasons for divine wrath against all of the small West Semitic nations. The house of Israel's neighbors have been like briers needling the house of Israel with contempt (v. 24). That is why God executes judgement against each of them, and shows his transcendent holiness in doing so (v. 22.)

Vv. 25-26 have nothing to do with Sidon or any of the other foreign nations. They form a pastoral interlude of promise for Israel in the midst of the stormy oracles of judgement against its neighbors. Despite all the wickedness of the house of Israel which provoked God's wrath and his punitive measures against Jerusalem and Judah (most of Ezek 1-24), the members of the house of Israel are God's elect. It is because they are his elect that he is angered by the attitude of the foreign neighbors (25:3, 8, 12, 15; 26:2). His vengeance on his own people has had its effect, and his fidelity in love for his people will in the long run be manifested. In the preceding and following oracles God says repeatedly: "Then they will know that I am the Lord." At the end of this pastoral interlude he says of the house of Israel, "Then they will know that I am the Lord *their* God."

EGYPT: A DRAGON AND A REED
29:1-16

29 In the tenth year, in the tenth month, on the twelfth day of the month, the word of the LORD came to me: ²"Son of man, set your face against Pharaoh king of Egypt, and prophesy against him and against all Egypt; ³speak, and say, Thus says the Lord GOD:
"Behold, I am against you,
    Pharaoh king of Egypt,
the great dragon that lies
    in the midst of his streams,
that says, 'My Nile is my own;
    I made it.'
⁴I will put hooks in your jaws,
    and make the fish of your streams
        stick to your scales;
and I will draw you up out of the
        midst of your streams,
    with all the fish of your streams
    which stick to your scales.
⁵And I will cast you forth into the wilderness,
    you and all the fish of your streams;

you shall fall upon the open field,
and not be gathered and buried.
To the beasts of the earth and to the
birds of the air
I have given you as food.

6"Then all the inhabitants of Egypt shall know that I am the LORD. Because you have been a staff of reed to the house of Israel; 7when they grasped you with the hand, you broke, and tore all their shoulders; and when they leaned upon you, you broke, and made all their loins to shake; 8therefore thus says the Lord GOD: Behold, I will bring a sword upon you, and will cut off from you man and beast; 9and the land of Egypt shall be a desolation and a waste. Then they will know that I am the LORD.

"Because you said, 'The Nile is mine, and I made it,' 10therefore, behold, I am against you, and against your streams, and I will make the land of Egypt an utter waste and desolation, from Migdol to Syene, as far as the border of Ethiopia. 11No foot of man shall pass through it, and no foot of beast shall pass through it; it shall be uninhabited forty years. 12And I will make the land of Egypt a desolation in the midst of desolated countries; and her cities shall be a desolation forty years among cities that are laid waste. I will scatter the Egyptians among the nations, and disperse them through the countries.

13"For thus says the Lord GOD: At the end of forty years I will gather the Egyptians from the peoples among whom they were scattered; 14and I will restore the fortunes of Egypt, and bring them back to the land of Pathros, the land of their origin; and there they shall be a lowly kingdom. 15It shall be the most lowly of the kingdoms, and never again exalt itself above the nations; and I will make them so small that they will never again rule over the nations. 16And it shall never again be the reliance of the house of Israel, recalling their iniquity, when they turn to them for aid. Then they will know that I am the Lord GOD.

The date in 29:1 is the equivalent of 7 January 587. The Babylonian siege of Jerusalem was then under way, but the city had not yet been taken. When Zedekiah sought help from Egypt, Hophra (Apries), Pharaoh since 589, sent to Judah an army which managed to get the Babylonians to abandon the siege temporarily. The Judean reliance on Egyptian aid was sadly misplaced, however, for the Egyptian army eventually withdrew, and the siege of Jerusalem began anew (Jer 37:5-10). This is the historical background of 29:1-16. After the general introduction in vv. 1-2, a compound oracle follows in three parts, each concluded by the formula: "Then (the inhabitants of Egypt) will know that I am the Lord." Each part can stand formally as an oracle in itself, but all three parts have some thematic links to one another.

The first part, vv. 3-6a, is an oracle of judgement, as far as its co-ordination of structure and meaning goes, but the accusation of guilt is somewhat untypically made by citing words put in the mouth of Pharaoh himself, and the words "because" introducing the accusation of guilt, and "therefore" introducing the announcement of punishment, usual in Ezekiel, are absent. Just as all of Tyrian society was represented in chapter 28 by its prince or ruler, drawn with mythical traits rather than with those of a discernible historical king, so is all of Egypt represented in 29:3-6a by a rather symbolic and mythical pharaoh. Like the king of Tyre in chapter 28, the pharaoh's great sin for which he will be punished is a sin of insolent pride offensive to God. Pharaoh is likened to a dragon in the Nile and its Delta branches, a mythical dragon of the sort which presides over the waters of chaos and who says in v. 3 that it was he who created the waters of the Nile, that it is he, consequently, who is the Nile's master. This can only be offensive to Yahweh, creator and lord of the Nile as he is of all the universe. The degrading penalty which Yahweh will inflict will reduce the dragon from a mythical and mysterious monster to an absurd and ugly river beast whose carcass will be heaved out of the water and thrown onto the desert sands. Pride will be punished by reduction to ignominy.

The second part, vv. 6b-9a, is another oracle of judgement. In this one, the grounds for Egypt's punishment are historical and political. As someone foundering in water grasps the stalk of a nearby plant to save himself, Judah in its anti-Babylonian rebellion has appealed to Egypt for help. Egypt has failed Judah; the reed grasped for support has broken in Judah's hand and left Judah in terror greater than before. For this, Egypt will be punished.

The third part, vv. 9b-16, begins as another oracle of judgement. The reason for Egypt's judgement (v. 9b) is that given in the mythically colored first part (v. 3), but the punishment (vv. 10-12) is to be the political and military one given in the second part (vv. 8-9a), with the addition of the Egyptians' dispersion in exile for forty years. Egypt's punishment thus begins to look like that of Judah's, with the people scattered in exile after a foreign army has devastated the homeland. This third part of the composite oracle moves on unexpectedly into consoling words of deliverance, just as oracles of woe for the house of Israel are often followed in Ezekiel by words of deliverance. This is the only oracle of deliverance for any foreign nation in our entire book. As Egypt and Judah will both suffer misfortune for their anti-Babylonian stand, so shall they both see the restoration of their homelands, but by divine decree Egypt will not again be important enough to tempt small neighbors like Judah to seek her unreliable aid. Never will the salvation of the house of Israel lie in political alliances.

GOD CHANGES A CONDITIONAL THREAT
29:17-21

[17]In the twenty-seventh year, in the first month, on the first day of the month, the word of the LORD came to me: [18]"Son of man, Nebuchadrezzar king of Babylon made his army labor hard against Tyre; every head was made bald and every shoulder was rubbed bare; yet neither he nor his army got anything from Tyre to pay for the labor that he had performed against it. [19]Therefore thus says the Lord GOD: Behold, I will give the land of

> Egypt to Nebuchadrezzar king of Babylon; and he shall carry off its wealth and despoil it and plunder it; and it shall be the wages for his army. [20]I have given him the land of Egypt as his recompense for which he labored, because they worked for me, says the Lord GOD.
>
> [21]"On that day I will cause a horn to spring forth to the house of Israel, and I will open your lips among them. Then they will know that I am the LORD."

The date of this oracle, the latest clear date given in the book, corresponds to 26 April 571. The thirteen-year Babylonian siege of Tyre has come to an end (see 26:7-14 and commentary thereon), but the utter destruction of Tyre announced in the prophetic oracles of chapters 26-28 has not come to pass. Since the threat announced by those earlier oracles had not come to pass, Ezekiel's hearers could be expected to call his prophetic credibility into question, and they were no doubt doing so. The oracle which we have here meets that problem. God has altered his plans, so to speak. The fate which he announced for Tyre has been transferred from Tyre to Egypt. God remains entirely free to say at one moment in history that he proposes a certain course of action and then to change his proposal, or even to revoke it, as he sees fit. In this instance, that is just what he has done. In prophecy there is often an unexpressed condition. A certain thing will happen "if" a certain situation prevails, but if it does not — if those to be punished, for example, have a change of heart — then God may revoke his decision, or change the penalty. In this case, it is the nation to be punished which has been changed, for reasons not revealed. To this transfer, announced in vv. 17-20, a double promise has been added in v. 21. When Egypt's power is broken, the house of Israel will receive a horn, symbolic of an aggressive power and force, individually or collectively possessed, which can save and protect (1 Sam 2:1; Pss 75(74):5-6, 11; 89(88):17, 24; 92(91):10). The horn marks a rise in Israel's inner strength as a people, and at that time God's words, uttered through Ezekiel, will be a constructive force in Israel's renewed history. God's decrees for the rise and fall of nations is ultimately in Israel's interest, and so are the words which he speaks to the house of Israel through Ezekiel, whether they are words of judgement and punishment or words of promise and hope. God adapts his historical proposals and his oracular utterances to the changing situations through which his own elected people passes.

EGYPT'S DEFEAT
30:1-26

30 The word of the LORD came to me: [2]"Son of man, prophesy, and say, Thus says the Lord GOD:

"Wail, 'Alas for the day!'

[3] For the day is near,
    the day of the LORD is near;
   it will be a day of clouds,
    a time of doom for the nations.
[4]A sword shall come upon Egypt,
    and anguish shall be in Ethiopia,
   when the slain fall in Egypt,
    and her wealth is carried away,
    and her foundations are torn down...

[20]In the eleventh year, in the first month, on the seventh day of the month, the word of the LORD came to me: [21]"Son of man, I have broken the arm of Pharaoh king of Egypt; and lo, it has been bound up, to heal it by binding it with a bandage, so that it may become strong to wield the sword. [22]Therefore thus says the Lord GOD: Behold, I am against Pharaoh king of Egypt, and will break his arms, both the strong arm and the one that was broken; and I will make the sword fall from his hand. [23]I will scatter the Egyptians among the nations, and disperse them through the countries. [24]And I will strengthen the arms of the king of Babylon, and put my sword in his hand; but I will break the arms of Pharaoh, and he will groan before him like a man mortally wounded. [25]I will strengthen the arms of the king of Babylon, but the arms of Pharaoh shall fall; and they shall know that I am the

LORD. When I put my sword into the hand of the king of
Babylon, he shall stretch it out against the land of Egypt;
²⁶and I will scatter the Egyptians among the nations and
disperse them throughout the countries. Then they will
know that I am the LORD."

In the first part of this chapter there are several short
oracles made up of stereotyped phrases expressing threats
of destruction of a nation. They are applied loosely to Egypt
by the haphazard inclusion of names of Egyptian cities. We
have omitted most of this material from the English text
above. "Ethiopia" (Hebrew *Kush*), mentioned in v. 4, is not
the land which we call Ethiopia today. It is Egypt's immediate neighbor to the south, Nubia, or today's Sudan. The
political fortunes of Egypt and Nubia were intertwined,
even dynastically, in the centuries leading to Ezekiel's own
time, and in the Old Testament *Kush* ("Ethiopia") and
Egypt often seem not to be clearly distinguished.

The point of the oracle in vv. 20-26 is determined by the
politics and the events of the moment in which it was given.
There is in vv. 22-26 what looks like the threat of punishment in an oracle of judgement; it is not, however, preceded
by an accusation of the guilt for which the punishment is to
be dealt out, but by a declaration of the fact of an Egyptian
defeat (v. 21). The date in v. 20 corresponds to 29 April 587,
and Pharaoh's already broken arm is certainly the Egyptian
army, routed by the Babylonian invaders and driven back to
Egypt after it had come to relieve the beleaguered Judeans
in Jerusalem. The declaration that the broken arm will not
be healed so that it can fight again effectively refutes Judean
hope of further aid from Egypt. From the threat in vv. 22-26
it is clear that the political alignments of Judah are not those
of Judah's God. Judah has rebelled against Babylon and put
its hope in Egypt. God is against Egypt with its Pharaoh,
and he strengthens the arm of the king of Babylon against
Egypt as well as Judah. In politics and policies, God's ways
are not necessarily our ways, because our political goals
may be incompatible with God's designs. God is resolved to
use the arm of the king of Babylon in order to punish Judah.

Judah resorted to Egypt in order to avert that punishment. God, unwilling to have his resolution thwarted, proceeded to break the arm of Pharaoh. The execution of divine judgement against Judah will advance. Egypt, because of its alliance with Judah to thwart God's plan, will share Judah's punishment. Both will be scattered among the nations (see 29:9b-12), a fate which Ezekiel's exiled hearers understand only too well.

THE MIGHTY CEDAR WILL FALL
31:1-18

31 In the eleventh year, in the third month, on the first day of the month, the word of the LORD came to me: ²"Son of man, say to Pharaoh king of Egypt and to his multitude:

"Whom are you like in your greatness?
³Behold, I will liken you to a cedar
in Lebanon,
with fair branches and forest shade,
and of great height,
its top among the clouds.
⁴The waters nourished it,
the deep made it grow tall,
making its rivers flow
round the place of its planting,
sending forth its streams
to all the trees of the forest.
⁵So it towered high
above all the trees of the forest;
its boughs grew large
and its branches long,
from abundant water in its shoots.
⁶All the birds of the air
made their nests in its boughs;
under its branches all the beasts of the field
brought forth their young;
and under its shadow
dwelt all great nations.

7It was beautiful in its greatness,
   in the length of its branches;
for its roots went down
   to abundant waters.
8The cedars in the garden of God could not rival it,
   nor the fir trees equal its boughs;
the plane trees were as nothing
   compared with its branches;
no tree in the garden of God
   was like it in beauty.
9I made it beautiful
   in the mass of its branches,
and all the trees of Eden envied it,
   that were in the garden of God.

10"Therefore thus says the Lord God: Because it towered high and set its top among the clouds, and its heart was proud of its height, 11I will give it into the hand of a mighty one of the nations; he shall surely deal with it as its wickedness deserves. I have cast it out. 12Foreigners, the most terrible of the nations, will cut it down and leave it. On the mountains and in all the valleys its branches will fall, and its boughs will lie broken in all the water-courses of the land; and all the peoples of the earth will go from its shadow and leave it. 13Upon its ruin will dwell all the birds of the air, and upon its branches will be all the beasts of the field. 14All this is in order that no trees by the waters may grow to lofty height or set their tops among the clouds, and that no trees that drink water may reach up to them in height; for they are all given over to death, to the nether world among mortal men, with those who go down to the Pit.

15"Thus says the Lord God: When it goes down to Sheol I will make the deep mourn for it, and restrain its rivers, and many waters shall be stopped; I will clothe Lebanon in gloom for it, and all the trees of the field shall faint because of it. 16I will make the nations quake at the sound of its fall, when I cast it down to Sheol with those who go down to the Pit; and all the trees of Eden, the choice and best of Lebanon, all that drink water, will be comforted in the nether world. [17]They also shall go down to Sheol with it, to those who are slain by the sword; yea, those who dwelt under its shadow among the nations shall perish. [18]Whom are you thus like in glory and in greatness among the trees of Eden? You shall be brought down with the trees of Eden to the nether world; you shall lie among the uncircumcised, with those who are slain by the sword.

"This is Pharaoh and all his multitude, says the Lord GOD."

The date in v. 1 is 21 June 587. In this oracle Pharaoh is likened to a great cedar, described in vv. 3-9. The cedar surpasses all other trees, even those of Eden "in the garden of God" (vv. 8-9) — a mythic element, as are the cedar's drawing its nourishment from the cosmic deep, and the life-giving waters flowing out from the cedar to all the trees of the forest (v. 4). The cedar is a life-giving cosmic tree, having "its top among the clouds" (v. 3), and all great nations dwell under it (v. 6). In order to understand better how this is related to the imagery of death and the nether world introduced later in the oracle, we may observe that in the Ancient Near East the cedar was associated with longevity, and that a longing for longevity may raise its goal, to become a longing for immortality. We see how aptly Pharaoh is likened allegorically to a cosmic tree at the center and source of life when we note that in the royal ideologies of the Ancient Near East a king was often felt to be so deeply integrated with the forces of nature that he radiated abundance and fertility on the land and its people. Some clear traces of this are found in Ps 72(71), especially in 72(71):3, 6, 16, and there is a prayer for what, literally taken, amounts to immortality in 72(71):5. We have seen mythic elements applied to the king of Tyre, the better to convey the enormity of his downfall, in Ezek 28:11-19. The mythic elements in the allegorical representation of the Egyptian Pharaoh here in Ezek 31 have a similar function.

In vv. 10-14 the cosmic cedar, so proudly described in the preceding verses, has been cut down by a mighty foreigner,

an allegorical reference to the vanquishing of the Pharaoh
Hophra (Apries) and the land which is identified with him.
(It should be noted that the Hebrew verbs in this section,
translated in the future tense in the Revised Standard Version, are actually past, but they may perhaps be taken as
examples of the "prophetic perfect," expressing God's determination already made to do something in the future.) The
divine motive in bringing this political event about is given
in v. 14. It is not a motive based on Egyptian political or
military behavior but on the mythic pride of the nation
identified with its king. Pharaoh, the cosmic tree, had
usurped qualities which befit gods better than mortals, and
God would not tolerate this. Once again, as in the story of
paradise and the fall in Gen 2:4b-3:24, we meet the motif of
human strivings toward divine prerogatives, thwarted by
divine resistance. As in Gen 3:22, and elsewhere in Ancient
Near Eastern literature, the divine prerogative at issue is
immortality, although here in Ezek 31 that is not stated
directly.

Images of death, already introduced in v. 14, govern vv.
15-18 (in which the Hebrew verbs continue to be past rather
than future): when the great cedar which is Pharaoh had
been cut down, it descended into the nether world, Sheol,
where it found all the once proud trees of Eden, "comforted"
in their misery (v. 16) by the companionship of the new
arrival which had been the greatest of them all. The basic
thought of vv. 15-18 will be taken up again in 32:17-32.

The relation of the entire oracle in chapter 31 to historical
events is slight. It serves as a warning that not only Egypt
represented by Pharaoh but all mighty nations with their
kings come to an end. Proud kings, who in the ancient way
of looking at things assured life and prosperity in the land,
have to remember that they are mortal, and that the life of
their nations will not endure forever.

CONCLUDING ORACLES AGAINST EGYPT
32:1-32

32 In the twelfth year, in the twelfth month, on the first day of the month, the word of the LORD came to me: ²"Son of man, raise a lamentation over Pharaoh king of Egypt, and you say to him:

"You consider yourself a lion among the nations,
but you are like a dragon in the seas;
you burst forth in your rivers,
   trouble the waters with your feet,
   and foul their rivers.
³Thus says the Lord GOD:
I will throw my net over you
with a host of many peoples;
and I will haul you up in my dragnet.
⁴And I will cast you on the ground,
on the open field I will fling you.
and will cause all the birds of the air to settle on you,
and I will gorge the beasts of the whole earth with you.
⁵I will strew your flesh upon the mountains,
and fill the valleys with your carcass.
⁶I will drench the land even to the mountains
with your flowing blood;
and the watercourses will be full of you.
⁷When I blot you out, I will cover the heavens,
and make their stars dark;
I will cover the sun with a cloud,
and the moon shall not give its light.
⁸All the bright lights of heaven
will I make dark over you,
and put darkness upon your land,
         says the Lord GOD.

⁹"I will trouble the hearts of many peoples, when I carry you captive among the nations, into the countries which you have not known. ¹⁰I will make many peoples appalled at you, and their kings shall shudder because of you, when I brandish my sword before them; they shall tremble every moment, every one for his own life, on the

day of your downfall. [11]For thus says the Lord GOD: The sword of the king of Babylon shall come upon you. [12]I will cause your multitude to fall by the swords of mighty ones, all of them most terrible among the nations.

"They shall bring to nought the pride of Egypt,
    and all its multitude shall perish.
[13]I will destroy all its beasts
    from beside many waters;
and no foot of man shall trouble them any more,
    nor shall the hoofs of beasts trouble them.
[14]Then I will make their waters clear,
    and cause their rivers to run like oil,
            says the Lord GOD.
[15]When I make the land of Egypt desolate
    and when the land is stripped of all that fills it,
when I smite all who dwell in it,
    then they will know that I am the LORD.
[16]This is a lamentation which shall be chanted; the daughters of the nations shall chant it; over Egypt, and over all her multitude, shall they chant it, says the Lord GOD."

[17]In the twelfth year, in the first month, on the fifteenth day of the month, the word of the LORD came to me: [18]"Son of man, wail over the multitude of Egypt, and send them down, her and the daughters of majestic nations, to the nether world, to those who have gone down to the Pit: [19]'Whom do you surpass in beauty?

Go down, and be laid with the uncircumcised.'
[20]They shall fall amid those who are slain by the sword, and with her shall lie all her multitudes. [21]The mighty chiefs shall speak of them, with their helpers, out of the midst of Sheol: 'They have come down, they lie still, the uncircumcised, slain by the sword.'

[22]"Assyria is there, and all her company, their graves round about her, all of them slain, fallen by the sword; [23]whose graves are set in the uttermost parts of the Pit, and her company is round about her grave; all of them slain, fallen by the sword, who spread terror in the land of the living.

[24]"Elam is there, ...

²⁶"Meshech and Tubal are there, . . .

²⁹"Edom is there, her kings and all her princes, . . .

³⁰"The princes of the north are there, all of them, and all the Sidonians, who have gone down in shame with the slain, . . .

³¹"When Pharaoh sees them, he will comfort himself for all his multitude, Pharaoh and all his army slain by the sword, says the Lord GOD. ³²For he spread terror in the land of the living; therefore he shall be laid among the uncircumcised, with those who are slain by the sword, Pharaoh and all his multitude, says the Lord GOD."

In this chapter there are two oracles against Egypt. The first (vv. 1-16) is dated with the equivalent of 3 December 586. Jerusalem had by then fallen to the Babylonians, but there is no reference to this in the oracle. This oracle is supposed to be a lament (vv. 2, 16). A lament is uttered for a person already dead, with his qualities and his deeds recalled in the past tense, with the dead person himself addressed possibly in the present tense. This oracular lament starts out, indeed, as a lament, but it shifts already in v. 3 to a threat for the future. As in 28:11-19, the threat of punishment which is a characteristic of an oracle of judgement is expressed in a poem showing some of the formal characteristics of a lament. The grounds for Egypt's punishment have, again, to do with pride, but the accusation of pride is not very well developed. Most of the oracle is devoted to threat. At the beginning, Pharaoh, although he thinks of himself as a regal lion, is likened instead to a water dragon, as in 29:3-6a. The dragon will be killed, with cosmic effects (vv. 5-8). With v. 9 there is a move from the bestiary symbolism to historical allusion: Hophra (Apries) of Egypt will be overcome by Nebuchadrezzar of Babylon. In v. 12b pride is at least stated clearly as the reason for God's causing the desolation of Egypt evoked in the rest of the oracle.

The date of the second oracle, 27 April 586, is earlier than that of the oracle preceding it. In this oracle (vv. 17-32) the thought of 31:15-18 is restated, with the tree symbolism replaced by direct allusion to historical nations which have now come to an end and which lie in their graves, in Sheol, in the Pit of the nether world — Assyria, which had been absorbed by her closely related southern neighbor, Babylonia; Elam to the east, in Iran; Meshech and Tubal, which were in Asia Minor; Judah's Transjordanian neighbor and rival, Edom; the Phoenician city-state of Sidon and all other states to the north of Judah. Their place in the nether world is not even an honorable one. It is the place of the uncircumcised and of those who have been "slain by the sword," which means those who have suffered the shame of death at the hands of another person. There Egypt will join them, "comforted" by the companionship of other dead nations, just as the trees of Eden were comforted by the arrival of the symbolic Egyptian cedar in 31:16. In this oracle, the instrument through which God will bring about the imminent descent of Egypt to the nether world of nations is not the sword of the king of Babylon but Ezekiel's efficacious prophetic word (v. 18).

Here end the oracles against Egypt, and here also ends the entire series of oracles against foreign nations which constitute the second part of the Book of Ezekiel.

PART THREE

DELIVERANCE FOR
THE HOUSE OF ISRAEL

A WATCHMAN TO WARN OF LIFE AND DEATH
33:1-20

33 The word of the LORD came to me: [2]"Son of man, speak to your people and say to them, If I bring the sword upon a land, and the people of the land take a man from among them, and make him their watchman; [3]and if he sees the sword coming upon the land and blows the trumpet and warns the people; [4]then if any one who hears the sound of the trumpet does not take warning, and the sword comes and takes him away, his blood shall be upon his own head. [5]He heard the sound of the trumpet, and did not take warning; his blood shall be upon himself. But if he had taken warning, he would have saved his life. [6]But if the watchman sees the sword coming and does not blow the trumpet, so that the people are not warned, and the sword comes, and takes any one of them; that man is taken away in his iniquity, but his blood I will require at the watchman's hand.

[7]"So you, son of man, I have made a watchman for the house of Israel; whenever you hear a word from my

mouth, you shall give them warning from me. ⁸If I say to the wicked, O wicked man, you shall surely die, and you do not speak to warn the wicked to turn from his way, that wicked man shall die in his iniquity, but his blood I will require at your hand. ⁹But if you warn the wicked to turn from his way, and he does not turn from his way; he shall die in his iniquity, but you will have saved your life.

¹⁰"And you, son of man, say to the house of Israel, Thus have you said: 'Our transgressions and our sins are upon us, and we waste away because of them; how then can we live?' ¹¹Say to them, As I live, says the Lord GOD, I have no pleasure in the death of the wicked, but that the wicked turn from his way and live; turn back, turn back from your evil ways; for why will you die, O house of Israel? ¹²And you, son of man, say to your people, The righteousness of the righteous shall not deliver him when he transgresses; and as for the wickedness of the wicked, he shall not fall by it when he turns from his wickedness; and the righteous shall not be able to live by his righteousness when he sins. ¹³Though I say to the righteous that he shall surely live, yet if he trusts in his righteousness and commits iniquity, none of his righteous deeds shall be remembered; but in the iniquity that he has committed he shall die. ¹⁴Again, though I say to the wicked, 'You shall surely die,' yet if he turns from his sin and does what is lawful and right, ¹⁵if the wicked restores the pledge, gives back what he has taken by robbery, and walks in the statutes of life, committing no iniquity; he shall surely live, he shall not die. ¹⁶None of the sins that he has committed shall be remembered against him; he has done what is lawful and right, he shall surely live.

¹⁷"Yet your people say, 'The way of the Lord is not just; when it is their own way that is not just. ¹⁸When the righteous turns from his righteousness, and commits iniquity, he shall die for it. ¹⁹And when the wicked turns from his wickedness, and does what is lawful and right, he shall live by it. ²⁰Yet you say, 'The way of the Lord is not just.' O house of Israel, I will judge each of you according to his ways."

This section has two parts, related to one another and integrated with one another here, although material of each part occurs elsewhere in the book independently of material from the other part. Vv. 2-9 have to do with Ezekiel's role as a watchman; of this part, vv. 7-9 have a close parallel at 3:16-19. Vv. 10-20 have to do with the moral responsibility of the individual person and the justice of God's punishment; these matters are the topics of chapter 18, and 33:17-20 is roughly parallel to 18:25-30a.

The first part (vv. 2-9) can be subdivided. In vv. 2-6, a case is presented: if God makes someone the people's watchman, there will be certain consequences. In vv. 7-9, Ezekiel himself is appointed watchman for the house of Israel. In vv. 2-6, the situation presumed is that of a land besieged by an enemy. If an appointed watchman blows the trumpet to warn of an approaching army's attack, those who do not heed the warning are responsible for their own death at the enemy's hands, but if the watchman himself fails to sound the warning, then he is responsible for the death of those who perish. (Idiomatically, the person on whose head a slain person's blood lies is the person who must bear the guilt for the slain person's death.) In vv. 7-9, though, the situation evoked is that in which Ezekiel receives the word of God announcing death as punishment for a wicked person's sinfulness. If Ezekiel, having received such a word, warns the sinner to turn from his ways, the sinful person who does not heed the warning is responsible for his or her own death, but if Ezekiel does not give the warning, then it is he himself who will have to bear guilt for the sinner's death, understood as the consequence of sin. We have here a good illustration of the conditional element in prophecy. In the case envisaged, God says, "O wicked man, you shall surely die," but it is clear that the sentence of death is not definitive and irrevocable, and that what God really wants is the sinner's change of heart, so that he will *not* die. It is only *if* he or she persists in wickedness and remains laden with guilt that the death sentence will be carried out.

The matter of repentance and failure to repent, already introduced in vv. 7-9, serves as a thematic link between the first part of this section (vv. 2-9) and the second part (vv. 10-20). This second part, like its broad parallel, chapter 18, shows characteristics of an authoritative lecture on norms of life, in which elements of a scholastic disputation are used. Both in chapter 18 and in 33:10-20 the topic is set up by a quotation expressing an idea currently held, which is then immediately refuted by an authoritative statement of principle. Here, in 33:10, the idea set up to be refuted is that once the burden of sin and guilt lies upon people there is not much hope of having the burden lifted so that the people can enjoy their full share of life. This sentiment of despair is different from the more cynical idea set up at the beginning of chapter 18 in the quoted proverb on the fathers who eat sour grapes and the children whose teeth are set on edge, but it is found, nevertheless, in 18:23, 30, 32. The principle serving as refutation of the idea expressed in the quotation is also different in the two passages. Here, the idea is refuted by God's declaration that his fundamental will is not that people die because of their sins but that they live (v. 11); for a sinner to live, he or she must freely turn from an orientation towards sin to an orientation which is in conformity with God's will, expressed in his law. In vv. 12-20, just as in the structurally corresponding part of chapter 18, the "lecture" continues with cases used as the basis of declarations of the mind of the divine lawgiver, and it is concluded with an objection and the divine answer to the objection.

The integrating factors in the union of vv. 10-20 with vv. 2-9 are the motifs of personal responsibility and of life. A watchman must warn people, so that they can escape death and live. Ezekiel is a watchman who must give people God's warnings, so that they can escape death as divine punishment and enjoy the fullness of life divinely allotted to them. If an individual person does not turn from his or her fundamentally sinful option, someone — either the sinner or the watchman who has shirked his duty — will have the sinner's blood on his head, but God's will is that the sinner live, and Ezekiel's mission is to favor the accomplishment of that will.

Placement of one account of Ezekiel's call to be a watchman at 3:16-21, in the general call-narrative at the beginning of the entire book, includes watchmanship as an element of his general vocation. Placement of another account of the same call here, at the beginning of the third major part of the book, indicates the validity of Ezekiel's vocation to be a life-saving watchman as it was exercised even when the period of collectively unheeded warnings and threats of death for Jerusalem, found mainly in part one of the book, had yielded, after the disaster in Judah, to a period in which the house of Israel had to face a very uncertain future. In that new period, Israel still needed correction, but it also needed the oracles of deliverance and hope and new life which are typical of parts three and four of the book. Ezekiel the watchman will now proclaim God's will that the house of Israel not die because of its sins but that it live.

JERUSALEM HAS FALLEN
33:21-22

> [21]In the twelfth year of our exile, in the tenth month, on the fifth day of the month, a man who had escaped from Jerusalem came to me and said, "The city has fallen." [22]Now the hand of the LORD had been upon me the evening before the fugitive came; and he had opened my mouth by the time the man came to me in the morning; so my mouth was opened, and I was no longer dumb.

Ezekiel reports the arrival of a refugee from Judah who has reached Babylonia, bearing the news of Jerusalem's fall. Jerusalem's walls were breached in July of 586 (Jer 39:2; 52:6-7), and the Temple was destroyed a month later (2 Kgs 25:8-9; Jer 52:12). The date of the refugee's meeting with Ezekiel (v. 21) is 8 January 585.

The setting of Ezekiel's life and work in the historical vicissitudes of his own people reappears, after the interruption caused by the insertion of the series of oracles against foreign nations between the end of chapter 24 and the beginning of chapter 33. At the end of chapter 24, Ezekiel was struck dumb with grief over the death of his wife, but the arrival of the refugee was announced there as the moment when Ezekiel's dumbness would end (24:25-27). Here, Ezekiel's dumbness is released by God's personal action, as the refugee arrives. Symbolically, Ezekiel's mouth is opened anew, to utter the new oracles which are to follow.

LESSONS GO UNHEEDED
33:23-33

²³The word of the LORD came to me: ²⁴"Son of man, the inhabitants of these waste places in the land of Israel keep saying, 'Abraham was only one man, yet he got possession of the land; but we are many; the land is surely given us to possess.' ²⁵Therefore say to them, Thus says the Lord GOD: You eat flesh with the blood, and lift up your eyes to your idols, and shed blood; shall you then possess the land? ²⁶You resort to the sword, you commit abominations and each of you defiles his neighbor's wife; shall you then possess the land? ²⁷Say this to them, Thus says the Lord GOD: As I live, surely those who are in the waste places shall fall by the sword; and him that is in the open field I will give to the beasts to be devoured; and those who are in strongholds and in caves shall die by pestilence. ²⁸And I will make the land a desolation and a waste; and her proud might shall come to an end; and the mountains of Israel shall be so desolate that none shall pass through. ²⁹Then they will know that I am the LORD, when I have made the land a desolation and a waste because of all their abominations which they have committed.

³⁰"As for you, son of man, your people who talk together about you by the walls and at the doors of the houses, say to one another, each to his brother, 'Come, and hear what the word is that comes forth from the LORD.' ³¹And they come to you as people come, and they sit before you as my people, and they hear what you say but they will not do it; for with their lips they show much love, but their heart is set on their gain. ³²And lo, you are to them like one who sings love songs with a beautiful voice and plays well on an instrument, for they

hear what you say, but they will not do it. [33]When this comes — and come it will! — then they will know that a prophet has been among them."

This passage is a sort of diptych with two distinct panels, each showing people who do not heed God's will, despite what he has done to get them to understand him and to modify their lives accordingly. In each, there is a divine comment on the group's unheeding attitude.

In the first panel (vv. 23-29), we see "the inhabitants of the waste places in the land of Israel" (v. 24), a fairly evident reference to the Judean homeland, recently devastated by the Babylonian army. They keep on thinking about their right to the promised land, and they appeal to sacred history, to God's promises to Abraham, in order to justify their right. In the quotation in v. 24 this attitude is set up for demolition. God then demolishes it by contradiction, reminding the Judeans of their violations of ethical requirements expressed in his law, and he brings the point home with the rhetorical questions. His promises to Abraham and his descendants are subject to the condition of Abraham's descendants' doing God's will. The inhabitants of Judah have in general not conformed to that will by their behavior, and so how, indeed, can they expect the promised reward? The disputation concludes with a threat of further punishment with a new desolation, perhaps that of the twenty-third year of Nebuchadrezzar (582/81) mentioned in Jer 52:30. From that fresh penalty they should at least realize that God is acting, and that he has good reason to act.

In the second panel (vv. 30-33), we see Ezekiel's own neighbors in exile. God's words are given to Ezekiel without a mandate to hand them on to any hearers, but they are, nevertheless, set down here in written record. The exilic neighbors like to hear Ezekiel pronounce his oracles, but they do not act upon them when action, or some kind of initiative, is called for. Perhaps the oracles which they like to hear are the consoling oracles of deliverance characteristic of the period after the arrival of the news of Jerusalem's fall and destruction, but Ezekiel, in this time of search for a new future, remains the watchman with a divine commission to warn the wicked to repent (see 33:7-20). The exiles, like basically religious people in all times and places, enjoy religious words which provide aesthetic enjoyment, or which make them feel good, but they do not bother to take seriously words which call for action and change in their lives. As far as they are concerned, Ezekiel might as well not be a prophet, for they do not take his prophetic words seriously. In this short divine message addressed to Ezekiel himself, there is divine sarcasm for the exilic neighbors and divine sympathy for Ezekiel. God tells his spokesman that when his prophetically uttered words on the future have been fulfilled, be they words of promise or words of threat, the people will know that he is indeed a prophet.

OF SHEPHERDS AND FLOCKS
34:1-31

34 The word of the LORD came to me: [2]"Son of man, prophesy against the shepherds of Israel, prophesy, and say to them, even to the shepherds, Thus says the Lord GOD: Ho, shepherds of Israel who have been feeding yourselves! Should not shepherds feed the sheep? [3]You eat the fat, you clothe yourselves with the wool, you slaughter the fatlings; but you do not feed the sheep. [4]The weak you have not strengthened, the sick you have not healed, the crippled you have not bound up, the strayed you have not brought back, the lost you have not sought, and with force and harshness you have ruled them. [5]So they were scattered, because there was no shepherd; and they became food for all the wild beasts. [6]My sheep were scattered, they wandered over all the mountains and on every high hill; my sheep were scattered over all the face of the earth, with none to search or seek for them.

[7]"Therefore, you shepherds, hear the word of the LORD: [8]As I live, says the Lord GOD, because my sheep have become a prey, and my sheep have become food for all the wild beasts, since there was no shepherd; and because my shepherds have not searched for my sheep,

but the shepherds have fed themselves and have not fed my sheep; [9]therefore, you shepherds, hear the word of the LORD: [10]Thus says the Lord GOD, Behold, I am against the shepherds; and I will require my sheep at their hand, and put a stop to their feeding the sheep; no longer shall the shepherds feed themselves. I will rescue my sheep from their mouths, that they may not be food for them.

[11]"For thus says the Lord GOD: Behold, I, I myself will search for my sheep, and will seek them out. [12]As a shepherd seeks out his flock when some of his sheep have been scattered abroad, so will I seek out my sheep; and I will rescue them from all places where they have been scattered on a day of clouds and thick darkness. [13]And I will bring them out from the peoples, and gather them from the countries, and will bring them into their own land; and I will feed them on the mountains of Israel, by the fountains, and in all the inhabited places of the country. [14]I will feed them with good pasture, and upon the mountain heights of Israel shall be their pasture; there they shall lie down in good grazing land, and on fat pasture they shall feed on the mountains of Israel. [15]I myself will be the shepherd of my sheep, and I will make them lie down, says the Lord GOD. [16]I will seek the lost, and I will bring back the strayed, and I will bind up the crippled, and I will strengthen the weak, and the fat and the strong I will watch over; I will feed them in justice.

[17]"As for you, my flock, thus says the Lord GOD: Behold, I judge between sheep and sheep, rams and he-goats. [18]Is it not enough for you to feed on the good pasture, that you must tread down with your feet the rest of your pasture; and to drink of clear water, that you must foul the rest with your feet? [19]And must my sheep eat what you have trodden with your feet, and drink what you have fouled with your feet?

[20]"Therefore, thus says the Lord GOD to them: Behold, I, I myself will judge between the fat sheep and the lean sheep. [21]Because you push with side and shoulder, and thrust at all the weak with your horns, till you have scattered them abroad, [22]I will save my flock,

they shall no longer be a prey; and I will judge between sheep and sheep. 23And I will set up over them one shepherd, my servant David, and he shall feed them: he shall feed them and be their shepherd. 24And I, the LORD, will be their God, and my servant David shall be prince among them; I, the LORD, have spoken.

25"I will make with them a covenant of peace and banish wild beasts from the land, so that they may dwell securely in the wilderness and sleep in the woods. 26And I will make them and the places round about my hill a blessing; and I will send down the showers in their season; they shall be showers of blessing. 27And the trees of the field shall yield their fruit, and the earth shall yield its increase, and they shall be secure in their land; and they shall know that I am the LORD, when I break the bars of their yoke, and deliver them from the hand of those who enslaved them. 28They shall no more be a prey to the nations, nor shall the beasts of the land devour them; they shall dwell securely, and none shall make them afraid. 29And I will provide for them prosperous plantations so that they shall no more be consumed with hunger in the land, and no longer suffer the reproach of the nations. 30And they shall know that I, the LORD their God, am with them, and that they, the house of Israel, are my people, says the Lord GOD. 31And you are my sheep, the sheep of my pasture, and I am your God, says the Lord GOD."

This chapter records a composite oracle having to do with shepherds (vv. 2-16, 23-24) and with the sheep entrusted to their care (vv. 17-22, 25-30). The shepherds are first and foremost the political rulers of the house of Israel, but what is said of them in vv. 2-16 can also be said of other persons in positions of high responsibility. The oracle begins with an accusation of the evil shepherds (vv. 2-6). They have been attentive to what they could themselves gain from having all the sheep at their disposition, to do with them what they willed to do (vv. 2b-3), and in doing so they have failed seriously in their duties toward the sheep, whom they have neglected, and whom they have ruled harshly (v. 4). Because of their egoism and their incompetence, the people of Judah have fallen prey to foreign violence and have been dispersed in exile (vv. 5-6). What is said of these rulers could be said of any ruler or of any autocratic oligarchy supposed to work for the welfare of the people but guilty of exploiting the people instead. On them judgement is passed in vv. 7-10. God will take the sheep away from the wicked shepherds' control. But what then? The question of Israel's future rises, and it is answered with a promise (vv. 11-16). God will be the good shepherd of the house of Israel. He will bring his people from dispersion in exile to new gathering in the promised land, and there he will assure their welfare, strengthening the weak and keeping a just eye on the strong. There is obviously an echo of this in the image of Jesus, the good shepherd, in Jn 10:1-21.

Words of judgement are then addressed to the members of the flock itself, those members of the house of Israel who are not in positions of authoritative responsibility. Although they have all been neglected and exploited by their shepherds, not all of them are innocent of antisocial behavior of their own. Some of them have ridden roughshod over their neighbors, showing irresponsible carelessness, tyrannizing or bullying their weaker fellows (vv. 17-22). As God has judged the rulers, so will he judge the ruled, for God, the good shepherd, is too great and just to fall into facile condemnation of irresponsible and self-seeking governors without condemning self-seeking exploiters among the governed as well. The ruled he will judge, though, not as a group but as individuals, distinguishing "between sheep and sheep, rams and he-goats" (v. 22), for the weak and the downtrodden among them need divine support, not divine judgement.

These words of selective judgement of individual members of the flock are followed by an unexpected promise of a new David to care for the flock. This future David is promised as a shepherd in v. 23, while Yahweh has already promised himself as a shepherd in vv. 11-16. It is as Israel's God that Yahweh will be Israel's shepherd, while the future David will be shepherd as prince over the people and as servant under God (v. 24). The identity of this new David of the future is left unspecified and open. He is probably called "David" because, just as the original David ruled over all Israel, before the nation's division into two separate kingdoms after Solomon's death, this future David will be "one shepherd," the sole ruler of the house of Israel united again. This seems to be the reason for his being called "David" in 37:24a too, for the central issue in 37:15-24a is the regained unity of all Israel. His being called "David" lends him the first royal David's aura of personal grandeur and of fidelity to Yahweh, and it may also suggest that he is to be of the royal house of David, whose promised continuation was to have no temporal limit (2 Sam 7). Whether this Davidic person was meant to be an eschatological or messianic figure or not in the original sense of the oracle can be debated, but he does lend himself well to such an interpretation, even if the interpretation is secondary.

To the end of this oracle on the shepherds and the flock there has been appended a promise of peace and prosperity whose description also lends itself well to an eschatological interpretation, for some of its elements are almost paradisiac (vv. 25-30). God's people will live in freedom in a rich land of abundance and fertility, without fear of wild beasts within the land or of predators from without. When this comes to pass, the members of the house of Israel will have yet another reason to know that all their blessings are from Yahweh, their God, who cares for them. V. 31, a late addition to the Hebrew text, serves to identify this blessed people with the allegorical flock of the preceding verses, thus integrating vv. 25-30 into the rest of the oracle. The promised shepherd David of vv. 23-24 thereby acquires a ruler's role in assuring the blessings of nature in vv. 25-30. This ancient association of the king with cosmic blessings is echoed in Ps. 72(71).

JUDGEMENT AGAINST MOUNT SEIR
35:1-15

35 The word of the LORD came to me: [2]"Son of man, set your face against Mount Seir, and prophesy against it, [3]and say to it, Thus says the Lord GOD: Behold, I am against you, Mount Seir, and I will stretch out my hand against you, and I will make you a desolation and a waste. [4]I will lay your cities waste, and you shall become a desolation; and you shall know that I am the LORD. [5]Because you cherished perpetual enmity, and gave over the people of Israel to the power of the sword at the time of their calamity, at the time of their final punishment; [6]therefore, as I live, says the Lord GOD, I will prepare you for blood, and blood shall pursue you; because you are guilty of blood, therefore blood shall pursue you. ...

[10]"Because you said, 'These two nations and these two countries shall be mine, and we will take possession of them,' although the LORD was there — [11]therefore, as I live, says the Lord GOD, I will deal with you according to the anger and envy which you showed because of your hatred against them; and I will make myself known among you, when I judge you. [12]And you shall know that I, the LORD, have heard all the revilings which you uttered against the mountains of Israel, saying, 'They are laid desolate, they are given us to devour.' [13]and you magnified yourselves against me with your mouth, and multiplied your words against me; I heard it. [14]Thus says the Lord GOD: For the rejoicing of the whole earth I will make you desolate. [15]As you rejoiced over the inheritance of the house of Israel, because it was desolate, so I will deal with you; you shall be desolate, Mount Seir, and all Edom, all of it. Then they will know that I am the LORD.

Mount Seir is the entire mountainous region southeast of the Dead Sea, the homeland of the Edomites. In 25:12-14 judgement is passed on Edom because of the spirit of revenge which the Edomites showed towards Judah in her time of trial. Here in chapter 35 that same attitude towards

Judah appears again as a reason for divine judgement. The revenge taken by Edom is rooted in a long history of "perpetual enmity" culminating in Edom's collaboration with the invaders of Judah (v. 5). Worse yet, Edom, when this oracle was delivered, intended to annex territory belonging to the house of Israel while Judah, recently ravished, was down and out (v. 10, in which the "two nations" are the two historically divided kingdoms of Judah and Israel). Yahweh is angry because those two countries, whether divided or united, belong to the house of Israel. They are Yahweh's land. Even though he has recently brought about the devastation of Judah as punishment for the sins of the house of Israel, he is faithful to his people, and besides, he intends to restore his people in that same land which he once promised to them. This oracle of judgement against the mountain country of Edom should be understood in relation to the immediately following 36:1-15, in which hope is proclaimed for the mountains of Israel.

JUDGEMENT IN FAVOR OF THE MOUNTAINS OF ISRAEL
36:1-15

36 "And you, son of man, prophesy to the mountains of Israel, and say, O mountains of Israel, hear the word of the LORD. ²Thus says the Lord GOD: Because the enemy said of you, 'Aha!' and, 'The ancient heights have become our possession,' ³therefore prophesy, and say, Thus says the Lord GOD: Because, yea, because they made you desolate, and crushed you from all sides, so that you became the possession of the rest of the nations, and you became the talk and evil gossip of the people; ⁴therefore, O mountains of Israel, hear the word of the Lord GOD: Thus says the Lord GOD to the mountains and the hills, the ravines and the valleys, the desolate wastes and the deserted cities, which have become a prey and derision to the rest of the nations round about; ⁵therefore thus says the Lord GOD: I speak in my hot jealousy against the rest of the nations, and against all

Edom, who gave my land to themselves as a possession with whole-hearted joy and utter contempt, that they might possess it and plunder it. [6]Therefore prophesy concerning the land of Israel, and say to the mountains and hills, to the ravines and valleys, Thus says the Lord GOD: Behold, I speak in my jealous wrath, because you have suffered the reproach of the nations; [7]therefore thus says the Lord GOD: I swear that the nations that are round about you shall themselves suffer reproach.

[8]"But you, O mountains of Israel, shall shoot forth your branches, and yield your fruit to my people Israel; for they will soon come home. [9]For behold, I am for you, and I will turn to you, and you shall be tilled and sown; [10]and I will multiply men upon you, the whole house of Israel, all of it; the cities shall be inhabited and the waste places rebuilt; [11]and I will multiply upon you man and beast; and they shall increase and be fruitful; and I will cause you to be inhabited as in your former times, and will do more good to you than ever before. Then you will know that I am the LORD. [12]Yea, I will let men walk upon you, even my people Israel; and they shall possess you, and you shall be their inheritance, and you shall no longer bereave them of children. [13]Thus says the Lord GOD: Because men say to you, 'You devour men, and you bereave your nation of children,' [14]therefore you shall no longer devour men and no longer bereave your nation of children, says the Lord GOD; [15]and I will not let you hear any more the reproach of the nations, and you shall no longer bear the disgrace of the peoples and no longer cause your nation to stumble, says the Lord GOD."

This oracle is the counterpart of the oracle of judgement against Edom which immediately precedes it. The previous oracle is addressed to Mount Seir, the mountain country of Edom, which is condemned. This one is addressed to the mountains of Israel, which receive a promise of new hope. The mountains of Israel were also addressed in 6:2-3, but there they were judged and condemned. Here they are the

beneficiaries of divine favor. In the first part of this oracle
(vv. 2-7) this favor is expressed to the mountains of Israel in
an oracle of disfavor towards the foreign nations around
about them, their enemies, with Edom mentioned particularly. As in the preceding oracle of chapter 35, the enemy is
accused of contributing to the unmentioned Babylonians'
work of laying Judah waste, and of plotting to annex part of
Judah after Jerusalem's fall. As in the preceding oracle, the
enemy is threatened with punishment for that. The reasons
for Yahweh's anger are the same in both of these comple-
mentary oracles: Judah, the final independent kingdom of
the house of Israel, has at its darkest moment been treated
badly by the neighboring nations, when it deserved help
rather than additonal exploitation; the land of Israel,
moreover, is Yahweh's own land (36:5).

In vv. 8-15 the oracle moves from condemnation of hostile neighbors to promise for Israel. The mountains of Israel,
devastated by their enemies and deprived of hope in the
natural order of things, are promised a new hope beyond
their expectation. The mountains have seen the fulfillment
of the prophecy of destruction announced in chapter 6, but
now they learn that the penalties visited upon them because
of the sinfulness of their inhabitants will not last forever.
God will bring their people back from exile, the fields laid
waste will be tilled agin, the ruined cities rebuilt. The lord of
history will turn around completely the situation following
the destruction of 586, the situation supposed both by 35:1-
15 and by 36:1-15. He will cause Judah, victimized and
derided by Edom and the other neighboring nations, to
prosper, while the nations successfully gloating over Judah's misfortune will themselves suffer reproach. It is not
because of any merit enjoyed by the members of the house of
Israel, individually or collectively, that God will bring this
about, for their wickedness is what led God to bring about
the destruction of their land in the first place. It is rather
because of God's gratuitous election of Israel, and his fidelity to his promises to Israel, including his promise of the
land, that he will do what he now proposes to do.

GOD ACTS TO SAVE HIS HONOR
36:16-38

¹⁶The word of the LORD came to me: ¹⁷"Son of man, when the house of Israel dwelt in their own land, they defiled it by their ways and their doings; their conduct before me was like the uncleanness of a woman in her impurity. ¹⁸So I poured out my wrath upon them for the blood which they had shed in the land, for the idols with which they had defiled it. ¹⁹I scattered them among the nations, and they were dispersed through the countries; in accordance with their conduct and their deeds I judged them. ²⁰But when they came to the nation, wherever they came, they profaned my holy name, in that men said of them, 'These are the people of the LORD, and yet they had to go out of his land.' ²¹But I had concern for my holy name, which the house of Israel caused to be profaned among the nations to which they came.

²²"Therefore say to the house of Israel, Thus says the Lord GOD: It is not for your sake O house of Israel, that I am about to act, but for the sake of my holy name, which you have profaned among the nations to which you came. ²³And I will vindicate the holiness of my great name, which has been profaned among the nations, and which you have profaned among them; and the nations will know that I am the LORD, says the Lord GOD, when through you I vindicate my holiness before their eyes. ²⁴For I will take you from the nations, and gather you from all the countries, and bring you into your own land. ²⁵I will sprinkle clean water upon you, and you shall be clean from all your uncleannesses, and from all your idols I will cleanse you. ²⁶A new heart I will give you, and a new spirit I will put within you; and I will take out of your flesh the heart of stone and give you a heart of flesh. ²⁷And I will put my spirit within you, and cause you to walk in my statutes and be careful to observe my ordinances. ²⁸You shall dwell in the land which I gave to your fathers; and you shall be my people, and I will be your God. ²⁹And I will deliver you from all your unclean-

nesses; and I will summon the grain and make it abundant and lay no famine upon you. 30I will make the fruit
of the tree and the increase of the field abundant, that you
may never again suffer the disgrace of famine among the
nations. 31Then you will remember your evil ways, and
your deeds that were not good; and you will loathe yourselves for your iniquities and your abominable deeds. 32It
is not for your sake that I will act, says the Lord GOD: let
that be known to you . Be ashamed and confounded for
your ways, O house of Israel.

33"Thus says the Lord GOD: On the day that I cleanse
you from all your iniquities, I will cause the cities to be
inhabited, and the waste places shall be rebuilt. 34And the
land that was desolate shall be tilled, instead of being the
desolation that it was in the sight of all who passed by.
35And they will say, 'This land that was desolate has
become like the garden of Eden; and the waste and desolate and ruined cities are now inhabited and fortified.'
36Then the nations that are left around about you shall
know that I, the LORD, have rebuilt the ruined places,
and replanted that which was desolate; I, the LORD,
have spoken, and I will do it.

37"Thus says the Lord GOD: This also I will let the
house of Israel ask me to do for them: to increase their
men like a flock. 38Like the flock for sacrifices, like the
flock at Jerusalem during her appointed feasts, so shall
the waste cities be filled with flocks of men. Then they will
know that I am the LORD."

The problematic question to which 36:16-38 gives an
answer is the same as that implicit in 36:1-15: why should
God restore his unfaithful people to the land he promised
their ancestors, when he has just expelled them from that
land for righteous reasons? The problem is set up in vv.
16-21: the house of Israel, conscious of its divine election
and of the promise of the land attached to that election, has
throughout its history behaved evilly, thinking that God
would never reject them and that he would never deprive
them of their land. God, however, mindful of his promises,

but mindful also of the righteous behavior he exacts from his people as their part of the covenant with him, has judged them guilty of failure to behave that way, and he has banished them in exile as their penalty.

A result of this, though, is scandal for the pagan peoples among whom the Judeans are exiled. If those pagans have some knowledge of God's promise of a perpetual gift of the land to his people Israel, they can only conclude that God has reneged his promise. It is, then, the very presence of the heirs of the promise in the lands of their exile that "profanes God's holy name" (vv. 20-21), because it leads other peoples to question the fidelity and trustworthiness of Yahweh. God has decided to save his honor (v. 21), and from that decision flows all that follows.

The main consequence of this is an answer to the implicit question pointed out above: it is in order to vindicate his honor among the nations, as a god faithful to his promises, that Yahweh will restore his unfaithful people to the land from which he has just expelled them. The historical restoration of the house of Israel will take place not for the sake of Israel, now justly punished, but for God's own sake, for reasons having to do not with the behavior of human beings acting in earthly history, but with the transcendent holiness of God, who disposes history (vv. 22-23). Vv. 26-28 repeat the essentials of 11:19-20 and remind us of Jer 31:31-34. In Ezekiel's oracles a new heart is promised in place of the old heart of stone, while in Jeremiah's oracle a new covenant is promised, to be written interiorly on the heart, not on tablets of stone as was the prior covenant. In Ezekiel, but not in Jeremiah, a new spirit is also promised. Although the word "covenant," a key word in Jer 31:31-34, is not uttered in Ezek 11:19-20 or 36:26-28, the statutes and ordinances which, according to Ezekiel, God will have his people observe are in fact the stipulations of the covenant, and in both Ezekiel and Jeremiah the parties to the covenant are declared: "You shall be my people, and I will be your God."

The description of the future restoration in vv. 24-32 has all the initiative coming from God. In the realm of political history, it is God who will bring about the return from exile.

In the realm of that inner conversion which is to be an integral part of the restoration of the house of Israel, it is God who will accomplish the cleansing of the people from their sins, God who will replace their old heart with the new heart and the new spirit by which they will be able to live the kind of moral life which he expects from them. Without the effective action of God there would be no conversion. Even though all of this will flow from God's own free decision and be accomplished by his own action upon persons in their inner lives, God does call upon the members of the house of Israel for an interior act which they themselves are eventually to make, an act of repentance for their past sins (vv. 31-32).

Two supplements then follow. In the first (vv. 33-36) we see how the scandal indicated in vv. 20-21 will be removed from the foreign nations. When they see the cities of Israel restored, they will conclude that Yahweh is faithful, after all, to his promise of the land. In the second (vv. 37-38) the theme of Israel as a flock (chapter 34) is briefly taken up again and linked to the theme of the restored cities of the verses immediately preceding (36:33-36). Israel the flock will prosper in the cities, but only if Israel is humble enough to admit that prosperity comes from God, and to ask God for that favor.

OLD BONES, NEW LIFE
37:1-14

37 The hand of the LORD was upon me, and he brought me out by the Spirit of the LORD, and set me down in the midst of the valley; it was full of bones. ²And he led me round among them; and behold, there were very many upon the valley; and lo, they were very dry. ³And he said to me, "Son of man, can these bones live?" And I answered, "O Lord GOD, thou knowest." ⁴Again he said to me, "Prophesy to these bones, and say to them, O dry bones, hear the word of the LORD. ⁵Thus says the Lord GOD to these bones: Behold, I will cause breath to enter you, and you shall live. ⁶And I will lay sinews upon you, and will cause flesh to come upon you, and cover you with skin, and put breath in you, and you shall live; and you shall know that I am the LORD."

⁷So I prophesied as I was commanded; and as I prophesied, there was a noise, and behold, a rattling; and the bones came together, bone to its bone. ⁸And as I looked, there were sinews on them, and flesh had come upon them, and skin had covered them; but there was no breath in them. ⁹Then he said to me, "Prophesy to the breath, prophesy, son of man, and say to the breath, Thus says the Lord GOD: Come from the four winds, O Breath and breathe upon these slain, that they may live." ¹⁰So I prophesied as he commanded me, and the breath came into them, and they lived, and stood upon their feet, an exceedingly great host.

¹¹Then he said to me, "Son of man, these bones are the whole house of Israel. Behold, they say, 'Our bones are dried up, and our hope is lost; we are clean cut off.' ¹²Therefore prophesy, and say to them, Thus says the Lord GOD: Behold, I will open your graves and raise you from your graves, O my people; and I will bring you home into the land of Israel. ¹³And you shall know that I am the LORD, when I open your graves, and raise you from your graves, O my people. ¹⁴And I will put my Spirit within you, and you shall live, and I will place you in your own land; then you shall know that I, the LORD, have spoken, and I have done it, says the LORD."

This passage, so dramatic in its imagery manifesting the power of God over death, is one of the best known in the entire book of Ezekiel. Structurally, it consists of a description of a vision followed by the vision's interpretation.

In the vision (vv. 1-10), Ezekiel is first transported to the scene by the spirit of the Lord, by the power of the hand of the Lord (compare, at the beginning or end of other visions, 3:12, 22; 8:1, 3; 11:24; 40:1-2). The scene of the vision is a valley or plain whose location is left undefined, for the impact of the vision itself depends on its being abstracted from the limitations of time and place. In the valley are dry and bare bones, all that is left of persons utterly dead. God intends to cover them with sinews and flesh and skin, and to put in them the breath of new life. God carries out his intention, and he does so through his prophet. It is the prophetic word of command uttered by Ezekiel which actually effects the reconstitution of bodies around the bones (vv. 5-6) and which summons the breath by which the bodies come to life (v. 9).

In the interpretation (vv. 11-14), the vision is applied to the situation of the house of Israel, deprived of the life it once had, broken in spirit, bereft of hope. The despairing attitude of the members of the house of Israel is contradicted by the interpretation of the vision. Their attitude is expressed by the quotation in v. 11 (a procedure found also in 12:21; 18:2; 33:10). In what then follows, the imagery of the bones slips away into the imagery of the graves, but the analogies are clear. The bones represent the members of the house of Israel, dead and desiccated as a people. While the bones of the vision, strewn loosely over the floor of the valley, suggest collectivity with little individuation, the graves of the interpretation are individual graves, and their use as imagery opens the oracle to a secondary interpretation in which the resurrection of individuals may find a place. To the bones, or to the bodies in the graves, God's spirit or breath will give new life, and in the collective interpretation, which belongs to the primary sense of the oracle itself, that new life will be theirs as a people, living once again in their own land.

As in 1:4-28 and 2:1-3:15, there is ambiguity in the Hebrew word which means "wind," "breath," and "spirit," and it is not always possible to seize its meaning in translating by choosing one of those possible meanings. The "spirit" of the Lord which conveys Ezekiel from place to place (v. 1) may also be understood as a powerful divinely activated wind. It is surely "breath" which vivifies the reconstituted bodies, but in v. 9 that breath comes from the four winds, and the Hebrew reader would not miss the identity of the word meaning both "breath" and "wind." In v. 14 the breath which vivifies is translated "spirit," because it is of God, but in reading the translation we do well to remember the verbal identity of "spirit" and "breath" in Hebrew. The breath of life comes from God. So it was at the beginning of creation, when the "spirit/wind/breath" of God hovered over the waters of chaos (Gen 1:2), ready to infuse life into an inert universe, just as it would infuse new life into the old bones in the mysterious valley of the dead.

The account of the vision of the bones, with its interpretation or application, is an oracle of hope, of new life after a punitive death. As in 36:16-38, the restoration of Israel which is the point of the oracle in its literal and primary sense will come about as the result of a free decision of God, without merit of the people, individually or collectively. Unlike 36:16-38, the oracle of 37:1-14 contains no mention of any divine motive for the decision — not even that of Yahweh's saving his own honor as a god forever faithful to his word. As a result, his decision to infuse new life into the dried bones of Israel appears all the more gratuitous. Because that decision is so gratuitously made, all will know, when it has been carried out, that it was Yahweh who acted (v. 14). Yahweh will have manifested himself as a savior so mighty that he can free people even from the bonds of death. In the Christian Church, this oracle is often read with application to God's exercise of power over death in his raising Christ from the dead after the harrowing of hell, or in his bringing about the general resurrection of the dead at the end of time.

UNITY AND PERMANENCE
IN GOD'S NEW ISRAEL
37:15-28

[15]The word of the LORD came to me; [16]"Son of man, take a stick and write on it, 'For Judah, and the children of Israel associated with him'; then take another stick and write upon it, 'For Joseph (the stick of Ephraim) and all the house of Israel associated with him'; [17]and join them together into one stick, that they may become one in your hand. [18]And when your people say to you, 'Will you not

show us what you mean by these?' ¹⁹say to them, Thus says the Lord GOD: Behold, I am about to take the stick of Joseph (which is in the hand of Ephraim) and the tribes of Israel associated with him; and I will join with it the stick of Judah, and make them one stick, that they may be one in my hand. ²⁰When the sticks on which you write are in your hand before their eyes, ²¹then say to them, Thus says the Lord GOD: Behold, I will take the people of Israel from the nations among which they have gone, and will gather them from all sides, and bring them to their own land; ²²and I will make them one nation in the land, upon the mountains of Israel; and one king shall be king over them all; and they shall be no longer two nations, and no longer divided into two kingdoms. ²³They shall not defile themselves any more with their idols and their detestable things, or with any of their transgressions; but I will save them from all the backslidings in which they have sinned, and will cleanse them; and they shall be my people, and I will be their God.

²⁴"My servant David shall be king over them; and they shall all have one shepherd. They shall follow my ordinances and be careful to observe my statutes. ²⁵They shall dwell in the land where your fathers dwelt that I gave to my servant Jacob; they and their children and their children's children shall dwell there for ever; and David my servant shall be their prince for ever. ²⁶I will make a covenant of peace with them; it shall be an everlasting covenant with them; and I will bless them and multiply them, and will set my sanctuary in the midst of them for evermore. ²⁷My dwelling place shall be with them; and I will be their God, and they shall be my people. ²⁸Then the nations will know that I the LORD sanctify Israel, when my sanctuary is in the midst of them for evermore."

In the preceding oracle God announced the resurrection of the house of Israel. In the present oracle he shows some salient characteristics of that new Israel, which is soon to be brought to life. The oracle begins with instructions for yet another symbolic action to be performed by Ezekiel (vv.

16-17). Ezekiel is to take two sticks, inscribe one to Judah and associates, and the other to Joseph and associates, and he is then to join the two sticks so closely together that they will seem to be but a single stick. Judah, the most important of the southern tribes, is the former southern kingdom, called, in fact, the Kingdom of Judah. Joseph, never really a tribe (hence the parenthetical addition mentioning the important northern tribe of Ephraim), represents the former northern kingdom, which had actually been called the Kingdom of Israel. In Ezekiel, "Israel" is never used of the northern kingdom alone (see the commentary on 4:4-8 for the exception in the present, probably expanded, text of that passage); it may be used of Judeans, but even then it connotes the chosen people as such, in ethnic and religious wholeness. Here, it is pointedly used both of the northern tribes associated with Joseph and of the southern tribes associated with Judah, for their unity is the point of the symbolism. In v. 18 the usual question leading to an interpretation of a symbolic action is anticipated, and its answer follows. First, God reminds us of the relation of a prophet to God (v. 19): just as what a prophet says is what God says, so is the symbolic action performed by Ezekiel as prophet the action of God. For that reason, the events which it symbolizes will surely come to pass.

The actual interpretation of the symbolic action is then given in vv. 20-24a: when God brings the members of the house of Israel home from dispersion, all, those of both northern and southern tribes, will be a single, united nation. The old division into two kingdoms, often quarreling with one another, will be no more. The interpretation in vv. 20-24a goes further than the unity symbolized by the action with the two emblematic sticks, however. To the one nation is promised one king. Like the future shepherd and prince of 34:23-24, the future king is called "David." Neither in 34:23-24 nor here in 37:20-24a is it clear whether the future ruler is to be one person or the symbol of a series of rulers. That he is called "king" here, instead of the "prince" usual in Ezekiel is determined by the Hebrew linguistic need to pair the Hebrew word for "nation" with the Hebrew word for "king," and the resulting exception to Ezekiel's usage thus has no particular significance. The interpretation also goes beyond the symbolic action's expression of national unity when it describes God's activity in renewing the nation. Not only will God bring them all back to the promised land in unity: he will also save them from the consequences of their guilt, cleanse them, and engage himself again with them in the covenant by which they will be his people and he their God. Israel, in other words, will pass from centuries of schism to a new age of unity at whose center will be a Davidic political figure, for a society is normally united around some leading person; but for the nation to be the united people of God there must first be reform of the people's behavior, a cleansing of their interior attitudes so that they are capable of renewing their engaged relationship with God. This, God alone can bring about, and he will bring it about.

In vv. 24b-28 we have a supplement, with no intrinsic relation to the symbolic action, but with an importance all its own, for it promises the blessed future condition for which preparations will be seen in chapters 40-48. While unity is the theme of the symbolic action and its interpretation, permanence is the theme of the supplement. The restored nation will inhabit the promised land forever, the covenant will be everlasting, the sanctuary will be in the midst of the people for evermore. Like the covenant of paradisiac harmony and prosperity described in 34:25-30, the covenant which God will make with the restored nation will be a covenant of peace. The future David is mentioned again, but in the supplement the central figure in the restored nation is not so much the prince in his house, the palace, but rather God in his house, the sanctuary. God will sanctify Israel (v. 28), and in the Hebrew way of envisaging holiness this means that God will set Israel apart from the nations of the world so that it will be properly and peculiarly his. This, more than the royal splendor, will constitute the glory of Israel in the eyes of the nations. The model admits application to the society of the Church, reformed and cleansed and united, with a human person somehow at the center of its unity, with its real glory in the eyes of the world shining not from earthly splendor, fine though some of that may be, but from its being peculiarly set apart from the things of this world in order to be authentically the kingdom of God.

THE MORE DISTANT FUTURE:
GOG'S INVASION FROM THE NORTH
38:1-23

38 The word of the LORD came to me: ²"Son of man, set your face toward Gog, of the land of Magog, the chief prince of Meshech and Tubal, and prophesy against him ³and say, Thus says the Lord GOD: Behold, I am against you, O Gog, chief prince of Meshech and Tubal; ⁴and I will turn you about, and put hooks into your jaws, and I will bring you forth, and all your army, horses and horsemen, all of them clothed in full armor, a great company, all of them with buckler and shield, wielding swords; ⁵Persia, Cush, and Put are with them, all of them with shield and helmet; ⁶Gomer and all his hordes; Bethtogarmah from the uttermost parts of the north with all his hordes — many peoples are with you.

⁷"Be ready and keep ready, you and all the hosts that are assembled about you, and be a guard for them. ⁸After many days you will be mustered; in the latter years you will go against the land that is restored from war, the land where people were gathered from many nations upon the mountains of Israel, which had been a continual waste; its people were brought out from the nations and now dwell securely, all of them. ⁹You will advance, coming on like a storm, you will be like a cloud covering the land, you and all your hordes, and many peoples with you.

¹⁰"Thus says the Lord GOD: On that day thoughts will come to your mind, and you will devise an evil scheme ¹¹and say, 'I will go up against the land of unwalled villages; I will fall upon the quiet people who dwell securely, all of them dwelling without walls, and having no bars or gates'; ¹²to seize spoil and carry off plunder; to

assail the waste places which are now inhabited, and the people who were gathered from the nations, who have gotten cattle and goods, who dwell at the center of the earth. [13]Sheba and Dedan and the merchants of Tarshish and all its villages will say to you, 'Have you come to seize spoil? Have you assembled your hosts to carry off plunder, to carry away silver and gold, to take away cattle and goods, to seize great spoil?'

[14]"Therefore, son of man, prophesy, and say to Gog, Thus says the Lord GOD: On that day when my people Israel are dwelling securely, you will bestir yourself [15]and come from your place out of the uttermost parts of the north, you and many peoples with you, all of them riding on horses, a great host, a mighty army; [16]you will come up against my people Israel, like a cloud covering the land. In the latter days I will bring you against my land, that the nations may know me, when through you, O Gog, I vindicate my holiness before their eyes.

[17]"Thus says the Lord GOD: Are you he of whom I spoke in former days by my servants the prophets of Israel, who in those days prophesied for years that I would bring you against them? [18]But on that day, when Gog shall come against the land of Israel, says the Lord GOD, my wrath will be roused. [19]For in my jealousy and in my blazing wrath I declare, On that day there shall be a great shaking in the land of Israel; [20]the fish of the sea, and the birds of the air; and the beasts of the field, and all creeping things that creep on the ground, and all the men that are upon the face of the earth, shall quake at my presence, and the mountains shall be thrown down, and the cliffs shall fall, and every wall shall tumble to the ground. [21]I will summon every kind of terror against Gog, says the Lord GOD; every man's sword will be against his brother. [22]With pestilence and bloodshed I will enter into judgment with him; and I will rain upon him and his hordes and the many peoples that are with him, torrential rains and hailstones, fire and brimstone. [23]So I will show my greatness and my holiness and make myself known in

the eyes of many nations. Then they will know that I am the LORD.

In the general composition of the Book of Ezekiel, chapters 38-39 are unexpected and, at first sight, disconcerting. Chapters 40-48, with their provisions for the new sanctuary of the restored nation in its ancestral land, blessed abundantly under the rule of its prince, would follow admirably upon the closing verses of chapter 37. Instead, we have in chapters 38-39 a long interruption devoted to an expedition from lands far away to the north, led against Israel by a ruler named Gog, after Israel is thoroughly resettled in its homeland. Prophecy on such an expedition in the more distant future is "chronologically" out of place between the preceding part of the book of Ezekiel, with its prophecies of restoration yet to be accomplished, and the following part, with its plans to be carried out when the restoration is begun. Why are chapters 38-39 here?

Prophecies about invaders from the north are found already in Jeremiah (Jer 1:15; 4:6, 15-16; 5:15; 6:22). Some modern authors think of such invaders as Scythians, others think rather of Medes, but perhaps no specific people was intended, the fearsome invaders of these prophecies in Jeremiah and here in Ezekiel being meant simply as armies coming from places far away. The North for the inhabitants of the Ancient Near East, like the Orient for Europeans and Americans of ages closer to our own, was a mysterious region at the uttermost part of the known world. Gog's army is represented as an army drawn from many peoples (38:6, 15), and the names of the peoples mentioned in 38:2-6 serve to conjure up thoughts of peoples hardly heard of, thoughts enhanced by fear of the unknown. In the prophecies on Gog and his army, only one place mentioned, the land of Israel, would have been clearly defined in the minds of Ezekiel's hearers. The other places existed for the most part, but they would have been unfocused in the minds of Ezekiel's hearers. The time of Gog's invasion is unfocused too. This lack of focus in the historical dimensions of geographical space and future time are not untypical of the apocalyptic *genre* which was to flourish later in Jewish literary production, and, although what we find in Ezek 38-39 is not strictly speaking apocalyptic, there are in this section several elements found characteristically in apocalyptic narrative: a great battle pitting malicious forces from undefined places against God's elect in Palestine, taking place at a chronologically undefined moment "in the latter years" (38:8), accompanied by cataclysmic happenings in nature (38:19-22), ending with God's deliverance of his elect.

The preceding oracles in Ezekiel have to do with the near future. In chapters 38-39 the range of vision goes beyond the near future to a future undefined but in any case more distant, and this must be the reason why these chapters have been placed here after the oracles collected in Parts One to Three which deal with situations which are imminent. But why not after chapters 40-48, which also deal with a more immediate future? Perhaps for a reason of literary classification. Chapters 38-39, like the chapters preceding them, contain prophetic oracles, and that is perhaps the reason why they have not been separated from those preceding chapters of similar literary *genres* to be placed after chapters 40-48, which contain visions with plans and provisions rather than oracles of judgement and promise.

Although the prophetic words of chapters 38-39 are detached from actual history, past, contemporary, or future, they draw upon some geographic and perhaps even some historical information available when they were composed. The name Gog may well be that of the king of Lydia in eastern Asia Minor in the seventh century whose name the Greeks turned into Gyges, while the writers of Neo-Assyrian records gave it in a form Gagu which would easily reflect the historical equivalent of our present Hebrew form Gog. If so, that particular historical person, who died in 644 B.C., long before the time when Ezek 38-39 was composed, has done no more than provide a name here. No land of Magog is mentioned anywhere in ancient records, except here and in the late stratum of the Pentateuchal Table of Nations (Gen 10:2). Tubal and Meshech (mentioned together also in Ezek 27:13; 32:26) had once existed as small princedoms in Asia

Minor, but they were far apart from one another (Tubal in the Taurus Mountains of Cilicia, Meshech far to the northwest, in Phrygia), and both had been uprooted in the seventh century. Persia in southwestern Iran, Cush in the modern Sudan, and Put, probably in Libya, are widely separated, and if Gomer is to be equated with the Cimmerians, a warlike people who appeared in Transcaucasia at the end of the eighth century and then in various parts of Asia Minor during the seventh, one must note that the Cimmerians had been assimilated by the native populations of Asia Minor when the sixth century began. Obviously, then, names of peoples and places are used here without concern for historical or geographical coherence. There is abstraction from both past and present, and projection into an indeterminate future. The name of Gog and the names of the places mentioned do not lead us to historical circumstances prevailing when these oracles were composed, or prevailing at any time afterward. Their function is symbolic, and they evoke an emotive reaction to what is distant, unknown, and potentially dangerous.

The component parts of chapter 38 are less heterogeneous than those of chapter 39, but they do not constitute a whole which is completely logical in its unity. Some parts have probably been added to others already composed. In vv. 1-6 God declares himself to be against Gog and his associated hordes. In vv. 7-9 God seems to take the initiative in having Gog and his army prepare an expedition against Israel, but in vv. 10-12 the plans are put into Gog's own mind. Inclusion of the question about commercial booty from Israel to be put on the market in the trading centers of Sheba and Dedan in Arabia and of Tarshish in Spain (v. 13) makes it clear that the time envisaged in the oracle is one when Israel will be so solidly restored in Palestine that its commercial importance will again be known throughout the world of trade.

In vv. 14-17 we see best the basic nature and purpose of these oracular words addressed to Gog and his army. The time is an undetermined future time ("on that day"), when the exiles will already be settled securely in their homeland again. The invaders are from the equally vague limits of the known world ("the outermost parts of the north"). The invasion of the land of Israel has a very real purpose in God's historical plan, namely, that of letting all the nations know that God's jealous vindication of Israel as his own does not stop with his establishing his people again in the land he promised to them but that it extends beyond that, on into the more distant future. (With respect to v. 16, let us remind ourselves again that, in Hebraic thought-categories, what is holy is of God, set apart from all that belongs to the profane, the ordinary, the things of this world, and that God's freely making Israel his holy people amounts to his making it his own possession, whose violation by the forces of this world he will not tolerate.) V. 17 gives us a key to the purpose of this material's inclusion in the book of Ezekiel. There existed already a *corpus* of prophecy on invaders from the north, and the inspired compilers of the book — if not Ezekiel himself, as far as the nucleus of this section goes —found it good to take up that tradition, projecting it into the age which would follow the restoration of the exiles in the promised land. In vv. 18-23 we see the effect of God's wrath directed against Gog and his army, an effect described with dire imagery involving the forces of nature and all sorts of creatures. God bests the terrible nations and defends his own, that his greatness and holiness may be manifest.

In the oracular words on Gog's expedition Israel's moral worth is not evaluated, and Israel plays no active role at all in the description of Gog's attack and defeat. Unlike what we find in Part One of Ezekiel, the threat from foreign nations is not the result of any divine judgement on wickedness or infidelity within the house of Israel. Unlike what we find generally in the oracles against foreign nations in Part Two, Gog and his allies are threatened with bloody defeat not because of their own intrinsic wickedness but because they will attack the Israel of the future. Gog will come with his army because God wants him to attack Israel. God wants him to attack Israel so that God can defeat him. God's expressed reason for wanting to defeat him is not one having to do with the moral worth of either Israel or the peoples of the distant northlands, however. The reason is a personal reason of God's. God simply wills the occasion for manifesting to the nations his own greatness and for letting the nations know that he will not allow violation of the holy, of what is, like his people Israel, properly and peculiarly his, to go unpunished.

MORE ON THE END OF GOG
(AND OTHER MATTERS)
39:1-29

39 . . . ⁹"Then those who dwell in the cities of Israel will go forth and make fires of the weapons and burn them, shields and bucklers, bows and arrows, handpikes and spears, and they will make fires of them for seven years; ¹⁰so that they will not need to take wood out of the field or cut down any out of the forests, for they will make their fires of the weapons; they will despoil those who despoiled them, and plunder those who plundered them, says the Lord GOD.

¹¹"On that day I will give to Gog a place for burial in Israel, the Valley of the Travelers east of the sea; it will block the travelers, for there Gog and all his multitude will be buried; it will be called the Valley of Hamon-gog. ¹²For seven months the house of Israel will be burying them, in order to cleanse the land. ¹³All the people of the land will bury them; and it will redound to their honor on the day that I show my glory, says the Lord GOD. ¹⁴They will set apart men to pass through the land continually and bury those remaining upon the face of the land, so as to cleanse it; at the end of seven months they will make their search. ¹⁵And when these pass through the land and any one sees a man's bone, then he shall set up a sign by it, till the buriers have buried it in the Valley of Hamon-gog. ¹⁶(A city Hamonah is there also.) Thus shall they cleanse the land.

¹⁷"As for you, son of man, thus says the Lord GOD: Speak to the birds of every sort and to all beasts of the field, 'Assemble and come, gather from all sides to the

sacrificial feast which I am preparing for you, a great sacrificial feast upon the mountains of Israel, and you shall eat flesh and drink blood. [18]You shall eat the flesh of the mighty, and drink the blood of the princes of the earth — of rams, of lambs, and of goats, of bulls, all of them fatlings of Bashan. [19]And you shall eat fat till you are filled, and drink blood till you are drunk, at the sacrificial feast which I am preparing for you. [20]And you shall be filled at my table with horses and riders, with mighty men and all kinds of warriors,' says the Lord GOD.

[21]"And I will set my glory among the nations; and all the nations shall see my judgement which I have executed, and my hand which I have laid on them. [22]The house of Israel shall know that I am the LORD their God, from that day forward. [23]And the nations shall know that the house of Israel went into captivity for their iniquity, because they dealt so treacherously with me that I hid my face from them and gave them into the land of their adversaries, and they all fell by the sword. [24]I dealt with them according to their uncleanness and their transgressions, and hid my face from them.

[25]"Therefore thus says the Lord GOD: Now I will restore the fortunes of Jacob, and have mercy upon the whole house of Israel; and I will be jealous for my holy name. [26]They shall forget their shame, and all the treachery they have practiced against me, when they dwell securely in their land with none to make them afraid, [27]when I have brought them back from the peoples and gathered them from their enemies' lands, and through them have vindicated my holiness in the sight of many nations. [28]Then they shall know that I am the LORD their God because I sent them into exile among the nations, and then gathered them into their own land. I will leave none of them remaining among the nations any more; [29]and I will not hide my face any more from them, when I pour out my Spirit upon the house of Israel, says the Lord GOD."

In chapter 39, the lack of unity is all too evident. What is said in vv. 1-8, addressed to Gog, has almost all been said already in chapter 38, and so we have omitted vv. 1-8 from the printed text above; one could argue that the original oracle against Gog is contained in these verses rather than in chapter 38, but that question need not detain us. The oracle continues with a description of the Israelites' fabulous destruction of the invaders' weapons, whose wood will provide enough firewood to take care of the Israelites' needs for seven years (vv. 9-10). These verses could conceivably be addressed still to Gog, but vv. 11-16, on the Israelites' seven months of work purifying their holy land from its defilement by the corpses of the slain invaders, seem to be tacked on rather clumsily to the oracle addressed to Gog, for in v. 11 Gog is not addressed but is spoken of in the third person instead. Vv. 11-16, with their meticulous concern for the laws of purity (see Num 5:2; 19:16 for personal defilement by contact with a corpse, Num 35:33-34 for defilement of the land by bloodshed), are quite different in tone from the stormy war prose of chapter 38.

Vv. 17-20 are addressed not to Gog but to the birds and the beasts, who are summoned to feast on the flesh and the blood of Gog and his soldiers and of the horses on which they rode. The description of the gory feast has received some touches intended to make it look like a sacrificial feast. As a result, God's involvement in the feast is expressed, but the passage stands better as a straightforward description of the sequel to a moment of carnage, without the additional sacrificial traits. Vv. 21-22 may conceivably be a conclusion to the entire section on Gog's future expedition, but vv. 23-24, in which the divine motives for punishing Israel expressed in Part One of the book are recapitulated, carry us back logically to the time following the fall of Jerusalem. Vv. 25-29, on the other hand, contain a recapitulation of the promises of restoration of the exiles in their homeland and the divine motives for those promises, found in Part Three. After the interruption caused by the insertion of the material on the invasion from the north in a more distant future, found now in chapters 38-39, vv. 25-29 lead us logically back to the point at which chapter 37 closed, before we proceed onward into the view of restoration in chapters 40-48.

PART FOUR
A VISION OF THE
RESTORATION

Chapters 40-48, the last part of our book, are cast in the framework of a vision, although not everything set within that framework is really visionary. Ezekiel, in vision, sees the return of God's glory to the new Temple in Jerusalem. He also sees the ground plan of the new Temple, and "sees" regulations which will assure correct worship in the Temple, to the benefit of the community and the prosperity of the land, reorganized under the rule of a legitimate prince. The literary unity of this part of the book is established artificially. Set into the framework of Ezekiel's vision are sections which differ very much from one another in content, in tone, in intrinsic purpose. The material in some of these sections — the cultic regulations, for example — can by its very nature hardly be the proper object of a vision. One does not properly speaking "see" laws. By no means all of the elements in the present text of these chapters come necessarily from Ezekiel's own hand.

The text must have grown in several stages, until it reached its final form. Scholars differ on some points when they try to assign various elements of the present text to various successive stages. Perhaps the original nucleus was formed by the purely visionary passages, 40:1-2; 43:4-7a (and parts of 47:1-12?), with which were integrated, first, in an early stage, Ezekiel's descriptions of his tour of the Temple as he was led from place to place by a man taking the Temple's measurements in 40:3-37; 40:47-41:4, then, at a slightly later stage, 41:5-15a; 42:15-19; 43:1-3, 7b-12; 44:1-2 and at least some parts of 47:1-12. Still later (not necessarily at a single later moment), the growing text was augmented with unintegrated (and often unvisionary) passages — the supplements to the description of the Temple's measurement in 40:38-46; 41:15b-42:14; 42:20; 43:13-27; the regulations for worship, clerical persons, and the prince in 44:3-46:27; the instructions for the new division of the land in 47:13-48:36; various phrases added here and there to smooth out the seams in the patchwork text, or to make a point.

The different components of these chapters have different intrinsic purposes, but their inclusion in this part of the book fits them into a general purpose of Part Four as a whole. In some fundamental respects, chapters 40-48 are a counterpart of chapters 8-11. Both in 8-11 and in 40-48 Ezekiel reports a vision in which he is led around the Temple and in which he sees a movement of the glory of God. In the tour of the Temple in chapters 8-11 he is shown the cultic abominations of the people which lead to the glory's departure from the Temple, while in chapters 40-48 he is shown the symmetric measurements of the Temple to which the glory returns. The real notional counterpart in 40-48 of the cultic abominations seen in 8-11 is not the symmetric plan of the Temple but the orthodox cultic propriety of worship in the new Temple, prescribed in the cultic regulations. The purpose of the regulations for the Temple, for its forms of worship, and for its clerical personnel is that of safeguarding the various degrees of holiness and purity in the restored community engaged in the worship of God; that is brought out by the inclusion of those regulations within the framework or setting of Ezekiel's vision of the glory of God returning freely and willingly to his earthly dwelling in

Jerusalem, where holiness and purity will in the future be assured.

That editorial association of prescription with vision makes the liturgical regulations more than mere parts of a plan: it makes them parts of a whole visionary view of what God will do for his people after their purgation in siege and exile. The same purpose of showing the future blessings of God for his people is accomplished by the association of the provisions for the new division of the land (47:13-48:35) with the vision of the waters of fertility issuing from the new Temple and flowing out over the land (47:1-12). Just as regulations for worship and provisions for distribution of the promised land were once made in connection with the Exodus from Egypt and the entrance into the land, so are the new regulations for worship and the new provisions for distribution of the land, given in Ezek 40-48, signs of the fulfillment of the promise of a new exodus, a new passage through the wilderness, and a new occupation of the land, in which there will be a renewed worship acceptable to God — the promise made in 20:33-44.

Throughout Part Four we see a passion for clear-cut, orderly arrangements, both in spatial and architectural matters and in matters of human organization. Are these chapters a plan for practical reality or for utopian order? They are probably a plan for both, a mixture of idealism and of practical proposal. Nostalgia for Jerusalem and the land promised to the fathers moves onward to enthusiasm for a better order of things, in a new Jerusalem with God at the center of all.

THE VISION BEGINS
40:1-4

> **40** In the twenty-fifth year of our exile, at the beginning of the year, on the tenth day of the month, in the fourteenth year after the city was conquered, on that very day, the hand of the LORD was upon me, [2]and brought me in the visions of God into the land of Israel, and set me down upon a very high mountain, on which was a structure like

a city opposite me. [3]When he brought me there, behold, there was a man, whose appearance was like bronze, with a line of flax and a measuring reed in his hand; and he was standing in the gateway. [4]And the man said to me, "Son of man, look with your eyes, and hear with your ears, and set your mind upon all that I shall show you, for you were brought here in order that I might show it to you; declare all that you see to the house of Israel."

The introductory date is the equivalent of our modern and Western 28 April 573 B.C., at the beginning of the fourteenth year reckoned from the destruction of Jerusalem (with the year of that destruction reckoned as year one), thirty-five years before the Edict of Cyrus in 538 opened the possibility of an actual return of the Jewish exiles from Babylonia to Palestine. As in 8:1, the hand of the Lord, representing the active intervening power of the Lord, takes hold of Ezekiel and places him "upon a very high mountain" in the land of Israel (40:1-2). Ezekiel is transported in vision to Jerusalem, to Mount Zion, although, unlike the report of the vision beginning in chapter 8, this account does not name the city. The main object of the vision was originally that of manifesting the future return of God's glory to the new Temple to be built there (43:1-7), but other things have been added between 40:1-2 and 43:1-7, and beyond. In v. 3 a man is introduced who, like the "form that had the appearance of a man" in chapters 8-11 (see 8:2), will guide Ezekiel through the Temple area and show him things there. Here, the guide is called "a man," but his appearance like bronze, and the nature of his command in v. 4, make it clear that he is not an ordinary human guide, but a celestial emissary. He bears a measuring reed and, for measuring greater lengths, a line of flax. He will use both in measuring dimensions of the Temple before Ezekiel's visionary eyes. He is standing in a gateway which must be the gateway at which the tour and the measuring will begin in v. 6, i.e. the eastern gate through which one would pass from profane space outside the Temple area into the outer court of the Temple compound.

In v. 4 the "man" tells Ezekiel to look and to hear. Both

the visionary and the auditory perceptions of a prophet are involved. Usually, in prophecy as we find it in the Old Testament, a prophet hears the word of God and then passes on what he has heard. Here, after the initial command to look and to hear, no more is said about hearing, however. Ezekiel has been brought in vision to Jerualem in order that he might *see* what the man will show him and then declare to the house of Israel not what he has heard but what he has seen. Like any prophet, he must declare. Like a visionary prophet, he must declare what has been shown to him. The nucleus of what is now chapters 40-48 was a vision of the return of God's presence to the Temple in glory (40:1-2; 43:4-7a). In most of chapters 40-42, Ezekiel still sees much but hears little. Only in still later additions to chapters 40-42 is he given words with a pointed message (40:45-46; 42:13-14).

MEASUREMENT OF THE GATES
TO THE TEMPLE COURTS
40:5-37

> [5]And behold, there was a wall all around the outside of the temple area, and the length of the measuring reed in the man's hand was six long cubits, each being a cubit and a handbreadth in length; so he measured the thickness of the wall, one reed; and the height, one reed. [6]Then he went into the gateway facing east, going up its steps, and measured the threshold of the gate, one reed deep; [7]and the side rooms, one reed long, and one reed broad; and the space between the side rooms, five cubits; and the threshold of the gate by the vestibule of the gate at the inner end, one reed. [8]Then he measured the vestibule of the gateway, eight cubits; [9]and its jambs, two cubits; and the vestibule of the gate was at the inner end. [10]And there were three side rooms on either side of the east gate; the three were of the same size; and the jambs on either side were of the same size. [11]Then he measured the breadth of the opening of the gateway, ten cubits; and the breadth of the gateway, thirteen cubits. [12]There was a barrier before

the side rooms, one cubit on either side, and the side rooms were six cubits on either side. [13]Then he measured the gate from the back of the one side room to the back of the other, a breadth of five and twenty cubits, from door to door. [14]He measured also the vestibule, twenty cubits; and round about the vestibule of the gateway was the court. [15]From the front of the gate at the entrance to the end of the inner vestibule of the gate was fifty cubits. [16]And the gateway had windows round about, narrowing inwards into their jambs in the side rooms, and likewise the vestibule had windows round about inside, and on the jambs were palm trees.

[17]Then he brought me into the outer court; and behold, there were chambers and a pavement, round about the court; thirty chambers fronted on the pavement. [18]And the pavement ran along the side of the gates, corresponding to the length of the gates; this was the lower pavement. [19]Then he measured the distance from the inner front of the lower gate to the outer front of the inner court, a hundred cubits. ...

[28]Then he brought me to the inner court by the south gate, and he measured the south gate; it was of the same size as the others. [29]Its side rooms, its jambs, and its vestibule were of the same size as the others; and there were windows round about in it and in its vestibule; its length was fifty cubits, and its breadth twenty-five cubits. [30]And there were vestibules round about, twenty-five cubits long and five cubits broad. [31]Its vestibule faced the outer court, and palm trees were on its jambs, and its stairway had eight steps. ...

The description of Ezekiel's guided tour through the Temple area begins. What he sees is really not very visionary. The images are architectonic rather than poetic, and there is nothing ecstatic in his reaction. The only movement in the scene is that which is seen in the passage from place to place and in the guide's application of his measuring tools — movement which is not very dramatic. The basis of the description may have been a sketch, or memory of the

Temple of Solomon as it was before the destruction of 586, or both, idealized to some extent in any case, with symmetry carried to an idealistic extreme. In the general introduction to Part Four of Ezekiel we have noted that the description of the Temple was most probably joined to an account of Ezekiel's vision of the return of God's glory which already existed in some written form, and the integration of description and vision remains rather superficial.

The modern reader naturally asks himself repeatedly what the religious purpose of this description of the Temple might be. Ezekiel is told in 40:4 that he is to declare what he sees during his tour of the Temple, but just what is he, as a prophet, to declare? Hardly that the plan of the Temple and its dimensions, manifested to him during the visionary tour, are to be followed in the actual construction of the new Temple after the return from exile, for the ground plan itself is not complete enough for so material a purpose, and the elevation of walls above the ground plan is regularly omitted. One purpose of the presentation of the Temple's plan as something seen in vision is that of showing that the Temple is a building in whose planning God is himself directly interested. It is, after all, to be God's house on earth, and God has his own requirements for his house, which he communicates to those who are responsible for its material construction. In Exod 25:40 God tells Moses to construct the Tabernacle according to the model given to him on Sinai. In 1 Chr 28:11, 19 we read that God himself gave to David the detailed model of the Temple which David handed on to Solomon, while in Wis 9:8 Solomon, represented in prayer to God, recalls being told to construct a Temple building and an altar which would be an imitation of the Tabernacle prepared from the beginning. In ancient Mesopotamia, where Ezekiel was living with his fellow exiles, it was rare that a ruler would undertake the building of a new temple for a god without trying to follow the ground plan of an earlier one, and a god might himself be represented giving the plan for a new temple with details of its construction. All this lies behind the presentation of the

form and measurements of the Temple as objects of Ezekiel's vision, to be declared by him to the house of Israel.
Ezekiel is to declare the divine origin of a holy place, the sole
dwelling of Yahweh on earth, begun with the desert Tabernacle, fixed with the Temple of Solomon, and continued in
the new Temple to be built on the site of Solomon's.

The modern interpreter of Ezek 40-42 has to draw heavily
on the competence of archaeologists. To archaeologists and
to exegetes, the text presents some continuing problems of
obscure Hebrew vocabulary, of textual corruption, of
inconsistency resulting from the inclusion of material with
different origins, but by and large a good idea of the ground
plan traced in Ezekiel can be had. The reader may find it
helpful at times to refer to the diagram of the Plan of the
Temple provided at the end of this volume. As we are told in
40:5 and 43:13, the basic unit of linear measure used in the
dimensions given throughout the text is the long cubit,
which, to judge from the patterns emerging in the archaeological study of the dimensions of remains of buildings in
Palestine, was the Egyptian royal cubit of 52.5 centimeters
(20.6692 inches), the equivalent of a normal cubit of c. 45
centimeters (17.7165 inches) plus a handbreadth of c. 7.5
centimeters (2.9527 inches). After the thickness and the
height of the wall running all around the Temple area and
separating it from the totally secular space outside have
been given in 40:5, the dimensions of the Temple gates are
given, as Ezekiel and his guide go from one gate to another,
the guide using his measuring implements constantly as they
proceed. There were no west gates, either into the outer
court or into the inner court.

In vv. 6-27, the outer gates — those leading from the space
outside the Temple compound into the Temple's outer court
— are measured, the outer east gate first and in greater
detail (vv. 6-16), with some features of the outer court given
(vv. 17-19a) before the tour moves on to the outer north and
south gates (vv. 19b-27), given in less detail because their
plans and dimensions are those of the east gate, a fact which
allows our omission of vv. 19b-27 from the text printed
above. V. 14 might as well be passed over by the reader, for

the preserved text is in poor shape, and the details given in the Revised Standard Version pose problems of reconciliation with details given elsewhere. As one entered the Temple area from outside, he or she climbed the steps leading to the threshold and opening (vv. 6, 11), then passed on through a corridor flanked on each side by three rooms, one after the other (vv. 7, 10, 13), with a barrier of some kind (pierced surely by an opening) separating each of them from the corridor running along in front of them (v. 12). After passing through the corridor, the vestibule with its own threshold opening into the outer court was reached (vv. 7-9, 14). Windows pierced the rear walls of the six side rooms flanking the corridor, with the series of windows continued in a straight line along the walls of the vestibule (v. 16).

In vv. 28-37, the tour passes on to the inner gates — those gates leading from the outer court of the Temple area into its inner (and higher) court. The inner south gate is measured first (vv. 28-31), then the inner east and north gates (vv. 32-37, omitted from the text printed above because their plan and dimensions are the same as those of the inner south gate). The dimensions of these three gates into the inner court are the same, actually, as those of the three gates into the outer court given previously. The ground plan of these inner gates is also the same as that of the outer gates, except in their orientation: while the vestibule of the outer gates was not reached until one moving inward had passed through a gate and was coming out into the outer court, the vestibule of the inner gates is approached immediately when one is ready to pass through one of them from the outer court on towards the inner court. The vestibule of an outer gate, in other words, is at the inward end of the gate's corridor, while the vestibule of an inner gate is at the outward end. The inner court was on a higher level than the outer court. The eight steps leading up to the vestibule of an inner gate (v. 31) were called for by that difference of level, and the inner gates themselves stood entirely on the higher level of the inner court. The reader can safely ignore v. 30, and spare himself some confusion by doing so. That verse, with its muddled mathematics, is still absent in the ancient

Greek version, and it must be a fairly late addition to the Hebrew text.

SOME CHAMBERS AND FURNISHINGS
40:38-46

[38]There was a chamber with its door in the vestibule of the gate, where the burnt offering was to be washed. [39]And in the vestibule of the gate were two tables on either side, on which the burnt offering and the sin offering and the guilt offering were to be slaughtered. [40]And on the outside of the vestibule at the entrance of the north gate were two tables; and on the other side of the vestibule of the gate were two tables. [41]Four tables were on the inside and four tables on the outside of the side of the gate, eight tables, on which the sacrifices were to be slaughtered. [42]And there were also four tables of hewn stone for the burnt offering, a cubit and a half long, and a cubit and a half broad, and one cubit high, on which the instruments were to be laid with which the burnt offerings and the sacrifices were slaughtered. [43]And hooks, a handbreadth long, were fastened round about within. And on the tables the flesh of the offering was to be laid.

[44]Then he brought me from without into the inner court, and behold, there were two chambers in the inner court, one at the side of the north gate facing south, the other at the side of the south gate facing north. [45]And he said to me, This chamber which faces south is for the priests who have charge of the temple, [46]and the chamber which faces north is for the priests who have charge of the altar; these are the sons of Zadok, who alone among the sons of Levi may come near to the LORD to minister to him.

Vv. 38-46 were inserted here after the basic description of the Temple area had been written. The movement of Ezekiel and his guide from place to place and the communication of measurements, those elements characteristic of the basic description of the Temple in chapters 40-42, are almost entirely absent from this inserted section, which actually falls into two parts, each of which may well come from a different person.

In the first part, vv. 38-43, there is a surprising amount of detail quite untypical of the older parts of chapters 40-42, and the author's interest is fixed not on the architectonic features of the Temple which are the concern of those older parts but on the location of some accessory furnishings and their use in the preparation of sacrificial victims. The gate in question is an inner gate, and presumably the north inner gate, not mentioned until v. 40, is meant throughout the text, since this text's insertion occurs at the point where, in the older text of chapters 40-42, Ezekiel and his guide have reached that inner north gate and its measurements have been given (vv. 35-37, which we have omitted from the text printed). At the top of the steps leading up to that gate was the gate's vestibule, and inside the vestibule were four tables, two on either side of the entrance, on which were slaughtered the victims for three types of sacrifice: the burnt offering or holocaust given over entirely to God on the altar with no parts consumed by human beings (Lev 1:3-17), and two expiatory types, the sin offering (Lev 4:1-5:13) and the guilt offering (Lev 5:14-6:7), whose origins were surely different but whose distinction is blurred in the texts which have come down to us. These are the four tables *inside* the vestibule mentioned in v. 39. The four tables *outside* the vestibule, two of them on either side of the entrance, mentioned in v. 40, must have served the same purpose as those inside; v. 41 indicates that.

V. 42 introduces confusing factors. For one thing, it seems to suggest that there were four tables in addition to the eight (inside and outside the vestibule) mentioned in vv. 39-41 — twelve tables in all. That may be what was intended; if so, the four tables "for the burnt offering" of v. 42a served as surfaces on which to lay the slaughtering instruments of v. 42b for use with "the burnt offerings and the sacrifices (of other types)," if we take the text as it now stands. On the other hand, the "also" at the beginning of v. 42 in the English of the Revised Standard Version printed above — the word which locks the English reader into a view of twelve tables — is not in the text; when we remove that "also" we see more readily that the purpose of v. 42a may simply be that of giving the dimensions of the tables for the most important type of sacrifice, that of the burnt offering, i.e. four of the eight tables of vv. 39-41. (Vv. 42b-43 present problems of their own, with which we need not grapple here.)

Finally, there was in connection (somehow) with the vestibule a chamber "where the burnt offering was to be washed" (v. 38); the burnt offering, in fact, was the only type of sacrifice in which the extant ritual texts indicate a washing of certain parts of the victim (Lev 1:9).

Why this concern with the tables for slaughtering, at the vestibule of an inner gate? It is really an integral part of a more general concern with degrees of holiness of space, corresponding with degrees of holiness of persons, manifest in the later stages of the text of chapters 40-48. Laymen wishing to have a sacrifice offered had to get their sacrificial animals to the place of ritual slaughtering, but in the system visible in Ezek 40-48 no layman could go beyond the outer court into the inner gates, let alone enter the inner court where the sacrificial altar stood (46:3, 20). In these later texts of Ezek 40-48, in which such concerns are manifest, the eventually non-priestly levites, endowed as a class with a degree of holiness greater than that of the Israelite laity, were to slaughter the sacrificial animals, and they were to oversee the gates, making sure that no one lacking the required degree of holiness of state passed through them (44:11). The Ezekielian non-priestly levites were to be men of gates and of sacrificial slaughtering (and of other responsibilities too). This arrangement differs from that in the priestly laws of the Pentateuch in some respects, notably in Ezekiel's exclusion of the laity from the inner court altogether (while the priestly laws of the Pentateuch admit them to certain parts of the inner court), and in Ezekiel's reservation of all sacrificial slaughtering to a group of levites distinct both from priests on the one hand and from laypersons on the other (while the Pentateuchal regulations allow some slaughtering by the lay offerer, and do not yet provide for levites as a distinct intermediary class). The spatial point most important in the practical application of these novelties is the vestibule at the entrance to the inner north gate: beyond that point the laity in the outer court are to go no farther, and at that point — not in the inner court — the non-priestly levites are to do the slaughtering entirely reserved to them. The sacral provisions of 38-43 are new in Israel, but they are the expression of a timeless concern with the function of sacred spaces and their demarcation.

The second part (vv. 44-46) of this block of material inserted into the basic text describing Ezekiel's tour of the Temple with his guide, shows signs of a mind slightly different both from that of the composer of the basic text of chapters 40-42 and from that of the person who wrote the first part of the present insertion (vv. 38-43). In vv. 44-46, an architectonic interest is evident in the focus on the two chambers opening onto the inner court, but the basic text's focus on the Temple's ground plan is absent. Ground plan gives way here to function. The guide's silent measuring, without comment, so characteristic of the pattern of the basic text, is not found here any more than it was in vv. 38-43, and although the English translation above has the guide leading Ezekiel into the inner court in v. 44, that statement, first appearing in the Greek version, is totally lacking in the original Hebrew text, which mentions no movement at all. The interest in furnishings, obvious in vv. 38-43, is absent in vv. 44-46. Concern with distinctions of class, implicitly present in the background of vv. 38-43, is explicit in vv. 44-46.

The author of vv. 44-46 has the guide point out two chambers on opposite sides of the inner court. (We cannot know whether they should be to the west or the east of those north and south inner gates which they adjoined, but we have put them to the west of those gates on the Temple Plan accompanying this commentary.) The guide then makes a comment (something the guide does not do in the basic text of chapters 40-42): he declares that one of these chambers is reserved for the priests who have charge of the general work of the Temple, while the other is reserved for a particular class of priests called "the sons of Zadok," who alone may do work at the sacrificial altar of the Lord in the inner court, for they alone may "come near to the Lord to minister to him," which is to imply that they enjoy a degree of holiness superior to that of the non-Zadokite priests. Therein lies the real point of vv. 44-46. In the programmatic system taking shape in Part Four of Ezekiel there is to be a clear distinction of class among the cultic personnel. Here in 40:44-46 that distinction is still one between Levitical priests who were not accepted as Zadokites and Levitical priests who were so accepted. In a slightly later stage of evolution, reflected in Ezek 44, the first group, those who are to be in charge of the general work of the Temple, its gates, the ritual slaughtering, will be called "levites" but no longer "priests" (44:10-14), while the second group, that of "the sons of Zadok," will be confirmed in its exclusive right to all functions in the sanctuary building and at the altar in the inner court (44:15-16). While 40:38-43 was occasioned by the effect which the novel distinction of class holiness between levites and layfolk below them were to have on sacral spatial limits, 40:44-46 is occasioned by an interest in insisting directly on the distinction of class holiness in the opposite direction, i.e. between a lower clergy (Levitical priests becoming simply levites) and a higher, priestly, clergy above them.

MEASUREMENTS OF THE TEMPLE BUILDING
40:47-41:4

[47]And he measured the court, a hundred cubits long, and a hundred cubits broad, foursquare; and the altar was in front of the temple.

[48]Then he brought me to the vestibule of the temple and measured the jambs of the vestibule, five cubits on either side; and the breadth of the gate was fourteen cubits; and the sidewalls of the gate were three cubits on either side. [49]The length of the vestibule was twenty cubits, and the

breadth twelve cubits; and ten steps led up to it; and there
were pillars beside the jambs on either side.

41 Then he brought me to the nave, and measured the
jambs; on each side six cubits was the breadth of the
jambs. ²And the breadth of the entrance was ten cubits;
and the sidewalls of the entrance were five cubits on either
side; and he measured the length of the nave forty cubits,
and its breadth, twenty cubits. ³Then he went into the
inner room and measured the jambs of the entrance, two
cubits; and the breadth of the entrance, six cubits; and the
sidewalls of the entrance, seven cubits. ⁴And he measured
the length of the room, twenty cubits, and its breadth,
twenty cubits, beyond the nave. And he said to me, "This
is the most holy place."

At this point we return to the basic text of chapters 40-42,
with the tour of the Temple area and the guide's silent
measuring carried onward, after the interruption caused by
the inserted material of 40:38-46. Before the interruption,
Ezekiel and his supernatural guide were at the north inner
gate. Now they pass through that gate into the inner court of
the Temple, which the guide proceeds to measure (v. 47).
Originally, something like "Then he brought me into the
inner court" must have stood in the basic text just before our
present v. 47. It was presumably dropped here when the
material just preceding was inserted. We have already noted
that the missing phrase, "Then he brought me from without
into the inner court," has been added to the beginning of v.
44 in the ancient Greek version (surely in order to get
Ezekiel and his guide there in time to see what is to be seen
there in the inserted vv. 44-46) but that it has never been
restored to the Hebrew text, either before v. 44, where it
would clarify the situation caused by the inserted material,
or before v. 47, where it originally belonged. In the inner
court Ezekiel sees the open-air altar on which sacrifices were
burned, situated in front of the Temple building whose
entrance is on the west side of the inner court (v. 47). A
description of the altar was added later to Part Four of our
book, at 43:13-17, in connection with the account of its
consecration which follows in 43:18-27. In 40:48-41:4 we

find the measurements of the Temple building itself, called "the house" in the Hebrew text of Ezekiel, "the Temple" in the Revised Standard Version's English. This is the house of God, the Temple in the strict and narrow sense. It is only in an extended sense that we use the word "Temple" to designate the entire complex comprising not only the house itself but also the courts, the gates, and all the rest of the space in the Temple compound separated from the profane world outside by the great outer wall. The Temple building consists of three rooms, arranged in a series, one after the other as one proceeds from the entrance at the east end to the innermost room at the western end.

The first of these three rooms is the vestibule (V on the Plan at the end of this commentary) at the entrance (vv. 48-49), approached by steps leading up from the west side of the inner court. Outside the entrance, on either side, stands a pillar; these are the two pillars whose purpose escapes us, found in Solomon's Temple (1 Kgs 7:15-22) but not, as far as we know, in the post-Exilic Temple actually begun in the days of the governor Sheshbazzar (Ezra 5:14-16) and finished in the days of the governor Zerubbabel, urged on by the prophets Haggai and Zechariah (Ezra 5:1-6:15; Hag 1:1-2, 9; Zech 4:7-10).

In 41:1-2 Ezekiel and his guide pass on from the vestibule into the next room, the nave (N on the Plan), which the guide duly measures. In the nave of Solomon's Temple were the altar of incense, the table for the bread of the Presence, and ten golden lampstands, according to 1 Kgs 6:20-22 (after textual emendations of the end of 6:22 in that textually corrupt passage); 7:48-49. We know from a passage in the Hellenistic Letter of Aristeas that in the post-Exilic Temple there was a table for the bread of the Presence, and the description of the seven-branched lampstand prescribed as a furnishing for the desert Tabernacle in Exod 25:31-40 and Exod 37:17-24 may actually be based on the appearance of a lampstand which stood in the nave of the post-Exilic Temple. We cannot argue from the silence of the texts that there was no altar of incense in the nave of the post-Exilic Temple, for we know that there was such an altar in the nave of its successor, the Temple built by Herod the Great.

Finally, the guide moves on by himself into the innermost room of the house (I on the Plan), which he measures (41:3-4). As the celestial emissary does his measuring in the innermost room, Ezekiel remains in the nave — a way of expressing awe and reverence towards this most holy of all sacred spaces, into which the post-Exilic high priest himself, represented by Aaron in the ritual for the Day of Atonement, could not often enter without incurring divine punishment (Lev 16:2). In Solomon's Temple, the ark of the covenant had been kept in this innermost room of the house of God, and the ark, overshadowed by two winged figures with human heads (the cherubim), was the "footstool" of God (1 Chr 28:2), who was enthroned on the cherubim (1 Sam 4:4; 2 Sam 6:2; 2 Kgs 19:15; Isa 37:16). The ark perished certainly in the destruction of Solomon's Temple in 586. In the innermost room of the post-Exilic Temple was the "mercy seat" mentioned in the ritual for the Day of Atonement (Lev 16:2, 13-15), and the room itself is called the room of the mercy seat in 1 Chr 28:11. Here in v. 4 it is for the first time called the "most holy place" or "holy of holies."

MEASUREMENTS OF SOME ACCESSORY BUILDINGS AND SPACES
41:5-15a

⁵Then he measured the wall of the temple, six cubits thick; and the breadth of the side chambers, four cubits, round about the temple. ⁶And the side chambers were in three stories, one over another, thirty in each story. There were offsets all around the wall of the temple to serve as supports for the side chambers, so that they should not be supported by the wall of the temple. ⁷And the side chambers became broader as they rose from story to story round about the temple; on the side of the temple a stairway led upward, and thus one went up from the lowest story to the top story through the middle story. ⁸I saw also that the temple had a raised platform round about; the foundations of the side chambers measured a

full reed of six long cubits. [9]The thickness of the outer
wall of the side chambers was five cubits; [and the part of
the platform which was left free was five cubits. Between
the platform of the temple and the [10]chambers of the
court was a breadth of twenty cubits round about the
temple on every side.] [11]And the doors of the side
chambers opened on the part of the platform that was left
free, one door toward the north, and another door
toward the south; and the breadth of the part that was left
free was five cubits round about.

[12]The building that was facing the temple yard on the
west side was seventy cubits broad; and the wall of the
building was five cubits thick round about, and its length
ninety cubits.

[13]Then he measured the temple, a hundred cubits long;
and the yard and the building with its walls, a hundred
cubits long; [14]also the breadth of the east front of the
temple and the yard, a hundred cubits

[15]Then he measured the length of the building facing
the yard which was at the west and its walls on either side,
a hundred cubits.

This section gives us the measurements of some parts of
the Temple compound near the Temple house. It is replete
with difficulties of the sort which make Ezek 40-42 so difficult for the interpreter — technical terms whose exact sense
escapes us, and textual problems caused by ancient scribes
tampering with the text in an effort to get things "right,"
although they were themselves having a hard time understanding what was being described in the text. Let us just
delineate what actually appears on the ground plan of the
Temple compound in this passage, with a few textual cor-
rections necessary for making sense out of what would
otherwise be impossible. Reference will be made to the Plan
of the Temple at the end of this commentary.

Built against the outer walls of the Temple house is a
series of chambers in three stories (S on the Plan), running
along those three sides of the Temple house which do not
open onto the inner court (vv. 5-9). The purposes for which

these side chambers are to be used can only be guessed. From these side chambers doors, one on the north side and one on the south (v. 11), open out onto the level or platform on which the Temple house is built — the "platform" of v. 8. (We shall see in a moment that the Revised Standard Version's "platform" in v. 9 needs to be reconsidered.) Running along the entire length of the Temple house is an open space or passageway, one along the north side of the house and one along its south side; these passageways (f on the Plan) are "the part (of the platform) which was left free" (a single technical word in Hebrew) of vv. 9b, 11b in the English of the Revised Standard Version.

In order to make coherent sense of vv. 9b-11 — and to get the dimensions from the south edge of the platform to its north edge to come out right — we must perform the following operations:

a) On the basis of a good clue provided by the Greek version, followed to the solution, emend a Hebrew word in v. 11b, untranslated in the Revised Standard Version, to a Hebrew word meaning "wall," and insert that into the English text, so that v. 11b reads: "and the breadth of the wall of the part (of the platform) that was left free was five cubits round about (i.e. both to the north and to the south of the house)." This wall (there were two of them, one on the north edge of the platform and one on its south edge — both of them marked "w" on the Plan) separated the "part of the platform that was left free" from the slope falling down to the outer court beyond. This wall on both sides of the platform thus had its importance as a barrier separating the holy space of the platform from the markedly less holy space of the outer court (see the commentary on 42:1-20).

b) Remove from v. 10a the "chambers of the court." "Of the court" is an addition found neither in the Hebrew text nor in the ancient versions. The immediate context, as it can be deciphered in the Hebrew text and in the ancient versions, shows that the masonry construction originally designated in v. 10a is across "the part of the platform that was left free" from the walls of the side chambers of the Temple house. Any chambers there on the opposite side, alongside of the north and south edges of the platform, would lie beyond the width of the platform itself, and thus would leave five cubits unaccounted for on both sides, in the total of the spaces measured across the width of the platform itself. A reasoned solution lies in replacing the "chambers of the court" with the wall which we restored to the text of v. 11b in the preceding operation *a*. This wall, five cubits broad, built on top of the platform, upon the edge of the platform's north and south sides rather than alongside of them, fills the five cubits needed on each side to get the single measurements across the platform to meet exactly the platform's total breadth given in v. 14.

c) Abandon the Revised Standard Version of vv. 9b-10 (set off in square brackets in the text printed above) in favor of a translation following closely the Hebrew text and the Greek version, with the emendation made in operation *b* above: "and the part of the platform which was left free between the side chambers of the Temple house and the wall was a breadth of twenty cubits along the Temple house on either side." In other words, the distance on the Plan from S to w, across f, is twenty cubits.

West of the Temple house is a building (B on the Plan) called simply "the building" (vv. 12-13, 15), whose purpose is not known. "The building" is separated from the Temple house by a stretch of the platform running north and south between "the building" and the west end of the side chambers built up against the Temple house. This stretch of the platform (y^1 on the Plan) is called the "yard" in the Revised Standard Version (vv. 12-13, 15). In v. 14 a "yard" is also indicated at the east end of the Temple house, where a "yard" (y^2) must have flanked the vestibule of the house on either side. A "yard" may have been a part of the platform not encumbered by buildings but covered, nevertheless, by some kind of sheltering roof (a hypothesis built on a possible etymology of the Hebrew word translated "yard").

THE INTERIOR DECORATION
OF THE TEMPLE HOUSE
41:15b-26

15bThe nave of the temple and the inner room and the outer vestibule 16were paneled and round about all three had windows with recessed frames. Over against the threshold the temple was paneled with wood round about, from the floor up to the windows (now the windows were covered), 17to the space above the door, even to the inner room, and on the outside. And on all the walls round about in the inner room and the nave were carved likenesses 18of cherubim and palm trees, a palm tree between cherub and cherub. Every cherub had two faces: 19the face of a man toward the palm tree on the one side, and the face of a young lion toward the palm tree on the other side. They were carved on the whole temple round about; 20from the floor to above the door cherubim and palm trees were carved on the wall.

21The doorposts of the nave were squared; and in front of the holy place was something resembling 22an altar of wood, three cubits high, two cubits long, and two cubits broad; its corners, its base, and its walls were of wood. He said to me, "This is the table which is before the LORD." 23The nave and the holy place had each a double door. 24The doors had two leaves apiece, two swinging leaves for each door. 25And on the doors of the nave were carved cherubim and palm trees, such as were carved on the walls; and there was a canopy of wood in front of the vestibule outside. 26And there were recessed windows and palm trees on either side, on the sidewalls of the vestibule.

Unexpectedly, we move back to the interior rooms of the Temple house, whose measurements were given in 40:48-41:4, but the move is not accomplished by narrative. The usual narrative statement that the guide led Ezekiel to the next place in their tour of the Temple compound is entirely lacking here. The usual concern with measurements is also lacking. From this we conclude that this section does not belong to the basic text of chapters 40-42 but was added at a later stage of the text's evolution.

In this section we are told a few things about the decoration of the interior of the Temple house and about its furnishings. The text is not always intelligible, for it is incorrigibly corrupt in some places, and the meaning of some technical terms remains unknown. According to the translation of vv. 15b and 17 in the Revised Standard Version (which follows the Greek version), the decoration of the walls of all three rooms of the Temple house is being described, but the problematic Hebrew text seems to mention only the first two rooms —the vestibule (V on the Plan) and the nave (N), but not the inner room (I) which is the most holy place. It is impossible to make sense of the end of v. 26; in the Revised Standard Version the end of that verse is prudently omitted altogether from the translation. No one knows what the word translated "canopy" in v. 25 means. In any case, the two (or three?) rooms described have framed windows and are panelled from the floor to the level of the windows. On the panelling there is a frieze of palm trees alternating with cherubim. In the nave, in front of the opening into the inner room to the west, is the altar-like table for the bread of the Presence (vv. 21-22). The openings between the rooms are closed off by double doors on which the frieze of palm trees alternating with cherubim is continued. The person inspired to add this description to the text has left us with a testimony, eloquent despite its obscurity, to the care and taste fittingly devoted to the decoration of the interior of the house of God.

MORE CHAMBERS, AND A SUMMARY
42:1-20

42 Then he led me out into the inner court, toward the north, and he brought me to the chambers which were opposite the temple yard and opposite the building on the north. ²The length of the building which was on the north side was a hundred cubits, and the breadth fifty cubits. ³Adjoining the twenty cubits which belonged to the inner

court, and facing the pavement which belonged to the outer court, was gallery against gallery in three stories. ⁴And before the chambers was a passage inward, ten cubits wide and a hundred cubits long, and their doors were on the north. ⁵Now the upper chambers were narrower, for the galleries took more away from them than the lower and middle chambers in the building. ⁶For they were in three stories, and they had no pillars like the pillars of the outer court; hence the upper chambers were set back from the ground more than the lower and the middle ones. ⁷And there was a wall outside parallel to the chambers, toward the outer court, opposite the chambers, fifty cubits long. ⁸For the chambers on the outer court were fifty cubits long, while those opposite the temple were a hundred cubits long. ⁹Below these chambers was an entrance on the east side, as one enters them from the outer court, ¹⁰where the outside wall begins. ...

¹³Then he said to me, "The north chambers and the south chambers opposite the yard are the holy chambers, where the priests who approach the LORD shall eat the most holy offerings; there they shall put the most holy offerings — the cereal offering, the sin offering, and the guilt offering, for the place is holy. ¹⁴When the priests enter the holy place, they shall not go out of it into the outer court without laying there the garments in which they minister, for these are holy; they shall put on other garments before they go near to that which is for the people."

¹⁵Now when he had finished measuring the interior of the temple area, he led me out by the gate which faced east, and measured the temple area round about. ¹⁶He measured the east side with the measuring reed, five hundred cubits by the measuring reed. ¹⁷Then he turned and measured the north side, five hundred cubits by the measuring reed. ¹⁸Then he turned and measured the south side, five hunded cubits by the measuring reed. ¹⁹Then he turned to the west side and measured, five hundred cubits by the measuring reed. ²⁰He measured it

on the four sides. It had a wall around it, five hundred cubits long and five hundred cubits broad, to make a separation between the holy and the common.

The tour of Ezekiel and his guide continues. In vv. 1-14 we have a description of two blocks of chambers for priestly use, and of the passageways running along the long sides of each of those two blocks, with some concluding statements on the use of the chambers. The text is full of difficulties, but thanks especially to the work of the German Biblical scholar and archaeologist Karl Elliger, we have a fairly good idea of the architectural realities described in the difficult text. The two blocks of priestly chambers (P on the Plan) are at the extreme western edge of the Temple compound, against the western outer wall. Between the two of them are "the building" (B), itself built against the west wall of the Temple compound, and the "yard" (y^1), i.e. that part of the space twenty cubits wide running around the Temple house on the level of the inner, upper, court (v. 3a) which separates "the building" from the Temple house (41:12-13, 15). In v. 2a, remove the Revised Standard Version's "the building," not in the text, which confuses the picture; the dimensions given in v. 2 are those of a block of priestly chambers. Of the two blocks of priestly chambers the first one described, in vv. 1-10a, is the one to the north of "the building" and the "yard" (v. 1; at the end of that verse in the Revised Standard Version insert a comma after "the building," for the sense required is that the northern block of priestly chambers was "opposite the building, on the north [of the building]").

Vv. 10b-12, omitted from the text printed above, tell us that the arrangement of the block to the south and its relation to the adjacent passages and neighboring structures is the mirror image of the arrangement of the block to the north. Only the northern arrangement is actually described.

Running between the described northern chambers on the one side and "the building" and the "yard" on the other is a corridor — the "passage inward" of v. 4 (b on the Plan), from which doors lead north into the block of chambers. The block of chambers is built in three parallel sections (the "gallery against gallery in three stories"), each running from the west wall eastward for 100 cubits. On the plan, we have used broken lines to mark this division of the chamber block into the three sections. The three sections are on three distinct levels. Since the block is built on the slope rising from the level of the outer court up to the higher level of "the building" and the "yard" (which is also the level of the inner court and the Temple house), the highest of the three parallel sections of the block of priestly chambers is on the level of the inner court, the lowest of the sections on that of the outer court, and the middle section on an intermediate level (so on the basis of vv. 3b, 5-6). Beyond the priestly block, down on the level of the outer court, are chambers of another kind: some of those chambers for the laity (L on the Plan), built around the outer edge of the outer court, mentioned in 40:17, which, measured with the pavement (p on the Plan) running in front of them (the pavement mentioned in 42:3), extend outwards 50 cubits from the western outer wall (v. 8a). Between the last of these chambers for the laity and the block of chambers for the priests runs a passage 50 cubits long (because that is the length, measured from the western outer wall, of the lay chamber plus the pavement in front of it); that passage (c on the Plan) is extended farther eastward for the remaining 50 cubits of the priestly block (whose total length is 100 cubits) by the construction of a wall extended out eastward from the end of the portico in front of the last lay chamber. The passage thus formed finally opens into the outer court (vv. 7, 9-10).

The purpose of the priestly chambers just described is given in vv. 13-14. Once again, it is a matter of separation of the sacred from the profane, of the reservation of holy space for holy persons and holy things. Some of the chambers in the priestly blocks just described are to be used by the priests for eating those parts of sacrificial offerings which were theirs to eat by right (v. 13). In 46:19-20 kitchens for preparing those parts for eating are indicated at the western end of the priestly blocks (K on the Plan). Three types of sacrifice are mentioned: the cereal offering, the sin offering, and the guilt offering. The burnt offering, or holocaust, is not mentioned, because with it all of the victim is given over to God, with none of it consumed by the priests. V. 14 informs us of another purpose for which some of the chambers in these priestly blocks are to be used: when the priests pass from the holy space reserved to them into the markedly less holy space of the outer court, they must change clothing, leaving their holy clothing somewhere in the blocks of priestly chambers. This is said more clearly yet in 44:19. In the Ancient Near East as a whole, people felt that the passage from profane space into sacral space called for a change of clothing, in order to avoid the pollution of the sacral with things brought over from the realm of the profane. Conversely, what was holy could also spread dangerously to the realm of the profane by a kind of contagion, and it is in order to avoid this that the priests in Ezekiel's system must remove their holy clothes and leave them in one of the blocks of priestly chambers before they leave holy space. The holy space reserved to the priests is the entire upper level on which are the inner court (where the sacrificial altar is), the Temple house, "the building," the connecting passageways, and the two blocks of priestly chambers of which each descends in its three tiers from the holy upper level to the less holy lower level. When the priests have left their holy garments in the still holy space of the priestly chambers and have donned secular clothing, they pass out through the passageway (c) of vv. 7, 9-10 into the less holy space of the outer court, without bearing with them in their clothing the contagious force of the sacral. (The outer court itself possesses a certain minor degree of holiness, however, as we shall see in the concluding verses of this section.) The two blocks of priestly chambers at the border between the holy and the less holy space of the Temple area are buildings for holy persons (the priests), in which are refectories for eating holy foods and sacristies for depositing holy clothing. The sacred and the profane or common are to be kept separate.

In vv. 15-20 the tour of the Temple is concluded. The supernatural guide takes Ezekiel through the outer east gate into the space outside the Temple compound altogether. There they make a tour of the outer walls of the Temple compound on all four sides, measuring those outer walls as they go. The Temple compound turns out to be a perfect square, and idealistic symmetry triumphs. The end of v. 20 (later perhaps than the rest of vv. 15-20) should be noted, for it tells us that the outer walls of the Temple compound separated the entirely common or profane space of the world at large from the holy space inside the Temple compound. All space inside the compound is holy. This provides some refinement in the spatial and personal distinctions between the holy and the profane in Ezekiel's plan. Up to this point, only the upper level of the compound, on which are the inner court, the Temple house, and the other spaces reserved to priests, has been called holy, in clear distinction from the outer court where the lay Israelites are allowed to be. The end of v. 20 shows that the outer court itself, though less holy than the space reserved to the priests, is itself holy to a minor degree, while only the space altogether outside the Temple compound is entirely common or profane. The lay Israelites are a holy people because they are God's people. Within the compound surrounding God's house, the space proper to the lay Israelites has its own, minor, degree of holiness. No one who is not a member of the house of Israel should enter it.

GOD'S GLORY RETURNS TO THE TEMPLE
43:1-12

43 Afterward he brought me to the gate, the gate facing east. ²And behold, the glory of the God of Israel came from the east; and the sound of his coming was like the sound of many waters; and the earth shone with his glory. ³And the vision I saw was like the vision which I had seen when he came to destroy the city, and like the vision which I had seen by the river Chebar; and I fell upon my face. ⁴As the glory of the LORD entered the temple by the gate facing east, ⁵the Spirit lifted me up, and brought me into the inner court; and behold, the glory of the LORD filled the temple.

⁶While the man was standing beside me, I heard one

speaking to me out of the temple; [7]and he said to me, "Son of man, this is the place of my throne and the place of the soles of my feet, where I will dwell in the midst of the people of Israel for ever. And the house of Israel shall no more defile my holy name, neither they, nor their kings, by their harlotry, and by the dead bodies of their kings, [8]by setting their threshold by my threshold and their doorposts beside my doorposts, with only a wall between me and them. They have defiled my holy name by their abominations which they have committed, so I have consumed them in my anger. [9]Now let them put away their idolatry and the dead bodies of their kings far from me, and I will dwell in their midst for ever.

[10]"And you, son of man, describe to the house of Israel the temple and its appearance and plan, that they may be ashamed of their iniquities. [11]And if they are ashamed of all that they have done, portray the temple, its arrangement, its exits and its entrances, and its whole form; and make known to them all its ordinances and all its laws; and write it down in their sight, so that they may observe and perform all its laws and all its ordinances. [12]This is the law of the temple: the whole territory round about upon the top of the mountain shall be most holy. Behold, this is the law of the temple.

This passage, particularly, vv. 1-7a, is the most significant part of chapters 40-48, of Part Four of our book. In it, Ezekiel sees God, invisible, but manifest in his glory, returning to the new Temple, to dwell again in the midst of his people, thus marking definitively the end of the Exilic period and of the bad relations between the people and God which led God to bring about his own departure from the Temple and his people's departure for exile. The primitive nucleus of this section may have been vv. 4-7a, which could originally have followed 40:1-2. The visionary description in vv. 1-3 contains points having parallels in the already expanded reports of the earlier visions to which v. 3 alludes: those in chapters 8-11 ("the vision which I had seen when he came to destroy the city") and chapters 1-3 ("the vision which I had seen by the river Chebar"). Vv. 10-12 obviously presume the integration of the tour and its Temple measurements (the basic text of 40:3-42:20) with the vision of God's glory returning; these verses also presuppose the addition of later texts in which one sees all the concern with holiness and its separation from the profane or common (especially evident in 40:38-46; 42:13-20; 46:19-24), and for that matter, all of the ordinances and laws set down in 43:18-46:18.

When the glory of God departed from the city before the city's destruction it went to "the mountain which is on the east side of the city" (11:23), the mountain later called the Mount of Olives. Now it returns from the east (v. 2) and enters the Temple through the eastern gate (v. 4), proceeding then to the interior of the Temple house, surely, although that is not said in all clarity. Ezekiel is then taken to the inner court, which is just in front of the entrance to the Temple house. The man who stands beside him there (v. 6) is probably meant to be the celestial guide and measurer of 40:3-42:20, but he no longer has any function of his own in the narrative. From the interior of the Temple house comes a voice which is the voice of God himself, although for reverential reasons that is left unstated. God declares the Temple to be his dwelling once again. Although the Solomonic Temple's cherubim on which God was enthroned and ark which he used as his royal footstool are omitted entirely from the descriptions of the new Temple in Ezekiel, and were in fact absent from the post-Exilic Temple when it was finally built (see above on 40:47-41:4), the divine presence to which those objects once pointed has returned in vision, and will return in reality. The absence of those objects is not to call the effective reality of the divine presence into doubt. The Temple itself, not certain furnishings within it, will be the place of God's throne and the footstool for his feet (v. 7a). It will be the right place for seeking God and paying him homage, for there will he henceforth dwell in the midst of his people.

Vv. 7b-12 have been tacked on to the original account of the vision. In vv. 7b-9 we find a warning against defiling the Temple by having the burial place of the kings too close to it.

To speak of God's name dwelling in the Temple is to speak of God himself dwelling in the Temple, expressing that in such a way that his transcendence is safeguarded, his presence in the Temple being kept relative or modal by attribution to his name rather than to his person. The rebuke for past iniquities and the reminder of a divine punishment which is past (v. 8b) seems somewhat out of place in this context. So, too, does the connection of the plan of the Temple with the thought of the people's iniquities in vv. 10-11. The idea that the appearance and plan of the Temple might be a remedy against the people's iniquities strikes us as curious, to say the least. It is really an elliptical expression of a line of reasoning which runs like this: the past iniquities of the house of Israel which led God to bring about the devastation of Judah and the deportation of the people were cultic iniquities which will be avoided in the future if the cultic laws and ordinances given especially in 44:4-46:18 are observed and performed; since those cultic laws can best be observed and performed in a Temple built according to an appearance and plan which assure the careful separation of the holy from the less holy or from the profane (v. 12), it follows that the appearance and plan (and the cultic laws and ordinances) which afford that assurance should be communicated to the house of Israel, so that it will not repeat its past iniquities. This concern with separation of the holy is not found in the original plan of the Temple in 40:5-42:20. It is found in the later additions to that plan in 40:38-46; 42:1-14, 20b, and in the correspondingly late prescriptions of 44:4-46:24. It is also the concern found in these verses (43:10-12) added to the end of Ezekiel's account of his vision of the return of God's glory to the Temple. These added verses form a bridge between the preceding visionary sections of chapters 40-48, which present the return of the divine presence to a Temple built according to a plan divinely revealed, and the following prescriptive sections, which present sacral laws whose observance will assure the kind of worship which God wants in that Temple.

THE ALTAR AND ITS CONSECRATION
43:13-27

¹³"These are the dimensions of the altar by cubits (the cubit being a cubit and a handbreadth): its base shall be one cubit high, and one cubit broad, with a rim of one span around its edge. And this shall be the height of the altar: ¹⁴from the base on the ground to the lower ledge, two cubits, with a breadth of one cubit; and from the smaller ledge to the larger ledge, four cubits, with a breadth of one cubit; ¹⁵and the altar hearth, four cubits; and from the altar hearth projecting upward, four horns, one cubit high. ¹⁶The altar hearth shall be square, twelve cubits long by twelve broad. ¹⁷The ledge also shall be square, fourteen cubits long by fourteen broad, with a rim around it half a cubit broad, and its base one cubit round about. The steps of the altar shall face east."

¹⁸And he said to me, "Son of man, thus says the Lord GOD: These are the ordinances for the altar: On the day when it is erected for offering burnt offerings upon it and for throwing blood against it, ¹⁹you shall give to the Levitical priests of the family of Zadok, who draw near to me to minister to me, says the Lord GOD, a bull for a sin offering. ²⁰And you shall take some of its blood, and put it on the four horns of the altar, and on the four corners of the ledge, and upon the rim round about; thus you shall cleanse the altar and make atonement for it. ²¹You shall also take the bull of the sin offering, and it shall be burnt in the appointed place belonging to the temple, outside the sacred area. ²²And on the second day you shall offer a he-goat without blemish for a sin offering; and the altar shall be cleansed, as it was cleansed with the bull. ²³When you have finished cleansing it, you shall offer a bull without blemish and a ram from the flock without blemish. ²⁴You shall present them before the LORD, and the priests shall sprinkle salt upon them and offer them up as a burnt offering to the LORD. ²⁵For seven days you shall provide daily a goat for a sin offering; also a bull and a ram from the flock, without blemish, shall be provided.

²⁶Seven days shall they make atonement for the altar and purify it, and so consecrate it. ²⁷And when they have completed these days, then from the eighth day onward the priests shall offer upon the altar your burnt offerings and your peace offerings; and I will accept you, says the Lord GOD."

In the description of the Temple there was a bald statement that the altar was in the inner court, in front of the entrance to the Temple house (40:47), but the altar was not described there. In the editorial process of putting together Part Four of the book of Ezekiel someone was moved to put here, before the sacral laws, a description of the altar followed by the prescriptions for its rite of consecration. Since we have no other description of the sacrificial altar of the Temple, from either before or after the Exile, the description furnished here has special value, even though we cannot say to what extent it reflects or does not reflect the real appearance of one of the historical altars in the Temple of Jerusalem.

In the description (vv. 13-17) there are measurements, but there is no attempt to follow the pattern of touring and measuring used in presenting the description of the Temple in 40:5-42:20. The cubit used here, as in chapters 40-42 (see 40:5) is the royal cubit of 52.5 centimeters (20.6692 inches). A span (v. 13) is ½ cubit. The reader may find it helpful to consult the sketch of the altar in cross section (east to west) which accompanies the commentary at this point. Problems of obscure technical terminology and ancient textual disturbance flourish again here.

The altar described is, in any case, made up of three square sections or layers (I-II-III on the sketch), rising one above another from a square "base" (B). In the textual and archaeological interpretation worked out in recent years and followed here, the "base" is sunk into the ground, with its upper surface exposed around the lowest layer of the altar which rests on it. Its upper surface is itself a cubit below the surface level of the surrounding inner court (thus the words: "its base shall be one cubit high" in v. 13, but for the

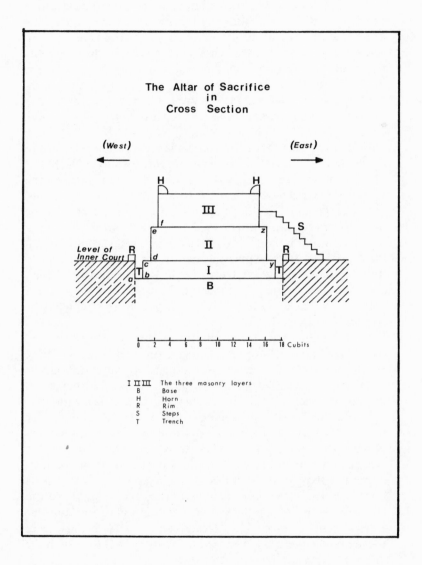

The Altar of Sacrifice
in
Cross Section

I Ⅱ Ⅲ   The three masonry layers
B   Base
H   Horn
R   Rim
S   Steps
T   Trench

English "high" read "deep" instead), so that around the altar is a trench (T) into which the blood of the sacrificial victims can flow without staining the level of the inner court. The altar is steplike, having its successively rising layers set on one another in such a way that a given layer is, on each of its four sides, set in one cubit from the sides of the layer below it. Set on the "base" (B) is the first layer (I), two cubits high, then above it, and set in one cubit from the lower layer's outer edges (the space from c to d repeated on all four sides), is the second layer (II), four cubits high (v. 14). Set in one cubit from the edges of the second layer (the space from e to f repeated on all four sides) is the uppermost layer (III), that of the altar hearth (v. 15), on whose upper surface the sacrificial victims were burned. Rising upward from each of the four corners of the hearth's upper surface is a stone projection (H), the "horn" (v. 15). Built against the altar's east side was a flight of steps (S) by which priests could reach the hearth (v. 17); a priest functioning at the altar would thus be facing westward, towards the Temple house, thereby avoiding the cultic abomination of worshiping eastward with one's back turned to the Temple house which was condemned in 8:16-18.

If the reader will make the following mental notes and adjustments, he will find the description in the English of the Revised Standard Version printed above understandable:

a) For the two "ledges" (v. 14), understand the horizontal upper surfaces of those two layers (I and II) which lie between the "base" and the hearth (i.e., the surfaces from c to y and from e to z). On each of these two "ledges" the mass of the next layer above rests, thus covering most of the "ledge" on which it rests. The outer part of a "ledge" is thus exposed all around the mass of the layer above which rests on it, and those exposed surfaces of the two "ledges" around the four sides of the layers above them give the altar its steplike appearance. The "ledge" of v. 17 is the upper of these two "ledges," i.e. the "ledge" (e to z) of II on which the mass of the altar hearth (III) rests.

b) In v. 14b, the "smaller ledge" would be more accurately called the "lower ledge." It is the "ledge" (c to y) of the lower layer (I) of the two layers which are placed between the "base" and the hearth. It is, as "ledge," not smaller but larger than the "ledge" above, in the horizontal dimensions which are properly those of the "ledges." It is accordingly smaller only in the improper sense that it is the "ledge" of the lower level whose dimension most evident to the beholder — its vertical dimension or height (two cubits) — is smaller than the vertical measurement of the layer above it (four cubits). In the same way, the "larger ledge" (e to z) is the "ledge" of the next layer upward (II), larger only in the sense that the height of that layer itself (but not the length and breadth of its "ledge") is greater than the height of the layer below.

c) The "broad" measurement of v. 13 and the measurements of "breadth" in v. 14 are horizontal measurements taken on the upper surface of a lower section, from the outer edge of that lower section inward to the point at which the vertical side of the section above meets the horizontal plane being measured — a to b in v. 13, c to d and e to f in v. 14. This measurement of breadth is in each case one cubit, but it is valid for each of the four sides. This means, at each level, a difference of two cubits (one on each side in cross section) in both length and breadth between the horizontal dimensions of two adjacent layers. Thus, the "ledge" of v. 17 (which is the "ledge" of II) measures 14 x 14 cubits, while the upper surface of the altar hearth (III) above it, measuring 12 x 12 cubits (v. 16) shows the difference of two cubits in square measurement from one layer to the next.

d)The rendering of v. 17 in the Revised Standard Version puts a "rim" around the upper "ledge," but the Hebrew text, with the archaic and ambiguous pronouns of this passage, does not actually express that connection. The "rim" of v. 17 may be the "rim" around the edge of the "base" already mentioned in v. 13 (R), for the text of v. 17 clearly returns to the "base." The Hebrew text of v. 17 does not have "broad" with the ½ cubit measurement of the "rim"; one of the two dimensions given for the "rim" — ½ cubit in v. 17, a span (= ½ cubit) in v. 13, may be its height, the other its width. That is the interpretation reflected in the dimensions of the "rim" as we have drawn it in our sketch of the altar in cross section.

The steplike altar described here could hardly have been put together with stones which were not hewn, and it has a flight of steps built against its east side (v. 17). Both of these details are expressly forbidden in the cultic law for an altar set down in Exod 20:25-26. Both Exod 20:25-26 and Ezek 43:13-17 are presented as divinely given instructions. They come from two different traditions, both of which are legitimate, but they contain contradictory provisions. When we notice this, we can conclude that liturgical law is never absolute. It can be changed, and in two different traditions there may be contradictory provisions governing the same thing. Both liturgical change and sharp liturgical difference between two traditions can be legitimate, with the difference, diachronically through change and synchronically in different traditions, enjoying divine sanction.

In vv. 18-27 we find the instructions for the consecration of the altar. The instructions have been drawn from a ritual of some kind, with alterations made in order to make the instructions fit the present context. Upon the altar a rite of expiation for sin has to be performed (vv. 20, 26). The reason for that is that the altar has to be transferred from the sphere of the profane and the sinful to the sphere of the holy and the pure. When that transfer has been accomplished, the altar can serve as the place where rites effecting a similar transfer in persons can take place. The peace offerings can then be shared by God (who receives his share from the altar) and by the offerers among the people (who eat their portions in the outer court). A result will be that God accepts the offerings (v. 27).

THE OUTER EAST GATE FOR GOD AND THE PRINCE 44:1-3

> **44** Then he brought me back to the outer gate of the sanctuary, which faces east; and it was shut. ²And he said to me, "This gate shall remain shut; it shall not be opened, and no one shall enter by it; for the LORD, the God of Israel, has entered by it; therefore it shall remain shut.

³Only the prince may sit in it to eat bread before the LORD; he shall enter by way of the vestibule of the gate, and shall go out by the same way."

The word translated "sanctuary" in the Revised Standard Version of these latter chapters of Ezekiel often designates the entire Temple compound, not the Temple house alone. So it is here. An unnamed person leads Ezekiel back to the outer east gate, the gate through which the glory of the Lord, in Ezekiel's vision, has entered the Temple (43:1-4). The dramatic procedure of having someone lead Ezekiel from place to place, established by the basic text of the Temple's description in chapters 40-42, is picked up in these later passages, but the guide's function no longer includes measuring. It includes, instead, verbal communication. The guide speaks authoritatively as an emissary from on high. In this short passage, he proclaims the general rule that the outer east gate of the Temple shall remain closed, adding then a partial exception to be made in the case of the civil ruler, the prince. The prince may enter that gate through the vestibule off the outer court, at the west end of the gatehouse, in order to eat his sacral food within the gatehouse but must then leave the way he came, by returning through the vestibule to the outer court. The exception does not provide for the opening of the doors at the east end of the gatehouse through which one might pass on out of the Temple into the countryside beyond.

Underlying the heavenly emissary's instructions is the ancient and noble idea that there should be royal doors through which only royal persons may pass. Since the Lord, the king of the universe, has passed through this gate and its outer doors, no one else should pass through them. Since the Lord intends to remain in the Temple forever (43:7a), the gate through which he has passed and which is reserved exclusively to him need never be opened gain. The prince, because of his earthly royalty, is admitted to the gatehouse, but he may not pass through the doors reserved to the Lord. In Christian typology, this gate, through which no one but the Lord may enter and leave, has been taken as a type of the virginal womb of Mary, into which Jesus, the Lord incarnate, alone entered, to leave it on the day of his birth.

RULES FOR LEVITES AND PRIESTS
44:4-31

⁴Then he brought me by way of the north gate to the front of the temple; and I looked, and behold, the glory of the LORD filled the temple of the LORD; and I fell upon my face. ⁵And the LORD said to me, "Son of man, mark well, see with your eyes, and hear with your ears all that I shall tell you concerning all the ordinances of the temple of the LORD and all its laws; and mark well those who may be admitted to the temple and all those who are to be excluded from the sanctuary. ⁶And say to the rebellious house, to the house of Israel, Thus says the Lord GOD: O house of Israel, let there be an end to all your abominations, ⁷in admitting foreigners, uncircumcised in heart and flesh, to be in my sanctuary, profaning it, when you offer to me my food, the fat and the blood. You have broken my covenant, in addition to all your abominations. ⁸And you have not kept charge of my holy things; but you have set foreigners to keep my charge in my sanctuary.

⁹"Therefore thus says the Lord GOD: No foreigner, uncircumcised in heart and flesh, of all the foreigners who are among the people of Israel, shall enter my sanctuary. ¹⁰But the Levites who went far from me, going astray from me after their idols when Israel went astray, shall bear their punishment. ¹¹They shall be ministers in my sanctuary, having oversight at the gates of the temple, and serving in the temple; they shall slay the burnt offering and the sacrifice for the people, and they shall attend on the people, to serve them. ¹²Because they ministered to them before their idols and became a stumbling block of iniquity to the house of Israel, therefore I have sworn concerning them, says the Lord GOD, that they shall bear their punishment. ¹³They shall not come near to me, to serve me as priest, nor come near any of my sacred

things and the things that are most sacred; but they shall bear their shame, because of the abominations which they have committed. [14]Yet I will appoint them to keep charge of the temple, to do all its service and all that is to be done in it.

[15]"But the Levitical priests, the sons of Zadok, who kept the charge of my sanctuary when the people of Israel went astray from me, shall come near to me to minister to me; and they shall attend on me to offer me the fat and the blood, says the Lord GOD; [16]they shall enter my sanctuary, and they shall approach my table, to minister to me, and they shall keep my charge. [17]When they enter the gates of the inner court, they shall wear linen garments; they shall have nothing of wool on them, while they minister at the gates of the inner court, and within. [18]They shall have linen turbans upon their heads, and linen breeches upon their loins; they shall not gird themselves with anything that causes sweat. [19]And when they go out into the outer court to the people, they shall put off the garments in which they have been ministering, and lay them in the holy chambers; and they shall put on other garments, lest they communicate holiness to the people with their garments. [20]They shall not shave their heads or let their locks grow long; they shall only trim the hair of their heads. [21]No priest shall drink wine, when he enters the inner court. [22]They shall not marry a widow, or a divorced woman, but only a virgin of the stock of the house of Israel, or a widow who is the widow of a priest. [23]They shall teach my people the difference between the holy and the common, and show them how to distinguish between the unclean and the clean. [24]In a controversy they shall act as judges, and they shall judge it according to my judgments. They shall keep my laws and my statutes in all my appointed feasts, and they shall keep my sabbaths holy. [25]They shall not defile themselves by going near to a dead person; however, for father or mother, for son or daughter, for brother or unmarried sister they may defile themselves. [26]After he is defiled, he shall count for himself seven days, and then he shall be clean. [27]And on

the day that he goes into the holy place, into the inner court, to minister in the holy place, he shall offer his sin offering, says the Lord GOD.

28"They shall have no inheritance; I am their inheritance: and you shall give them no possession in Israel; I am their possession. 29They shall eat the cereal offering, the sin offering, and the guilt offering; and every devoted thing in Israel shall be theirs. 30And the first of all the first fruits of all kinds, and every offering of all kinds from all your offerings, shall belong to the priests; you shall also give to the priests the first of your coarse meal, that a blessing may rest on your house. 31The priests shall not eat of anything, whether bird or beast, that has died of itself or is torn.

At this point, the cultic laws and ordinances of chapters 44-46 begin. They have been connected editorially with Ezekiel's vision as it was when it had already come to include his tour of the Temple compound, led by the heavenly emissary with his measuring tools (chapters 40-42). The editorial connection of this cultic material in chapters 44-46 with what already existed of Part Four of our book is made by having the nameless guide bring Ezekiel through the outer court of the Temple, from the place near the inner opening of the outer east gate given as the viewpoint for 44:1-3 to the inner north gate, and then on through that gate into the inner court, in front of the Temple house, which is filled by the Lord's glory (v. 4). Although the Hebrew text makes Yahweh, the Lord, the speaker in vv. 5-6a, the speaker is certainly the guiding emissary, just as in 40:4 (on which this material is based). The emissary then begins in v. 6b to function as a prophet, speaking words of the Lord God.

The words of the Lord which he speaks are laws, accompanied by words of blame or of praise for past behavior. The words of blame and of praise are fitting in a prophetic oracle of judgement, but they do not fit the literary genre of a legal code. Neither the laws nor the words of blame and praise are adequate objects of a vision, for that matter. This material has been inserted into Part Four of our book in order to have the provisions of cultic law made a part of Ezekiel's divinely revealed vision of what is to be the shape of the future. If we are not aware of what has happened here editorially, the legal provisions and the rebuke for past wickedness, in a happy context which is visionary, and which abstracts from the sinfulness of the past, may confuse us. The words of the Lord begin with an accusation of sinful behavior in the past, just as does an oracle of judgement (vv. 6b-8); the point of accusation important for what follows is the past practice of admitting to the Temple area as workers persons who are not Israelites. Then v. 9 begins with the formula normally introducing the threat of punishment in a prophetic oracle of judgement. What actually follows, however, is not a threat of punishment but a cultic prescription. The editor of this part of the book has introduced confusion of literary forms.

The cultic prescription of v. 9 is more accurately a cultic prohibition. No longer may any person who is not an Israelite enter the Temple. The entire Temple area is holy, and only persons who enjoy some degree of holiness may enter it. The Israelites, because they are God's people, are a holy nation or a holy people (Exod 19:6; Deut 7:6; 14:2, 21; 26:19; 28:9); they may, accordingly, enter the outer court, which is that part of the Temple to which the lowest degree of holiness is attached. Rules for two classes of Israelites possessing greater degrees of holiness — a priestly class and a class of levites whose intermediate degree of holiness puts them, in functions and in spaces, between the class of priests and the class of lay members of the house of Israel (44:11 with 40:38-46) — follow in vv. 9-31.

In this late stratum of chapters 40-48, there is a clear distinction made between priests and levites, with a clear bias in favor of the priests. The priests intended are those of the group whose members had the priestly establishment in Jerusalem firmly in their hands before the Exile. Many of them, along with members of other influential classes of Judean society, were taken off into Exile with members of their families, with Ezekiel among them.

Vv. 9-14 have to do with levites, members of a class of

cultic officials distinct from and inferior to the class of priests. When the word "levite" is used in this newly emerging sense in this commentary we write it without an initial capital, for its original sense in which a member of the tribe of Levi is meant is then no longer primary. The programmatic reduction of the men in this category to a position in which all priestly functions are closed to them is justified here in this passage with words of blame, of accusation of idolatry which are polemical, and which are not in conformity with historical reality.

Vv. 15-31 have to do with priests. They are called "Levitical priests," with the tribal sense of the word "Levitical" still primary. The idea that a legitimate priest ought to be a member of the tribe of Levi has been accepted, and the priests of the establishment are called "Levitical" in that sense. That, too, is a tendentious assertion with a polemic background, rather than a statement of totally historical fact. The duties reserved to these priests in the imminent restoration are given in vv. 16, 23-24. "Sanctuary" in v. 16 — the sanctuary into which the priests may enter — seems to designate the Temple house, from which levites are excluded, although in this part of Ezekiel generally "sanctuary" seems to refer to the Temple compound as a whole. In v. 11 "sanctuary" does refer to the Temple compound broadly, for according to v. 11 the levites do have the right to minister in it. Only priests may serve God at his table, the altar; only they shall give instruction on separation of the holy from the common, of the clean from the unclean; priests are to function as judges in controversies. On the evolution of these functions, before and after Ezekiel, and on the compromise in which all priests are henceforth reckoned as Levites while no levites (in the new sense, functional rather than tribal) are to be priests, see the excursus on the evolution of priesthood at the end of this commentary. The privileges of priests beyond those inherent in the reservation of certain duties to them are given in vv. 28-30. The stated justification for the privileges — the fact that they have no inheritance of land of their own but have Yahweh as their inheritance — is actually a traditional justification for special consideration to be given to members of the tribe of Levi (Num 18:20-24; Deut 18:1-2). A "devoted thing" (v. 29) is anything turned over to God, but in practice turned over to priests because they may appropriately deal with the things of God (Lev 27:21, 28-29; Num 18:14).

The rest of the rules for priests are rules meant to safeguard the separation of the holy from the common or profane, to avoid the contamination of what belongs to one of those domains by what might come from the other, whether by the condition of a priest's physical person or by his association or contact with persons and things (vv. 17-22, 24b-27). A comparison of the details in these rules with those having the same purpose in the late strata of the Pentateuch will reveal that some of the details in those two documents are contradictory, and that in other cases there is a difference, with the provisions in Ezekiel being more strict than those in the Pentateuch. The regulations governing ritual purity and the careful separation of the holy which we find in Ezekiel were set down before the restoration actually got under way in Judah. The less strict regulations which we find in the Pentateuch are those which were adopted in the realities of the restoration, and which stood the test of actual use in post-Exilic Judaism.

SPECIAL LANDS FOR THE HOLY, THE PRINCE, AND ALL ISRAEL
45:1-8

45 "When you allot the land as a possession, you shall set apart for the LORD a portion of the land as a holy district, twenty-five thousand cubits long and twenty thousand cubits broad; it shall be holy throughout its whole extent. [2]Of this a square plot of five hundred by five hundred cubits shall be for the sanctuary, with fifty cubits for an open space around it. [3]And in the holy district you shall measure off a section twenty-five thousand cubits long and ten thousand broad, in which shall be the sanctuary, the most holy place. [4]It shall be the holy portion of the land; it shall be for the priests, who minister in the sanctuary and approach the LORD to minister to him; and it shall be a place for their houses and a holy place for the sanctuary. ⁵Another section, twenty-five thousand cubits long and ten thousand cubits broad, shall be for the Levites who minister at the temple, as their possession for cities to live in.

⁶"Alongside the portion set apart as the holy district you shall assign for the possession of the city an area five thousand cubits broad, and twenty-five thousand cubits long; it shall belong to the whole house of Israel.

⁷"And to the prince shall belong the land on both sides of the holy district and the property of the city, alongside the holy district and the property of the city, on the west and on the east corresponding in length to one of the tribal portions, and extending from the western to the eastern boundary of the land. ⁸It is to be his property in Israel. And my princes shall no more oppress my people; but they shall let the house of Israel have the land according to their tribes.

In this section the partition of the land of the house of Israel (47:13-48:29) is anticipated. A part of the land near Jerusalem, the capital, is not to be assigned to any particular tribe but is to be divided into portions allotted to the priests of Jerusalem (vv. 3-4), to their associates of lower rank, the levites (v. 5), to the inhabitants of the capital (v. 6), and to the civil ruler, the prince (vv. 7-8a). The holy portion of this (v. 1), i.e. the portion allotted to the priests and to the levites, is to have the Temple compound within its boundaries (v. 2), and v. 3b locates the Temple precisely within the land allotted to the priests. The dimensions of the square plot of the Temple compound are those given in 42:15-20.

The provision for allotments given here is paralleled in 48:8-22, whose greater detail helps us to understand the arrangement of the parts in the whole. First, a square measuring 25,000 x 25,000 cubits is marked off. That square is then divided from north to south into three sections running parallel to one another. The length of each of the three sections is 25,000 cubits from east to west, for each extends from the eastern boundary of the 25,000 cubit square to its western boundary at the other side of the square. The breadth of each of the three sections is measured from north to south. The northernmost section, allotted to the levites, is 10,000 cubits broad. Adjacent to it on its south side is the middle section, allotted to the priests, which is also a strip 10,000 cubits broad and which has within its space the 500 cubit square Temple compound. The southernmost section, reserved for the secular, civil, persons living in Jerusalem, is 5,000 cubits broad, and according to 48:15-19 it contains both the city and an expanse of "open country" which is to be divided into small plots of land on which individual workers in the city can do their vegetable gardening. Both to the east and the west of the 25,000 cubit square is land reserved for the prince. Even though the power of the future civil ruler is limited in the view of the future found in Ezekiel, in which he is regularly called a prince instead of a king, the idea that a king should have his own royal demesne was too strongly rooted in the Ancient Near Eastern mind for it to be discarded. This entire scheme is utterly impractical, for it takes no account at all of the exigencies of the topography in and around Jerusalem, or of realistic demographic needs for space. The penchant for absolute symmetry of spatial plan which we have already encountered in the description of the Temple in 40:5-42:20 overrides all practical considerations.

To the literary critic, there are good reasons for taking 48:8-22 as the original description of these allotments, and 45:1-8 as a shortened form slightly reworked in order to make it conform better to what is said of priests in the passage immediately preceding (44:15-31). By "sanctuary" the entire Temple compound is certainly intended in v. 2, as it is in 48:8-10 and in chapters 40-48 regularly. In v. 4, however, priests are said to minister in the sanctuary; that is phraseology picked up from 44:16, where the sanctuary seems to be the Temple house specifically. In 48:8-22 nothing is said about the question whether anyone, or any society, is actually to hold possession of land or not, but in 45:5-7 the land allotted to the levites is explicitly called their

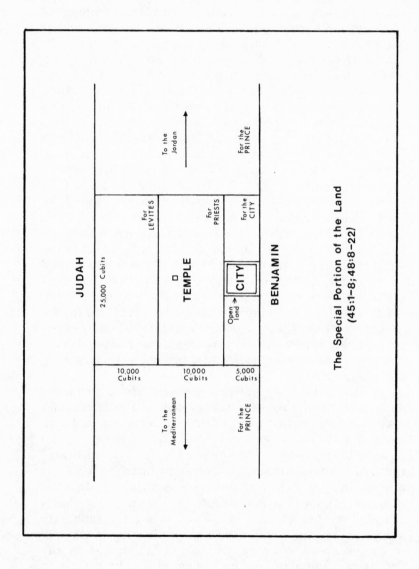

The Special Portion of the Land
(45:1-8; 48:8-22)

possession, as the city's land is its possession, while this is not said of the priests. This brings our present passage into conformity with the application of the old Levitical principle to the Zadokite priests in 44:28: the priests from now on, and not the definitively inferior levites, are to have no possession in Israel, for Yahweh is their possession. V. 8b anticipates the sentiments of v. 9, which belongs to an originally distinct and separate component of the book. V. 8b, in other words, is an editorial link joining the two originally separate and independent sections.

THE PRINCE AND PUBLIC LITURGY
45:9-25

9"Thus says the Lord GOD: Enough, O princes of Israel! Put away violence and oppression, and execute justice and righteousness; cease your evictions of my people, says the Lord GOD.

10"You shall have just balances, a just ephah, and a just bath. 11The ephah and the bath shall be of the same measure, the bath containing one tenth of a homer, and the ephah one tenth of a homer; the homer shall be the standard measure. 12The shekel shall be twenty gerahs; five shekels shall be five shekels, and ten shekels shall be ten shekels, and your mina shall be fifty shekels.

13"This is the offering which you shall make: one sixth of an ephah from each homer of wheat, and one sixth of an ephah from each homer of barley, 14and as the fixed portion of oil, one tenth of a bath from each cor (the cor, like the homer, contains ten baths); 15and one sheep from every flock of two hundred, from the families of Israel. This is the offering for cereal offerings, burnt offerings, and peace offerings, to make atonement for them, says the Lord GOD. 16All the people of the land shall give this offering to the prince in Israel. 17It shall be the prince's duty to furnish the burnt offerings, cereal offerings, and drink offerings, at the feasts, the new moons, and the sabbaths, all the appointed feasts of the house of Israel: he shall provide the sin offerings, cereal offerings, burnt offerings, and peace offerings, to make atonement for the house of Israel.

[18]"Thus says the Lord GOD: in the first month, on the first day of the month, you shall take a young bull without blemish, and cleanse the sanctuary. [19]The priest shall take some of the blood of the sin offering and put it on the doorposts of the temple, the four corners of the ledge of the altar, and the posts of the gate of the inner court. [20]You shall do the same on the seventh day of the month for any one who has sinned through error or ignorance; so you shall make atonement for the temple.

[21]"In the first month, on the fourteenth day of the month, you shall celebrate the feast of the passover, and for seven days unleavened bread shall be eaten. [22]On that day the prince shall provide for himself and all the people of the land a young bull for a sin offering. [23]And on the seven days of the festival he shall provide as a burnt offering to the LORD seven young bulls and seven rams without blemish, on each of the seven days; and a he-goat daily for a sin offering. [24]And he shall provide as a cereal offering an ephah for each bull, an ephah for each ram, and a hin of oil to each ephah. [25]In the seventh month, on the fifteenth day of the month and for the seven days of the feast, he shall make the same provision for sin offerings, burnt offerings, and cereal offerings, and for the oil.

This section begins with an admonition to princes (v. 9) which is inspired by negative memories of kings before the Exile. No matter how one might feel about kings, however, it is unthinkable that in the theocratic state envisaged here the king, or the prince who is to replace the king in the restoration after the Exile as it is envisaged in the book of Ezekiel, should not have a responsible role to play in assuring the offerings necessary for public sacrifice, the sacrifice which is that of the people headed by their prince rather than that of the individual, private, Israelite. The main purpose of this section is that of regulating that responsibility of the prince.

First of all, it is required that measures be "just," in other words, that they should have fixed standards. The ephah and the bath are equal in capacity, but the ephah is a dry measure (and so is the cor in other texts but not here, for in v. 14 the cor is mentioned as a liquid measure). The shekel, the gerah, and the mina are measures of weight. Some of these measures, and another liquid measure, the hin (v. 24), are then used in the specifications of offerings to be provided by the people or by the prince. The people are to deliver stated quantities of grain and oil and sheep to the prince (vv. 13-16). From these provisions the prince must furnish what is needed for public sacrifice, which is offered on the days when the people assemble for worship together: feasts, new moon days, and sabbaths (v. 17). When the specific offerings which the prince must provide on the festive days are listed (vv. 22-25), he-goats, not mentioned among the gifts required of the people, are included, as are young bulls, which ordinary people with their flocks of small cattle would be less likely to raise. The lists of offerings which the prince must provide on sabbaths and new moon days are not given here; they can be found in another context, at 46:4-7. The short paragraph formed by vv. 18-20 is intrusive. Instead of regulations on the quantity of sacrificial gifts it gives directions for a rite of expiation to be performed on the 1st and 7th days of the first month of the year, which in the calendric system used for dating in this section, is the month beginning with the new moon occurring in the latter part of March or the earlier part of April.

From this passage we can extract the liturgical calendar planned for the restoration. The weekly sabbaths and the monthly new moon days are to be observed after the return from the Exile as they were in ancient times (v. 17). The new moon day (the 1st day) of the first month and the 7th day of the same month are to be observed with special rites of expiation (vv. 18-20). The great feasts of the year are to be Passover on the 14th of the first month followed immediately by the Week of Unleavened Bread which was originally independent of Passover (vv. 21-23), and the unnamed feast (v. 25) which is in fact the autumnal Feast of Booths or Tabernacles, to be celebrated on the 15th of the seventh month with a prolongation of seven days, at the end of the harvest work (Lev 23:24; Num 29:12-28; Deut 16:13, 16). The festal calendar which finally prevailed in post-Exilic Judaism is that of Num 28-29, from which the festal calendar of Ezekiel 45:9-25 differs in some respects. The calendar in Ezekiel has no Feast of Weeks at the time of the gathering of the first fruits (the feast which was to become Pentecost), and it does not include the feasts of the 1st and the 10th of the seventh month. The feast of the 10th of the seventh month in post-Exilic Judaism is the Day of Atonement, whose ritual, given in Lev 16, has absorbed the expiatory rites of the 1st and 7th of the first month for which Ezek 45:18-20 does provide.

The lasting importance of this passage lies in the principles of responsibility from which the particular prescriptions flow: the responsibility which all the people have for contributing what is needed for the festal worship of God, and the responsibility of civil rulers to regulate the just administration of such contributions when there are administrative ties between religious society and the state.

MORE ON THE PRINCE AND PUBLIC LITURGY
46:1-24

46 "Thus says the Lord GOD: The gate of the inner court that faces east shall be shut on the six working days; but on the sabbath day it shall be opened and on the day of the new moon it shall be opened. ²The prince shall enter by the vestibule of the gate from without, and shall take his stand by the post of the gate. The priests shall offer his burnt offering and his peace offerings, and he shall worship at the threshold of the gate. Then he shall go out, but the gate shall not be shut until evening. ³The people of the land shall worship at the entrance of that gate before the LORD on the sabbaths and on the new moons. ⁴The burnt offering that the prince offers to the LORD on the sabbath day shall be six lambs without blemish and a ram without blemish; ⁵and the cereal offering with the ram shall be an ephah, and the cereal offering with the lambs shall be as much as he is able, together with a hin of oil to each ephah. [6]On the day of the new moon he shall offer a young bull without blemish, and six lambs and a ram, which shall be without blemish; [7]as a cereal offering he shall provide an ephah with the bull and an ephah with the ram, and with the lambs as much as he is able, together with a hin of oil to each ephah. [8]When the prince enters, he shall go in by the vestibule of the gate, and he shall go out by the same way.

[9]"When the people of the land come before the LORD at the appointed feasts, he who enters by the north gate to worship shall go out by the south gate; and he who enters by the south gate shall go out by the north gate: no one shall return by way of the gate by which he entered, but each shall go out straight ahead. [10]When they go in, the prince shall go in with them; and when they go out, he shall go out.

[11]"At the feasts and the appointed seasons the cereal offering with a young bull shall be an ephah, and with a ram an ephah, and with the lambs as much as one is able to give, together with a hin of oil to an ephah. [12]When the prince provides a freewill offering, either a burnt offering or peace offerings as a freewill offering to the LORD, the gate facing east shall be opened for him; and he shall offer his burnt offering or his peace offerings as he does on the sabbath day. Then he shall go out, and after he has gone out the gate shall be shut.

[13]"He shall provide a lamb a year old without a blemish for a burnt offering to the LORD daily; morning by morning he shall provide it. [14]And he shall provide a cereal offering with it morning by morning, one sixth of an ephah, and one third of a hin of oil to moisten the flour, as a cereal offering to the LORD; this is the ordinance for the continual burnt offering. [15]Thus the lamb and the meal offering and the oil shall be provided, morning by morning, for a continual burnt offering.

[16]"Thus says the Lord GOD: if the prince makes a gift to any of his sons out of his inheritance, it shall belong to his sons, it is their property by inheritance. [17]But if he

makes a gift out of his inheritance to one of his servants, it shall be his to the year of liberty; then it shall revert to the prince; only his sons may keep a gift from his inheritance. [18]The prince shall not take any of the inheritance of the people, thrusting them out of their property; he shall give his sons their inheritance out of his own property, so that none of my people shall be dispossessed of his property."

[19]Then he brought me through the entrance, which was at the side of the gate, to the north row of the holy chambers for the priests; and there I saw a place at the extreme western end of them. [20]And he said to me, "This is the place where the priests shall boil the guilt offering and the sin offering, and where they shall bake the cereal offering, in order not to bring them out into the outer court and so communicate holiness to the people."

[21]Then he brought me forth to the outer court, and led me to the four corners of the court; and in each corner of the court there was a court — [22]in the four corners of the court were small courts, forty cubits long and thirty broad; the four were of the same size. [23]On the inside, around each of the four courts was a row of masonry, with hearths made at the bottom of the rows round about. [24]Then he said to me, "These are the kitchens where those who minister at the temple shall boil the sacrifices of the people."

The first part of this chapter (vv. 1-15) contains more regulations having to do with the involvement of the prince in public worship. Already given in the preceding section were the general statement of his rights and duties in the matter of assuring the sacrificial offerings (45:13-17) and the lists of offerings which he must provide on the yearly feasts (45:21-25). Attention now turns from the feasts to the other days of liturgical assembly: the weekly sabbaths and the monthly new moon days (46:1-8). It is in this context that the lists of offerings are given which the prince must provide on sabbaths and new moon days (vv. 4-7).

Attention also moves from sacrificial offerings to cere-monial matters of movement and placement on days of liturgical assembly, with special attention to gates. On ordinary ferial weekdays, the east gate of the inner court is to be kept closed, but on sabbaths and new moon days it is to be opened and to be left open the entire day (vv. 1-2). The same regulation is valid when the prince has a votive sacrifice offered on an ordinary weekday, but then the inner east gate is closed as soon as the sacrifice is finished and the prince has left (v. 12). The prince goes to his proper place of worship by coming up from the outer court of the Temple to the vestibule of that inner east gate, through which he passes to reach the threshold at the other end of the gate, where he takes his place by the post of the threshold, at the point where the threshold opens onto the inner court in which the sacrificial altar is. The prince, in this plan for assuring liturgical propriety, may thus pass into an inner gate and through it, which is something lay people may not do (see the commentary on 40:38-43), but he may not pass beyond the threshold of that gate into the inner court, which only priests may enter. The sacrality of a king is to be retained by the post-Exilic prince, but the degree of his sacral holiness will not reach that of a priest. While the prince worships at the threshold of the inner east gate, the rest of the people worship in the outer court outside that gate (v. 3). Prince and people enter and leave the Temple area through the north and south outer gates (vv. 9-10); the outer east gate, through which God's glory passes, is closed, never again to be opened for use as a passageway by anyone else (44:1-3). These ceremonial regulations of a particular time and culture are intended to safeguard the timeless and universal value of reverent good order in sacral spaces at times of worship.

With vv. 9-10 attention is expanded to embrace all "appointed feasts," i.e. all days of general liturgical assembly — not only sabbaths and new moon days but also the festal days. V. 11 is largely superfluous after 45:24 and 46:5, 7. Attention then turns from the days of general liturgical assembly to the other days, the ferial weekdays, on which the prince may provide offerings for a private votive sacrifice of his own when he chooses to do so (v. 12), and on which he is obliged to provide the offerings specified for the daily morning sacrifice (vv. 13-14).

To these regulations governing the prince and worship in relation to one another some other things have been joined, either because they have to do with the prince (although not with worship) or because they have to do with worship (although not with the prince). Vv.16-18 contain regulations on the acquisition and alienation of the land of the crown (45:7-8; 48:21-22). The provisions of v. 18 are designed to prevent the princely family from gaining land at the expense of the other members of the house of Israel. The provision of v. 17, on the other hand, is designed to keep the crown land itself intact. It is perhaps best understood in the light of the utopian requirement that land which had been alienated should revert to its original owner in the next year of jubilee (Lev 25:10, 14-17). That requirement, meant evidently to protect small landowners from the encroachments of the rich and powerful, is turned on its head in this provision that a gift made by the prince to one of his servants should eventually revert from the servant to the prince. Vv. 19-24 treat not of princes but of kitchens. Ezekiel is led, by literary device now rather than by visionary experience, first to see kitchens (K on the Temple Plan at the end of this commentary) on the west end of the holy chambers described in 42:1-14, in which priests can cook those sacrificial elements which will be devoted to God or eaten by the priests in those chambers. The degree of holiness attached to those elements is too high for them to be taken out into the outer court for cooking, for in the outer court their holiness would contaminate the people dangerously (vv. 19-20). Finally, the prophet is led out into the outer court and over to the far corners of the Temple compound, in order to see the kitchens (k on our Temple Plan) in which the levites can cook those parts of the peace offerings (Lev 7:15-18) and of the Passover sacrifice (Deut 16:2-7) which will be eaten by the lay people who have brought their offering to the Temple, as a meal which they share with God (vv. 21-24).

WATERS OF LIFE FLOW FROM THE TEMPLE
47:1-12

47 Then he brought me back to the door of the temple; and behold, water was issuing from below the threshold of the temple toward the east (for the temple faced east); and the water was flowing down from below the south end of the threshold of the temple, south of the altar. ²Then he brought me out by way of the north gate, and led me round on the outside to the outer gate, that faces toward the east; and the water was coming out on the south side.

³Going on eastward with a line in his hand, the man measured a thousand cubits, and then led me through the water; and it was ankle-deep. ⁴ Again he measured a thousand, and led me through the water; and it was knee-deep. Again he measured a thousand, and led me through the water; and it was up to the loins. ⁵Again he measured a thousand, and it was a river that I could not pass through, for the water had risen; it was deep enough to swim in, a river that could not be passed through. ⁶And he said to me, "Son of man, have you seen this?"

Then he led me back along the bank of the river. ⁷As I went back, I saw upon the bank of the river very many trees on the one side and on the other. ⁸And he said to me, "This water flows toward the eastern region and goes down into the Arabah; and when it enters the stagnant waters of the sea, the water will become fresh. ⁹And wherever the river goes every living creature which swarms will live, and there will be very many fish; for this water goes there, that the waters of the sea may become fresh; so everything will live where the river goes. ¹⁰Fishermen will stand beside the sea; from En-gedi to En-eglaim it will be a place for the spreading of nets; its fish will be of very many kinds, like the fish of the Great Sea. ¹¹But its swamps and marshes will not become fresh; they are to be left for salt. ¹²And on the banks, on both sides of the river, there will grow all kinds of trees for food. Their leaves will not wither nor their fruit fail, but

they will bear fresh fruit every month, because the water
for them flows from the sanctuary. Their fruit will be for
food, and their leaves for healing."

The end of the mass of legal material and secondary
descriptions of the Temple placed editorially at 43:13-46:24
has been reached, and we return to the ecstatic atmosphere
of prophetic vision. For the secondary descriptions preceding, Ezekiel has been taken editorially from place to place in
the Temple area, most recently into the outer court (46:21).
He must now be brought back editorially to the inner court
of the Temple, where he saw the glory of the Lord filling the
house of God in the new Temple compound (43:5), and
where his visionary experience continues now with a new
episode recounted here. The editorial transportation is
accomplished in v. 1a, and the prophetic visionary account
then begins at once in v. 1b.

Ezekiel sees a stream of water rising from a hidden spring
beneath the house of God, issuing from beneath the entrance
of the house to flow eastward across the inner court past the
south side of the altar, then down to the level of the outer
court, across which it flows to leave the Temple compound
on the south side of the perpetually closed outer east gate
(vv. 1b-2) and move on eastward through the countryside.
(The measuring mentality evident elsewhere in chapters
40-48 expresses itself in vv. 3-5, probably secondary to the
original text; these verses detract from the impact of the
vision, and the reader can let them pass.) The stream of
water wends its way eastward from Jerusalem, through the
barren desert of Judah, until it reaches the cliffs looming
above the Dead Sea and falls through them to the Arabah
(the steppe lying to the north and south of the Dead Sea, and
in what little space there is between the Dead Sea's banks
and the surrounding cliffs which press hard upon them).
Continuing across the Arabah, the stream spends itself in
"the stagnant waters" of the Dead Sea (v. 8).

The course of the stream is significant. It issues from the
house of God on earth, on Zion, his holy mountain; it flows
through a region ever more barren as one goes eastward,

and it empties itself into a body of water with no outlet, far below sea level, whose salt content makes it utterly inimical to all life, so that no fish can possibly survive in it. The waters flowing from the mountain of God are waters which bring life to a lifeless region. Trees spring up along the banks of those waters, to give fruit for food and leaves for healing. The stagnant and noxious sea becomes fresh. It teems with fish like those of the "Great Sea" (the Mediterranean), while retaining the swamps and marshes at its southern end which obligingly continue to provide useful salt. The trees are marvelous trees. They keep their foliage all the year round, and they bear a new crop of fresh fruit every month.

In all of this, the poetry of myth enters the symbolic vision of the future. Like the waters of Gen 2:10-14, the waters which Ezekiel sees are paradisaic. To a wasteland they bring life. They bring it from the place where God, the source of life, dwells. As in Ps 46(45):4-5:

> There is a river whose streams make
>   glad the city of God,
>   the holy habitation of the Most High.
> God is in the midst of her, she shall
>   not be moved;
> God will help her right early.

Ezekiel's vision of the waters of life completes his vision of the restoration in symbol. The land of Judah, laid waste by the sword, by famine, and by pestilence because of the pervasive sinfulness of its people, will again flourish in a wondrous way. The flourishing of the land is a symbol of the flourishing of its people, a symbol understood all the more vividly when one has a sense of that mingling of the cosmic and the social, that mysterious interpenetration of the fates of human beings and the land on which they live, which we have noticed before in Ezekiel's world-view (see above on 6:1-14). Because God's glory will return to his earthly dwelling on Zion, his people will be blessed with prosperity and healed of their sins, as they thrive in their once lifeless land freshly flourishing with wondrous trees which constantly bear fruit for food and foliage for healing. Christians have found in this a type pointing to baptism, which brings healing and new life from God actively present in his new Temple, the Church.

With this we reach the conclusion of the primary visionary accounts (perhaps originally only 40:1-2; 43:4-7a; 47:1b-2 + much of vv. 6-12) which are the core from which Part Four of our book grew. Ezekiel's vision in chapters 40-48 is a vision of the promise of 37:24-28 fulfilled. In our present passage, 47:1-12, he sees that the return of God's presence seen in 43:4-7a will not remain static, that it will bring about the promised blessings. Even the sacral laws and laws for the prince added to his vision in 43:18-46:18 are related to elements of the promise in 37:24-25: the Israelites of the restoration will follow God's ordinances and observe his statutes, and the symbolic David shall be their prince for ever. All these blessings flow from one great divine favor: God's free decision to dwell again in his sanctuary "in the midst of them for evermore" (37:28).

THE NEW ISRAEL'S BOUNDARIES
47:13-48:29

[13]Thus says the Lord GOD: "These are the boundaries by which you shall divide the land for inheritance among the twelve tribes of Israel. Joseph shall have two portions. [14]And you shall divide it equally; I swore to give it to your fathers, and this land shall fall to you as your inheritance.

[15]"This shall be the boundary of the land: On the north side, from the Great Sea by way of Hethlon to the entrance of Hamath, and on to Zedad, [16]Berothah, Sibraim (which lies on the border between Damascus and Hamath), as far as Hazer-hatticon, which is on the border of Hauran. [17]So the boundary shall run from the sea to Hazar-enon, which is on the northern border of Damascus, with the border of Hamath to the north. This shall be the north side.

[18]"On the east side, the boundary shall run from Hazar-enon between Hauran and Damascus; along the Jordan between Gilead and the land of Israel; to the eastern sea

and as far as Tamar. This shall be the east side.

19"On the south side, it shall run from Tamar as far as the waters of Meribath-kadesh, thence along the Brook of Egypt to the Great Sea. This shall be the south side.

20"On the west side, the Great Sea shall be the boundary to a point opposite the entrance of Hamath. This shall be the west side.

21"So you shall divide this land among you according to the tribes of Israel. 22You shall allot it as an inheritance for yourselves and for the aliens who reside among you and have begotten children among you. They shall be to you as native-born sons of Israel; with you they shall be allotted an inheritance among the tribes of Israel. 23In whatever tribe the alien resides, there you shall assign him his inheritance, says the Lord GOD.

48 "These are the names of the tribes: Beginning at the northern border, from the sea by way of Hethlon to the entrance of Hamath, as far as Hazar-enon (which is on the northern border of Damascus over against Hamath), and extending from the east side to the west, Dan, one portion. 2Adjoining the territory of Dan, from the east side to the west, Asher, one portion. 3Adjoining the territory of Asher, from the east side to the west, Naphtali, one portion. 4Adjoining the territory of Naphtali, from the east side to the west, Manasseh, one portion. 5Adjoining the territory of Manasseh, from the east side to the west, Ephraim, one portion. 6Adjoining the territory of Ephraim, from the east side to the west, Reuben, one portion. 7Adjoining the territory of Reuben, from the east side to the west, Judah, one portion.

8"Adjoining the territory of Judah, from the east side to the west, shall be the portion which you shall set apart, twenty-five thousand cubits in breadth, and in length equal to one of the tribal portions, from the east side to the west, with the sanctuary in the midst of it. 9The portion which you shall set apart for the LORD shall be twenty-five thousand cubits in length, and twenty thousand in breadth. 10These shall be the allotments of the holy portion: the priests shall have an allotment measuring twenty-five thousand cubits on the northern side, ten thousand cubits in breadth on the western side, ten thousand in breadth on the eastern side, and twenty-five thousand in length on the southern side, with the sanctuary of the LORD in the midst of it. ¹¹This shall be for the consecrated priests, the sons of Zadok, who kept my charge, who did not go astray when the people of Israel went astray, as the Levites did. ¹²And it shall belong to them as a special portion from the holy portion of the land, a most holy place, adjoining the territory of the Levites. ¹³And alongside the territory of the priests, the Levites shall have an allotment twenty-five thousand cubits in length and ten thousand in breadth. The whole length shall be twenty-five thousand cubits and the breadth twenty thousand. ¹⁴They shall not sell or exchange any of it; they shall not alienate this choice portion of the land, for it is'holy to the LORD.

¹⁵"The remainder, five thousand cubits in breadth and twenty-five thousand in length, shall be for ordinary use for the city, for dwellings and for open country. In the midst of it shall be the city; ¹⁶and these shall be its dimensions: the north side four thousand five hundred cubits, the south side four thousand five hundred, the east side four thousand five hundred, and the west side four thousand five hundred. ¹⁷And the city shall have open land: on the north two hundred and fifty cubits, on the south two hundred and fifty, on the east two hundred and fifty, and on the west two hundred and fifty. ¹⁸The remainder of the length alongside the holy portion shall be ten thousand cubits to the east, and ten thousand to the west, and it shall be alongside the holy portion. Its produce shall be food for the workers of the city. ¹⁹And the workers of the city, from all the tribes of Israel, shall till it. ²⁰The whole portion which you shall set apart shall be twenty-five thousand cubits square, that is, the holy portion together with the property of the city.

²¹"What remains on both sides of the holy portion and of the property of the city shall belong to the prince.

Extending from the twenty-five thousand cubits of the holy portion to the east border, and westward from the twenty-five thousand cubits to the west border, parallel to the tribal portions, it shall belong to the prince. The holy portion with the sanctuary of the temple in its midst, ²²and the property of the Levites and the property of the city, shall be in the midst of that which belongs to the prince. The portion of the prince shall lie between the territory of Judah and the territory of Benjamin.

²³"As for the rest of the tribes: from the east side to the west, Benjamin, one portion. ²⁴Adjoining the territory of Benjamin, from the east side to the west, Simeon, one portion. ²⁵Adjoining the territory of Simeon, from the east side to the west, Issachar, one portion. ²⁶Adjoining the territory of Issachar, from the east side to the west, Zebulun, one portion. ²⁷Adjoining the territory of Zebulun, from the east side to the west, Gad, one portion. ²⁸And adjoining the territory of Gad to the south, the boundary shall run from Tamar to the waters of Meribath-kadesh, thence along the Brook of Egypt to the Great Sea. ²⁹This is the land which you shall allot as an inheritance among the tribes of Israel, and these are their several portions, says the Lord GOD.

Already in 47:1-12 attention moved from the Temple out to the countryside. Now the land of Israel is the main object of attention, as its outer borders are set and its interior divisions are made. The borders and divisions are prefaced (47:13) and concluded (48:29) with a formula which gives them the character of instructions emanating from God. As the exodus from Egypt in the days of Moses was followed by entry into the promised land divided among the twelve tribes, so must the restoration of the house of Israel after the Exile, a restoration which is the term of a new exodus (20:33-44), entail a new and better distribution of the land, with special provision made for holy land around the Temple, for the city of Jerusalem, and for the prince who will be the heir of the promises made to David.

First, in 47:15-20, the boundaries of the land of Israel are traced. The location of most of the places mentioned is far from certain today. The northern boundary seems to run along, or near, the northern border of the modern Republic of Lebanon, from the Mediterranean (the "Great Sea") eastward, skirting the northern ends of the coastal mountains of Lebanon and of the valley lying beyond them, as far as the Anti-Lebanon range. From that point, the eastern border runs south along the Anti-Lebanon with the lands of Hamath and Damascus to the east, then on down the Jordan Valley and along the Dead Sea (the "eastern sea") with the Transjordanian states to the east, as far as Tamar, which must be south-southwest of the Dead Sea. From Tamar, the southern border passes through the steppe and the desert south of Palestine to the stream bed forming the Egyptian frontier, along which it runs northward to the Mediterranean, which forms the western border. Although these boundaries partly reflect such geopolitical realities as the existence of the non-Israelite states of Ammon, Moab, and Edom beyond the Jordan and beyond the Dead Sea, both before and after the Exile, they also express an expansionistic ideal, for they include in Israelite territory the Phoenician coast with cities like Tyre and Sidon and Byblos which were never subject to Israelite domination, and they push the northern border far beyond territory ever occupied by Israelites of any tribe.

In 47:21-48:29 the land within the borders just traced is divided among the Israelites. The divisions made are far too ideal to be realized. That taste for topographical symmetry in which no account is taken of the inescapable realities of the lay of the land, evident in the ground plan of the Temple traced in 40:5-42:20, reappears. The land of Israel is divided into thirteen strips of land, each of which runs lengthwise across the country from the eastern border traced in 47:18 to the western border, the Mediterranean Sea. Twelve of these strips are given to the twelve tribes singly (48:1-7, 23-28). Although the tribe of Levi does not share in this allotment of the ordinary land, the division of the tribe of Joseph into the two separate tribes of Ephraim and Manasseh keeps the tribes twelve in number. Each of the twelve tribes receives an equal share of the land, for in this utopian project social and economic equality is an ideal to be promoted with legislative conviction. That equality of the twelve tribes admits special provisions for those who stand apart from ordinary society — the priests and levites, because of their heightened holiness as God's particular servants, and the prince because of his position as the Davidic shepherd of the house of Israel. These special persons, and those who dwell in Jerusalem which is a city belonging to all tribes and to none (48:19), receive their special allotments in the thirteenth strip of land, which lies between Judah on the north and Benjamin on the south (48:8-22). This special strip contains the square whose land is allotted, respectively (from north to south), to the levites, to the priests, and to the city of Jerusalem, with the crown lands allotted to the prince running eastward and westward from the square to the eastern and western borders of Israel. (For an examination of the details, see the commentary on 45:1-8.) The portion of the levites and priests is God's portion, the holy portion (48:10, 12, 14), and the Temple is placed within it, in the "most holy" section of land reserved for priests.

In this project we also find a social concern for the "alien" (47:22) — any person who is not an Israelite but who has a domicile in Israel. An alien is to receive his property, too, from the land of the tribe in whose territory he and his family reside. This utopian distribution of the land is made with a sense of open demographic hospitality which is all the more striking when one remembers that the land which the alien is to receive is land promised to the house of Israel.

THE CITY WHERE THE LORD IS
48:30-35

> 30"These shall be the exits of the city: On the north side, which is to be four thousand five hundred cubits by measure, 31three gates, the gate of Reuben, the gate of Judah, and the gate of Levi, the gates of the city being named after the tribes of Israel. 32On the east side, which is to be four thousand five hundred cubits, three gates, the

gate of Joseph, the gate of Benjamin, and the gate of Dan. [33]On the south side, which is to be four thousand five hundred cubits by measure, three gates, the gate of Simeon, the gate of Issachar, and the gate of Zebulun. [34]On the west side, which is to be four thousand five hundred cubits, three gates, the gate of Gad, the gate of Asher, and the gate of Naphtali. [35]The circumference of the city shall be eighteen thousand cubits. And the name of the city henceforth shall be, The LORD is there."

Throughout chapters 40-48 attention has been fixed on the new Temple of the future restoration. The new city, Jerusalem, was not even mentioned until land assigned to none of the twelve tribes was set aside for it (48:15-20, from which 45:6 was later derived). Now, at the very end of the book, a design for the city of the future restoration unexpectedly appears. This brief concluding section seems to be an addition to the project for the division of the land in 47:13-48:29, but, as is so often the case in the growth of the Book of Ezekiel, the ideas of the immediately preceding section, and even of a large part of the book, are carried over into the supplementary addition. The city's twelve gates stress symbolically the principle that the city belongs to none of the twelve landholding tribes but is open to all of them, to the whole house of Israel. That idea was already present in 48:19.

The city's essential characteristic, conferring upon it its real importance in the history of God's dealing with his people, is that all important characteristic of the Temple which was revealed to Ezekiel in the vision constituting the core of chapters 40-48, and which is developed in the rest of the material progressively added to that core: God's earthly presence is focused there. Now we can understand why the name Jerusalem has not been mentioned in the primary visionary accounts since the moment when Ezekiel, having been brought "to Jerusalem" by the Spirit (8:3) to see the wickedness of the "inhabitants of Jerusalem" (11:15), saw the glory of the Lord departing, not "from Jerusalem" but "from the city" (11:22). The old faithless city is no more, and the new one will be radically different. So radical a change calls for abandonment of the old name, Jerusalem, and conferment of a new name which will fit the city's new character better. The vital element in the city's new character, the transcendental fact which will determine its place in the future history of the whole house of Israel, is expressed in the city's symbolic new name: "The Lord is there." We do not know whether Ezekiel with his earthly eyes ever saw the city of his origins rising from its ruins. Perhaps that no longer mattered to him. He had already seen God's glory there, with the eyes of a visionary.

AN EXCURSUS ON PRIESTHOOD IN ISRAEL

Many of the laws and ordinances in Ezekiel which have to do with priests stand at a watershed in the evolution of Israelite priesthood. To trace that evolution, we add here a brief excursus on priesthood.

Already in the period of the Judges, when we get our first glimpses of priests in Israel, a priest was a man set apart for functions which entailed more immediate access to God's presence. In order to function as a priest he had first to be made holy, like all persons and things set apart from the ordinary functions and uses of this world and given over to God for his service or for his use. When the men of Kiriath-jearim put the son of Abinadab in charge of the ark, they "made him holy" (1 Sam 7:1) — the literal sense of the Hebrew, rather than the conventional English rendering "consecrated him" or "ordained him." Thus the son of Abinadab, like all priests, was set apart for the personal service of God, for no one who was not a priest could perform such service.

Since the divine presence was intensely concentrated on the ark, wherever it happened to be, the ark was intensely holy, and its care, consequently, called for the service of priests, even when it was being carried out to battle by the sons in Eli's priestly family (1 Sam 4:4, 11) or transported to another place (2 Sam 15:24-29). God was strongly present in his sanctuaries, too. A sanctuary, in Israel and elsewhere, was the house of a god, who, like the lord and master of an earthly mansion, required the services of his household attendants; the attendants serving the holy God of Israel in his sanctuaries had to be priests (Judg 17-18; 1 Sam 1-3; 21-22). We know little of the ordinary duties of a priest in a sanctuary in this early period. A trace of the ancient and widespread practice of bringing food before a god in his sanctuary was surviving in the bread which Ahimelech and other priests set before God in the sanctuary at Nob (1 Sam 21:4-7). Sacrifice, in this early period, did not of itself require the service of a priest, but when sacrifice was offered at a sanctuary we presume that it was the sanctuary's priests who performed the rites of offering God's portions to him, and it is evident from 1 Sam 2:12-17 that certain parts of the sacrificial animals went to the priests by right.

A function of priests which was more significant in this early period was their oracular consultation of God. If someone had a question to put to God, he did so by resorting to a priest. That God should be consulted through a priest, and should respond through a priest, is consonant with the role of a priest as a holy person. Since a holy person was, by definition, a person set apart for close contact with God and for the direct service of God, he could approach God to serve as a mediator between God and secular persons. Just as ordinary persons would present questions to an earthly ruler through his household attendants or courtiers, or through his aide-de-camp when he was leading the army on an expedition, and receive answers through them, so did secular persons ask questions of God, and receive answers from him, through the mediation of those who ministered to God as his priestly attendants, either at his residence, the sanctuary (Judg 18:5-7; 1 Sam 22:10, 13, 15), or in the field with a military company fighting for the cause of Israel, which was also Yahweh's cause (1 Sam 14:18-19, 36-42; 23:9-12; 30:7-8).

During the four centuries of the monarchical period in Israel (from the middle of the tenth century to the beginning of the sixth), the role reserved to priests in sacrifice increased significantly, while their function as oracular consultors of God evolved almost beyond recognition. By the end of the monarchical period, any sacrificial action requiring contact with the altar had to be performed by a priest. The simple manifestation of divine will and divine intentions through answers to questions communicated through priests in oracular consultation evolved into a more complex manifestation of God's will in priestly pronouncements or decisions on what was pleasing or displeasing to God in matters of ritual purity, of distinction between what was to be done and what was to be avoided in matters of separation between the holy and the profane. This kind of priestly pronouncement was called a *torah*. Collections of such decisons, in both ritual and ethical matters, formed bodies of sacral law, and as evolution went further the word *torah* came to be almost synonymous with law itself. All law in Israel was looked upon as the expression of God's regulating will, whether it dealt with the specifically religious aspects of life or not. *Torah* in Deut 31:9, in a passage written when the monarchical period was at its end, certainly refers to the entire legal code of Deut 12-26. Jer 18:18, written in the same period, shows us that *torah* was by then seen to be just as characteristic of a priest as the word was of a prophet, or counsel of a wise man.

The extension of priestly *torah* beyond cultic decisions towards something more properly legal led to the involvement of priests in the official tribunals set up in the monarchical period. When King Jehoshaphat, in the second quarter of the ninth century, established a court of appeals in Jerusalem, he put on that court a priest, who was to be responsible for the affairs of Yahweh, and a lay judge who was to be responsible for the affairs of the king (2 Chr 19:4-11) — a distinction corresponding to that between sacral *torah* and civil customary law. Later, towards the end of the monarchical period, Deut 17:8-13 shows that the older distinction between the respective competences of the priestly judge and the lay judge on the tribunal was no longer cut clearly: a priest could be involved in handing down a decision on the basis either of *torah* or of customary law dealing with cases which were in no way cultic in themselves.

In the period of the monarchy the importance of the priests in charge of the royal sanctuaries, the Temple of Jerusalem in Judah and the sanctuaries of Bethel and Dan in the northern kingdom (until its fall in the eighth century), was quite naturally greater than that of priests of other sanctuaries. Priests in charge of the Temple belonged to the royal cabinet already in the reigns of David and Solomon (2 Sam 8:17; 20:25; 1 Kgs 4:2; 1 Chr 18:16). The ark of God's presence was installed in the Temple built by Solomon (1 Kgs 6:9; 8:1-9), where it remained until the destructive upheavals of Ezekiel's time. With the passing of the centuries, the priesthood of Jerusalem began to move from a position of predominance in fact towards one of exclusivity by right.

Other sanctuaries of Yahweh had continued to exist, with their own priests, and members of the tribe of Levi had been successful in asserting their claims to a particular right to occupy priestly positions. Thanks to Deuteronomy, this ideological success of the Levites extended to Jerusalem itself, where the established priests of the Temple had probably not been Levites. Deuteronomy also called for the abolition of all sanctuaries apart from the Temple. When all the other sanctuaries were abolished by King Josiah around the year 622, the priests of the abolished country shrines of Judah were allowed to come to Jerusalem, but they were not allowed to "go up to the altar of Yahweh in Jerusalem." They could function only as cultic workers of inferior rank around the Temple (2 Kgs 23:8-9). This was the situation obtaining when the Temple was destroyed by the Babylonian invaders in 586. The established priests of Jerusalem, with some individual exceptions, perhaps, were not historically members of the tribe of Levi, but they would have to be absorbed within its ranks if they were to retain their aura of legitimacy. The other priests of the realm, many of them authentic Levites, were being excluded from access to priestly positions in the Temple, the only sanctuary at which priests might legitimately officiate since Josiah's reform, but they were making claims to a right to officiate in the Temple, nevertheless, on grounds of their Levitical ancestry.

This tension between the priests who had been established in the Temple and the Levites who had been excluded from the exercise of priestly functions is the background against which the provisions for priests and levites in Ezek 44:6-31 and in the phrases added at 40:45-46; 43:19; 45:1-8; 46:19-24; 48:11 have to be understood. These texts, among the latest in chapters 40-48, were most probably composed in Babylonia before the return to Judah had really reached notable proportions. Since the exiles in Babylonia were drawn mainly from the influential classes of people in Judah, many representatives of priestly families (like Eze-kiel himself), but few of the disadvantaged Levites, must have been among them.

The author of the provisions for priests and levites in Ezek 40-48 strongly favors the priests of the traditional establishment. He calls them the "sons of Zadok" (40:46; 43:19; 44:15; 48:11), thereby appealing to their historical connection with Zadok, one of David's priests, the one who was victorious in the palace intrigue at the beginning of Solomon's reign (1 Kgs 2:35). In forensic work, priests are to be judges in controversies; the lay judge of the pre-Exilic tribunals is not mentioned in Ezek 44:24. The idea that legitimate priests should be Levites is now fully accepted among the exiles, for the Zadokites are themselves called "Levitical priests" (43:19; 44:15), included among the "sons of Levi" (40:46). They alone, in this plan for the imminent restoration in Judah, are to have the right to officiate at the altar and to receive the gifts and offerings which go to priests by right (40:46; 43:19; 44:15-17, 29-30).

According to this same plan, all other cultic persons must accept a position of inferiority in which they are allowed to do various things in the service of God in the Temple, but nothing which entails service at the altar. In 40:45 (perhaps earlier than the rest of these texts) these inferior cultic persons are called "priests." Elsewhere, they are called "levites" but not "priests." The word "levite" has acquired a new sense, that of a cultic functionary of inferior degree who is not a priest. In this sense the word can be written in English without the initial capital letter still called for when "Levite" designates a member of the tribe of Levi. The service of the Temple which levites are allowed to perform (44:11-14; 45:4-5; 46:20-24) is not to be considered priestly in the strict sense — (44:13) at least after 40:45 was written. The comments accompanying the prescriptive rules compare the levites unfavorably with the priests. The levites are tendentiously and unfairly accused of abandoning the worship of Yahweh for the worship of idols (44:10, 12), while the (Zadokite) priests are praised for having taken care of Yahweh's sanctuary (44:15). The Levites had managed to impose acceptance of the principle that all priests should be Levites but the Zadokite priests had managed successfully both to float the idea that they were themselves Levites and to reduce all other Levitical claimants to non-priestly status.

When Judah was restored, and the Temple rebuilt, the Zadokite priesthood became politically as well as "ecclesiastically" supreme. By 520 Zerubbabel, grandson of King Jehoiachin, and the Zadokite priest Joshua were respectively civil governor and chief priest (Hag 1:1; Zech 4:11-14; 6:13), but before long Zerubbabel disappeared from the scene. From that time onward, the restored Jewish community functioned primarily as a religious community. A new civil governor, like Nehemiah, might be appointed by the Persian authorities, but the highest authority in Judah, both civil and religious, was usually the high priest of the Temple. From the latter part of the second century until the reign of Herod the Great in the latter part of the first century B.C. the Hasmonean rulers of Judah retained the office of high priest for themselves.

Lev 10:10-11 shows that priests in the restored community were responsible for *torah* both in the ancient cultic sense of making distinctions between the holy and the profane or common (cf. also Hag 2:11-13) and in the extended sense of making known to the people the legal statutes of the Law. The lay judge of the pre-Exilic court of appeal is no longer mentioned; it is the priests who are to act as judges in controversies (so, already, Ezek 44:24). In the Temple, priests alone took care of the sacrificial blood rites, the service of the altar, the rites of expiation, and the libations (Lev 1-6; 16), and they alone might bless the people (Num 6:22-27). They were in charge of the sacred vessels and of the furnishings inside the Temple house (Num 3:31).

The levites in the restored community took care of the liturgy of praise and thanksgiving, the ritual purifications of holy things, and the making of ritual bread; they were also in charge of the Temple's supply rooms (1 Chr 9:26-32; 23:25-32). The administration of the Temple and its finances, as well as the supervision of construction work in the sacred area, were left to the post-Exilic levites (2 Chr 24:5-6; 34:9, 12-13), doubtlessly under the general administrative supervision of the high priest. The insistence of Ezek 44:11 that only levites, not the lay offerers, should slaughter the victims for a holocaust or for a sacrifice in which the people would share the meat was not heeded in the actual practice after the Exile (Lev 1:5; 3:2).

In the portrait of a priest drawn in the praises of Aaron and Phinehas written by Jesus ben Sirach toward the beginning of the second century B.C., we see a man who offers sacrifices and incense, performs rites of expiation, and blesses the people (Sir 45:6-26), and who makes statutes and legal judgements — components of living *torah* — known to the people (Sir 45:14-17). By then the real exegetes and theologians who interpreted the Law were the wise and learned scribes (Sir 39:1-11), a few of whom were also priests. The priests remained responsible for worship and for all duties of mediation between the holy and the profane, between God and the people. In New Testament times, members of what can be called a priestly nobility were associated with upper classes of the laity in the party of the Sadducees, politically conservative, and culturally "enlightened." Strongly opposed to priests of that sort were the pietistic and rather fundamentalistic Essenes known best today from what they left behind them at Qumran, persons who thought of themselves as the true heirs of the exilic community led by Zadokite priests in the time of Ezekiel. When the Romans destroyed the Temple in 70 A.D., all active priesthood came to an end in Judaism, but the hopeful expectance of its restoration at the end of this present era has not been lost.

FURTHER READING

Commentaries:

Carley, Keith W., *The Book of the Prophet Ezekiel*. The Cambridge Bible Commentary on the New English Bible (Cambridge University Press, 1974).
Short, not technical, but learned and perceptive.

Cooke, G. A., *A Critical and Exegetical Commentary on the Book of Ezekiel* (New York: Charles Scribner's Sons, 1937).
Dated, but still of real value for its sober critical approach and its religious sense.

Eichrodt, Walther, *Ezekiel: a Commentary*. The Old Testament Library (London: SCM Press, 1970).
A theologically oriented commentary built on solid scholarship.

Greenberg, Moshe, *Ezekiel, 1-20*. The Anchor Bible, Vol. 22 (Garden City: Doubleday & Co., 1983).
A scholarly commentary accessible to readers who are not themselves biblical scholars. Particularly attentive to problematic details. Ezekiel, 21-48 is in preparation.

Wevers, John W., *Ezekiel*. The Century Bible (London: Nelson, 1969).
Valuable particularly for its critical evaluation of the Revised Standard Version in the light of the ancient texts.

Zimmerli, Walther, *Ezekiel*. Hermeneia (Philadelphia: Fortress Press, 1979-1983).

The most important commentary on Ezekiel in any language today.

We might also mention two recent works on neglected parts of Ezekiel:

Boadt, Lawrence, *Ezekiel's Oracles against Egypt: a Literary and Philological Study of Ezekiel 29-32.* Biblica et Orientalia 37 (Rome: Biblical Institute Press, 1980).
Technical, but the serious general reader too can appreciate the fresh insights into style and ideas.

Levenson, Jon Douglas, *Theology of the Program of Restoration of Ezekiel 40-48.* Harvard Semitic Monograph Series 10 (Missoula, Montana: Scholars Press, 1976).
Essays bringing new life to the study of these chapters.

Background Reading:
Ackroyd, Peter R., *Israel under Babylon and Persia.* New Clarendon Bible (Oxford University Press, 1970).

Clements, R. E., "The Ezekiel Tradition: Prophecy in a Time of Crisis," in Richard Coggins, Anthony Phillips and Michael Knibb (eds.), *Israel's Prophetic Tradition: Essays in Honour of Peter Ackroyd* (Cambridge University Press, 1982), 119-36.

Malamat, A., "The Twilight of Judah: in the Egyptian-Babylonian Maelstrom," in *Supplements to Vetus Testamentum* 28 (Leiden: E. J. Brill, 1975), 123-45.

Vaux, Roland de, *Ancient Israel: its Life and Institutions.* London: Darton, Longman and Todd, 1961).
Information on the religious and cultural phenomena appearing in Ezekiel can be found by using the references to Ezekiel in the index of Biblical references.

KEY TO THE PLAN OF THE TEMPLE

(Capital letters designate enclosed buildings.)

B   "The building" (41:12-13, 15)
G   Gates
H   Priestly chambers (40:44-46)
I   Inner room ("most holy place") of Temple house
      (41:3-4, 15b-20, 23)
K   Kitchens for priests' parts of victims (46:19-20)
L   30 Chambers for lay use (40:17; 42:8a);
      exact arrangement unknown
N   Nave of Temple house (41:1-2, 15b-25)
P   Chambers for priestly use (42:1-14)
S   Side chambers of Temple house (41:5-9, 11)
V   Vestibule of Temple house (40:48-49; 41:15b-16, 25-26)
Z   Zadokite chambers (40:44-46)
a   Altar of sacrifice (40:47; 43:13-27)
b   "Passage inward" (42:4)
c   Passage prolonged by wall (cf. 42:7, 9-10)
f   "The part of the platform which was left free" (41:9, 11)
i   Inner court
k   Kitchens for laity's parts of victims (46:21-24)
o   Outer court
p   Pavement (40:17-18); perhaps roofed and fronted with
      columns to form a portico (cf. 42:6)
v   Vestibules of gates
w   Separating wall or parapet (restored to 41:10, 11)
y^1 "Yard" of 41:12-13, 15
y^2 "Yard" of 41:14

Thickness of walls is indicated only where it is measured in the text. When all the interior dimensions are co-ordinated, they allow no thickness of the western outer wall, despite 40:5 with 42:15-20.

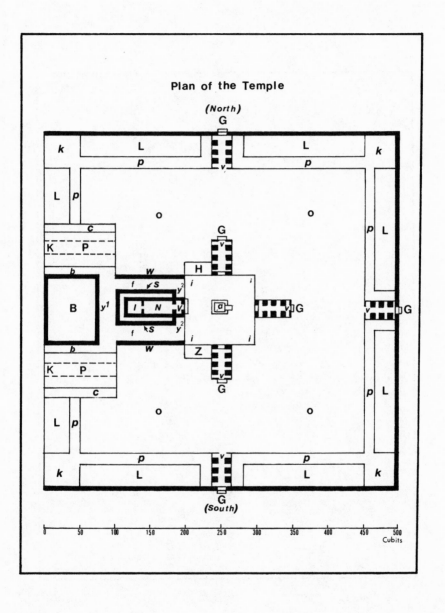

Plan of the Temple

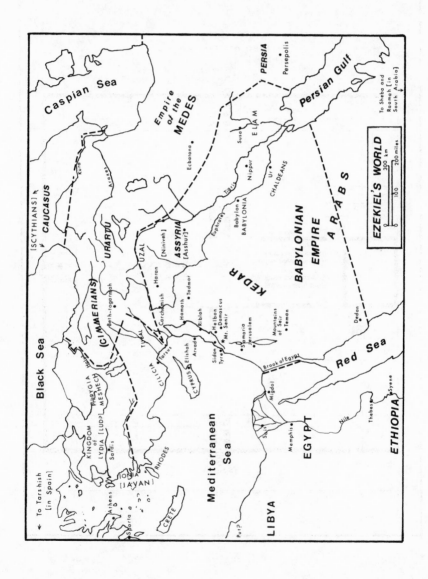

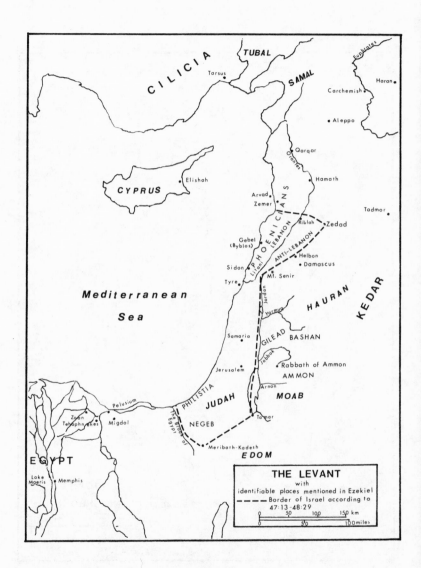

THE LEVANT
with
identifiable places mentioned in Ezekiel
Border of Israel according to
47:13-48:29

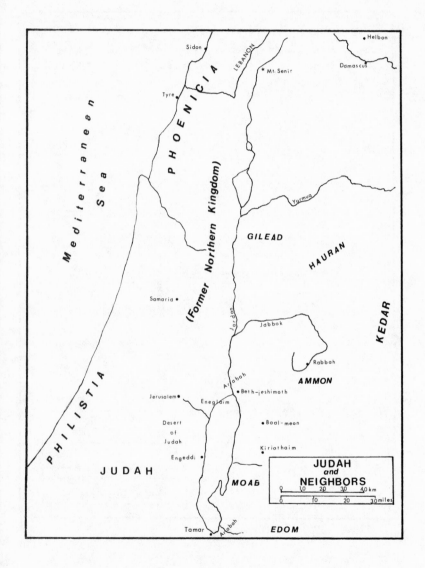

JUDAH
and
NEIGHBORS

OLD TESTAMENT MESSAGE
A Biblical-Theological Commentary

Editors:

Carroll Stuhlmueller, C.P. and Martin McNamara, M.S.C.

DISCUSSION QUESTIONS

1. During Madeline and Steve's twenty-six-year wedding anniversary celebration, Madeline recalls how the past year and a half had been difficult and that "it had reframed an entire lifetime of memories." Do you think that difficult moments in life can completely change how you remember the past? Are the difficulties something you work to forget or are they something that affects your future as well?

2. What do you think about Max and Millie's relationship? How did the emotional prologue set the tone of the novel?

3. When Avery, Nicole, Kyra, and Deirdre arrive at Bella Flora to tape *Do Over*, they find themselves as part of a reality show instead of a show about a renovation. What are your opinions about reality shows? Do you think they have value in our society? Should those featured have the right to have "off-limits" areas?

4. Do you think Nicole made the right decision when she turned her brother in to Special Agent Joe Giraldi? Could you have done that? Do you think it was a conflict of interest that Joe romantically pursued Nicole after her brother went to jail?

5. How did you feel when Daniel Deranian was introduced? Do you feel like his feelings were genuine regarding Dustin and Kyra? Do you sympathize with Tonja at all?

6. Why did Deirdre ask Madeline to teach her how to be a real mother? Can someone be taught how to be a parent? How can one better prepare to become a parent?

7. Is there a correlation between renovating The Millicent and the characters' personal lives? What role does Max's character play in regard to their development?

8. Describe the changes in Avery and Deirdre's relationship throughout the novel. Was the shooting the turning point or were there signs of change before that incident?

9. Prior to reading this novel, what did you know about cold case investigations? How long would you continue to search for someone you loved?

10. How did Aaron's disappearance shape Max and Millie's lives? How would their lives have been different if he had never disappeared?

11. Were you surprised when Steve said he wasn't going to see his family after the shooting? What do you think his actual motivations were for not doing this? Was it because he never wanted Madeline to do the show to begin with?

12. When Aaron's true identity was revealed, what was your reaction?

13. Imagine the lives of the characters after the novel. How do they unfold? Do Madeline and Steve stay married? Will Daniel come back into Kyra's life? Do Avery and Deirdre continue to stay close? What happens with Nicole's business?